The Makeover in Movies

The Makeover in Movies

Before and After in Hollywood Films, 1941–2002

Elizabeth A. Ford *and*
Deborah C. Mitchell

McFarland & Company, Inc., Publishers
Jefferson, North Carolina, and London

LIBRARY OF CONGRESS CATALOGUING-IN-PUBLICATION DATA

Ford, Elizabeth A., 1946–
   The makeover in movies : before and after in Hollywood
films, 1941–2002 / by Elizabeth A. Ford and Deborah C.
Mitchell.
      p.   cm.
   Includes bibliographical references and index.

   ISBN 0-7864-1721-8 (softcover : 50# alkaline paper)

   1. Beauty, Personal, in motion pictures.   2. Motion
pictures—United States.   I. Mitchell, Deborah C., 1951–
II. Title.
PN1995.9.B42F67   2004
791.43'653—dc22   2004000957

British Library cataloguing data are available

Cover image: ©2004 Corbis

Manufactured in the United States of America

McFarland & Company, Inc., Publishers
   Box 611, Jefferson, North Carolina 28640
      www.mcfarlandpub.com

For our mothers,
who love us the way we are

Acknowledgments

This project began in a small way, really, with a simple observation. About two years ago, we began to notice that America was obsessed with the "makeover"—that physical transformation of self, home, corporation.

We watched television shows springing up everywhere showing the before and after. Oprah was always taking some poor soul and making her over, much to the delight of her audiences. Regis and Kelly's ratings soared whenever they did a makeover show. MTV created a makeover series for teens called *Made*, which became a big hit. *This Old House* transformed entire homes, while *Trading Places* focused on the metamorphosis of individual rooms.

We saw the concept in newspapers where headlines proclaimed that people, organizations, cars, sports teams, government offices—you name it—were getting makeovers. We read magazines that devoted entire issues to the makeover of body and soul.

Even Colleen Rowley, the FBI whistleblower who stood defiantly on the cover of *Time* magazine, couldn't escape makeover scrutiny. After her televised testimony, fashion consultants and hairdressers wrote to her, offering their assistance and expertise in refurbishing her appearance.

Our thoughts turned to feature films. Hadn't Hollywood always manufactured beauty? Hadn't we seen the makeover—that one moment of transformation when the ugly duckling becomes the beautiful swan—played out on the silver screen countless times, decade after decade? The makeover, we knew, had deep roots in that old Cinderella story with the happily-ever-after ending.

When we tested our ideas about the makeover's evolution at conferences and in presentations, we found so much support and enthusiasm for our project that a lengthier study seemed inevitable. We would like to acknowledge all of those interested voices—our colleagues, our students, our friends, our families—who listened to our theories with excitement, adding their own excellent observations about makeover movies and makeover heroines.

We gratefully acknowledge our student assistants: Amanda Kengersky, who worked on the filmography; Jennifer Bechtel, who searched for source material; and Ashley Mondale, who shaped our presentations with an expert technical hand. Thanks also go to Jeremy Megraw and Tom Lisanti at the New York Public Library for the Performing Arts, Ned Comstock at USC's Cinema and Television Library, and Janet Lorenz at the Motion Picture Academy in Beverly Hills, who assisted in finding the before and after photographs; and, especially, Lou Giannetti, whose own work so clearly guided ours.

Table of Contents

Introduction:
Makeover Mania

Easy to Use: Just Click and Watch Yourself Transform.
   —*Cosmopolitan* Virtual Makeover 2003, Deluxe Suite

Annie Leibovitz's landmark show *Women,* held over at the Corcoran Gallery from November 1999 to March 2000, proved amazingly popular with female viewers. Women reveled in the chance to look at the results of Leibovitz looking at all kinds of other women. Here is Susan Sontag's take on the collection of photographs: "The ensemble says, so this is what women are now—as different, as varied, as heroic, as forlorn, as conventional, as unconventional, as this."

Women may have been drawn by a unique chance to examine the variety of our sex, but, both times we saw *Women,* the largest knots of viewers formed in front of two side-by-side photographs that detailed a process as old as the folktale: the first, a head shot of a short-haired, pale, thirty-something woman; the second, a headdress-to-toe photo of a Las Vegas showgirl in full regalia. Only the titles make it clear that the plain Jane and the beauty queen are both Susan McNamara. Although the choice of subjects and the intriguing positioning of all the photos provoked conversation—for example, a portrait of Barbara Bush was placed in the center of a wall that also featured a bearded hermaphrodite, AIDS activists and victims of domestic abuse—the compelling before and after sequence featuring Susan McNamara drew crowds.

It's easy to understand why viewers clustered before these two photographs. A continuing fascination with the transition from woman to goddess holds us in thrall. Cinderella-like tales, dating from an 850 AD Chinese version, show that the spell is neither recent nor located in any single culture. Apparently, the pull has never lessened; modern American women are inundated by and obsessed with images of *becoming.* Our language even provides a word for the act of transforming one's surface appearance: *makeover*.

It's difficult to avoid daily exhortations to revamp. Women's magazines, like *Glamour's* January 2003 makeover issue, routinely feature step-by-step instructions for improving hair, makeup, and clothing, and *Cosmopolitan* now offers software to help women envision makeover results before trying anything permanent. Conventional small-screen wisdom says that any makeover format draws viewers. The rash of new makeover shows include *This Old House* which makes over entire homes and *Trading Spaces*, a show where rooms get makeovers. Talk shows in search of ratings hire *Glamour* before and after guru Suze Yalof Schwartz to remake deserving and fashion-needy viewers. "There's always a bump," says Regis and Kelly's producer, Michael Gelman, when they do a makeover show (La Ferla, "Need a Ratings Boost?" 1). Certainly viewer appetite helped spawn shows like MTV's *Made*, the Style Network's *How Do I Look?*, and ABC's *Extreme Makeover*.

The last decade offers convincing evidence that not only the anonymous provide grist for the makeover mill. The mirror of media often fixates on prominent women and their changing looks. Oprah Winfrey's search for a new physical self rivaled her show's content for attention, while Britney Spears grabbed the look-of-the-minute torch Madonna once wielded so powerfully. During her husband's first year as president, Hilary Clinton cut her hair and upscaled her wardrobe, and *Vogue* featured her makeover in an article and on its cover. Just six years later, when Linda Tripp and Paula Jones—two women who had provoked two separate sex scandals in the Clinton administration—appeared before the press with dramatically different, obviously expensive looks, the result was a flood of spiteful speculation about what had been done to whom, and who paid the bill. To cap the decade, fashion-forward critics of first lady Laura Bush's dowdy appearance struck a nerve, precipitating attempts to render her ensembles and hairdo slightly more with-it, a process detailed in *Woman's Day*.

This seemingly endless media focus on *who* is looking *how* right *now* hasn't slaked our thirst for makeover details in the new millennium. Katie Couric's multi-million dollar contract with NBC sparked not quite as much buzz as her decision to lighten and lengthen her hair, while Rosie O'Donell's harder, tougher new look had her audience wondering who she really is. *Every* woman who finds herself in the public eye is seen as makeover material. Whistleblower FBI agent Colleen Rowley's damning post–September 11 testimony at a Senate hearing unleashed "a flurry of concerned letters from fashion consultants, hairdressers and ophthalmologists who yearned to make her over" (Ripley and Sieger 39).

Not only in real life do makeovers make fascinating stories. What better venue for transformation than the movies, where a change in coiffure or eyebrow shape can fill a screen? Long tuned in to the appeal of female metamorphosis, Hollywood has provided it over and over again. Many big films of the thirties, such as *It Happened One Night* (1934), paralleled the position of women in Hollywood. They featured strong, attractive, wealthy heroines who must remake their psyches before they can choose the correct soul mates, real men, not effete, meaningless snobs. But change came with the changing times. During the war years, Hollywood launched the overexposed but under-examined genre we focus on here. Makeover films rest on this premise: the central female character makes the journey from blah to beautiful. Her *physical* self must be transformed before she can become an effective person. From the forties to the present, through years of change in Hollywood, changes in the standards of female beauty, and changes in American women's cultural status, the makeover film has remained a viable commercial product.

Still an eminently watchable film, *Now, Voyager* (1941), the first major makeover movie, established ground rules for the makeover genre. Male reviewers dismissed the film, adapted from Olive Higgins Prouty's novel of the same name, calling it a "weepy." Female audiences, however, relished the chance to follow Charlotte Vale's rebirth as she morphed from a chronically depressed, lackluster spinster into a glamorous and powerful heiress. In Chapter One, "Charting the Course," we describe and discuss Vale's journey from before to after, and we list the elements of her transformation that continue to characterize many films in this genre. *The Princess Diaries* (2000), a makeover film for teens, acts as a test case. Although it targets a different audience and has a much lighter tone, the more recent film repeats *Now, Voyager*'s list of before and after traits, down to the dark-rimmed glasses its heroine, Mia Thermopolis, wears. Similarities in these films, which were released 59 years apart, start our discussion about the way female beauty has been presented by Hollywood.

Most makeover films, like *The Princess Diaries*, draw on stock situations and details from earlier makeover films, but they have a more ancient, more magical source as well. Chapter Two, "So Many Cinderellas," begins with glances back at Charles Perrault and Jacob and Wilhelm Grimm, whose tales "The Glass Slipper" and "The Little Ash Girl" color most Cinderella-type films. The story has always attracted creative minds and unique approaches. Cinderella's makeover gets an assist from mice (an inheritance from the Brothers Grimm) in Walt Disney's *Cinderella* (1950), still the most watched film retelling of the folktale. Cinderella's fairy godmother (a character from the pages of Charles Perrault) sings

Cinderella a song written by America's most eminent musical comedy duo in Rodgers and Hammerstein's *Cinderella* (1965).

Some versions of Cinderella nod to Perrault and the Brothers Grimm while also providing star vehicles: Richard Chamberlain postures as Prince Charming in the politically-inflected *The Slipper and the Rose* (1976), Whitney Houston and Brandy give the tale a long overdue multicultural take in Disney's remake of Rodgers and Hammerstein's *Cinderella* (1997), and Drew Barrymore stars in the radical revision *Ever After* (1998). With support from Stockard Channing and Johnathan Pryce, Disney approaches "Cinderella" from a different perspective in *Confessions of an Ugly Stepsister* (2001).

After so many retellings, should Cinderella be laid to rest? To help ourselves (and you) begin to formulate an answer, we look at Cinderella's progress through film history, considering especially the issues of individuality and recognition that surround the makeover. Cinderella's different set of before and after signifiers fits her transition from poverty and servitude to wealth and position, and the change often parallels her shift from girl to woman. The crux of the transformation, however, is still the nature of female beauty. Because the Prince usually recognizes Cinderella only when she is richly dressed, her beauty resides in her gorgeous gown and expensive accessories. Even after their love-at-first-sight experience at the ball, the Prince depends upon the confirmation of a perfectly fitting dainty slipper to assure him he has the right woman. Besides suggesting some serious mental deficiencies in the royal male, "Cinderella," so deeply encoded into our culture, forces us to grapple with the relationship between female perfection and "perfect" romance. Conventions from *Now, Voyager* and tensions endemic to "Cinderella" continue in many makeover films, which we group into sub-genres.

Shades of Cinderella are certainly reflected in the films covered in Chapter Three, "Teen Makeovers." From childhood, through puberty, and into the teen years, American girls are bombarded with makeover images. Dolls, magazines, movies, and television shows ensure that the Cinderella story holds fast. The media flood of messages that suggest something is wrong with a girl if she doesn't look or act a certain way—and the options they offer her for "correcting" all her flaws and blemishes—is nothing short of amazing, if not a little scary. With more disposable income than ever before, teens spend and spend and spend in search of that perfect look. The cartoon-inspired *Josie and the Pussycats* (2001), which we discuss in this chapter, hits a makeover low in its shameless attempt to promote recreational consumption of beauty products (though it claims to be doing just the opposite).

In an effort to get its share of those teen dollars, Hollywood started cranking out flicks that would appeal to teenage girls. Most are highly forgettable, but a few stand out for their attempts to deliver strong female characters. In *She's All That* (1999), golden guy Zach Siler (Freddy Prinze, Jr.) *almost* makes a prom queen of the biggest nerd in the senior class, Lainie Boggs (Rachel Leigh Cook). Like *The Princess Diaries, She's All That* slavishly replicates the *Now, Voyager* formula for plainness, but this cliché-ridden film at least gives the heroine some Charlotte Vale determination and zest.

An encouraging breeze blows through the two teen makeover films directed by Amy Heckerling, *Clueless* (1995) and *Legally Blonde* (2001). The too-cool heroines in each of these comedies (Alicia Silverstone and Reese Witherspoon, respectively) are what most of us would call "afters" when the films begin, and indeed, they see themselves as perfect. In each case, the savvy, witty, and genuinely nice heroine deglams a little as she ruefully discovers just how much she's got besides that pretty face, gorgeous figure, and designer wardrobe.

An urban Cinderella tale, *Maid in Manhattan* (2002), starring Jennifer Lopez, recently caught some flack for retelling what many critics see as a threadbare narrative. We place *Maid in Manhattan* in Chapter Four, "The Ladder of Class," because it details the struggles of Marisa Ventura, a hotel maid from the Bronx who longs to improve her own life as well as her son's. Marisa crosses class boundaries to find a career *and* love, but not all heroines in class-inflected makeover films are so lucky.

The very American notion that class distinctions can be erased sounds healthy and patriotic, but most heroines experience difficulty and loss as they make their transitions. They learn that upward mobility isn't exactly free. For example, in *Sabrina* (1954), Sabrina Fairchild (Audrey Hepburn) makes marrying a rich man her *raison d'être*. She trades on her newly acquired Paris look, and she doesn't care that she steps on her target's fiancée to achieve her goal. A 1995 remake of *Sabrina* attempts to give her character some depth, but doesn't go far enough. Sabrina's "after" is still her entre into the glamorous world of mansions and champagne picnics.

It's hard to tell what self Sabrina Fairchild suppressed before storming the castle, but Jo (also played by Audrey Hepburn), the heroine of *Funny Face* (1957), has intellectual leanings. The film paints Jo's philosophic turn as silly, and her pursuit of truth halts when she finds love and glamour as a top fashion model. But then, isn't the elite existence of the beautiful people much more worth having than some moldy old thoughts? These films reflect the post-war, fifties elevation of brittle beauty as a woman's most important asset.

Not every heroine aspires to upper class grandeur. *Grease* (1978) demonstrates the strength of the environment to enforce its prevailing ideas of beauty. At Rydell High, *up* is *down* for the virginal Sandy (Olivia Newton-John), who allows her bad girl friends to replace her Sandra Dee sweetness with a persona that resembles a babe from a raunchy ZZ Top video. Of course, Sandy's semi-sleazy look, characterized by big hair, broad shoulders, tight pants, and stiletto heels, dominated not only Rydell High, but the real world of late-seventies fashion as well. Sandy's trampy transformation sent a message to women to "shape up" their sex appeal (ergo, buy more clothes and hair products) and signaled that a nice girl could *stay* nice and look ... well, hot. (We have to admit that around this time, we both got those God-awful perms.)

Like those hot *Grease* girls, Tess McGill (Melanie Griffith) sports big hair in *Working Girl* (1988), but she's also got a big brain. Although late sixties affirmative action policies forced companies to hire women and minorities, making them a significant part of the work force for the first time since the war, Hollywood was slow to envision working women as subjects of interest, and films like *Norma Rae* (1979) and *Silkwood* (1983) are few and far between. *Working Girl* considers the fate of a woman stuck in a class-inflected corporate ghetto and follows her quest to have the world see more than her outward appearance. Tess has the smarts, but her look screams Fluff Chick. How can she get out of the secretarial pool? Tess's boss gives her some makeover hints in return for her ideas. You might think that by 1988 Hollywood would be flooded with images of women helping women, but *Working Girl* just can't abandon the women-being-mean-to-women stereotype. It's there in *Maid in Manhattan* as well, and certainly in *Pretty Woman* (1990), probably the most popular makeover film of the nineties.

If you had only *Pretty Woman* to use as a cultural referent, you might think that being a prostitute wasn't such a bad job—think of all those colored condoms! To conclude this chapter, we propose that the ugly ramifications of *Pretty Woman* tower over its charming, class-transgressing heroine and hunky hero. After her transformation from prostitute to upper-class beauty, Vivian Ward (Julia Roberts) has only her relationship with Edward Lewis (Richard Gere) to validate her existence, which takes us back, full circle, to *Sabrina*. Class shifting is costly. In each of these films, while the male lead may have a change of heart, the heroine must adapt or be transformed to suit *his* needs or *his* world.

Follow that concept a little farther, and you've got the films in Chapter Five, "Pygmalion Problems," in which men try to control female transformations completely. George Bernard Shaw's play *Pygmalion*, which suggests that this scheme won't work, graced the London stage in 1914, but, as the films in this chapter demonstrate, Hollywood has largely ignored the hint. George Cukor's film adaptation of Lerner and Loewe's smash hit *My Fair Lady* (1964) amends Shaw's play by sweetening the heroine (Audrey Hepburn, again), and by giving Henry Higgins (Rex Harrison) an unhealthy dollop of power. *Shampoo* (1975) does a better job of revealing the futility of trying to maintain even so small a transformation as perfect hair. Like a one-knight crusader for stylish coiffures, hairdresser George Roundy (Warren Beatty) makes the weary rounds of his clients and lovers, only to find himself alone in the end. *Shampoo* forces us to consider America's ongoing obsession with image.

Both *Up Close and Personal* (1996) and *Miss Congeniality* (2000) feature female characters in professions long considered male strongholds: broadcast journalism and law enforcement. Change of image is everything to Tally Atwater (Michelle Pfeiffer). Monolithic newscaster Warren Justice (Robert Redford) wrenches her into a "perfect" anchor, using himself as a model. Hmm, does that sound a little narcissistic? Something worse than narcissism dominates *Miss Congeniality* (2000), a comedy that pretends to give a closer, kinder look at beauty pageant contestants. The assumption underlying this film suggests that a woman like Gracie Hart (Sandra Bullock), who works in a "man's world," like the FBI, becomes mannish. On special assignment, Gracie gets the full treatment, changing from slob to full-fledged pageant chick with the aid of Victor Melling (Michael Caine), a gay pageant coordinator who knows how to make Hart a perfect woman. The extreme before and after states Bullock assumes are both stereotypes, and so is every other character in this dreadful film: male and female, gay and straight.

At least *Miss Congeniality* isn't blood-curdling. Taken to its extreme, the Pygmalion plan—to create a perfect woman—dissolves into horror in *The Stepford Wives* (1975). Based on Ira Levin's 1972 bestseller of the same title, *The Stepford Wives* imagines a community in which men have figured out how to dictate female perfection. What men *want*, and what they *get* from their disgusting makeover "technique," are equally upsetting. All the films in this section take the Pygmalion myth a step further; we see what happens after the "perfect" woman comes to life, and it's not a pretty picture.

A more hopeful aura emanates from the female characters in Chapter Six, "Mid-life Makeovers." Sometimes a mature woman knows she needs a change. Sometimes she makes it happen. In *Alice Doesn't Live Here Anymore* (1974), *Moonstruck* (1987), *The Mirror Has Two Faces* (1996), and *My Big Fat Greek Wedding* (2002), we get to watch female characters make positive changes. The heroines in these films have something in common, and it's not the frenzied wish to get a better job or a richer man.

All of them, like Charlotte Vale, need to find themselves. Fortunately, most of them don't have to search alone, as do many of their makeover film sisters. They belong to loving families, or they find communities that welcome them. Men don't tell them *what* to change, *how* to change, or *why* they should change. Makeovers for these mid-life heroines grow from internal needs, and are, consequently, softer and much more believable.

All these films (and many more we haven't been able to include here) demonstrate the makeover story's staying power. The target of makeover films certainly has not changed. From *Now, Voyager* (1942) to *The Princess Diaries* (2001), Hollywood has aimed squarely at female audiences. In the chapters that follow, we examine makeover moments and their effects on the heroines and those around them. We direct our examinations at these questions: What does this genre's persistence imply? Why do makeover movies still draw enlightened female viewers?

One

Charting the Course

Now, voyager, sail thou forth to seek and find.
—Walt Whitman, "The Untold Want"

Those before and after photos of Susan McNamara in Annie Leibovitz's *Women* showed astonished viewers that an ordinary woman, someone you might pass in a supermarket, really *could* become a spangled bird of paradise. Makeover movies have never worked quite that way. The assumption that a star *never* could be an ordinary woman alters the makeover process profoundly into the following sequence: initial star status (a glamorous star is usually cast in a makeover role), before (the star masquerades as plain), after (the star's beauty is restored). Because the after is a given, the shock of the before and the drama of the makeover, more than the astonishing end product, provide the fascination.

Consider the interesting case of *Now, Voyager* (1942) starring Bette Davis, the first high profile film with a physical makeover at its center. As Lou Giannetti and Scott Eyman point out, Davis was never typecast as a beauty; she earned the title "actor-star" because she played "offbeat character roles" (*Flashback* 145). She had, however, played glamorous women, like Julie Marsten in *Jezebel* (1938), a performance that won her an Oscar. This doesn't appear to have been enough to keep Warner Bros. from worrying about the effect of casting her as Charlotte Vale, the frumpy and frustrated heroine of *Now, Voyager.*

To forestall any perception that, unembellished, Davis might actually *look* like pre-makeover Charlotte, the studio issued alerts. Promotional materials for *Now, Voyager* touted the costuming required for Davis to play Vale before transformation: "to make herself appear dowdy in the film's early sequences, Davis wore padding, glasses and heavy fake eyebrows." Studios still use such disclaimers to shield glamorous female stars who choose less than glamorous parts. *Time*'s blurb about Nicole Kidman's portrayal of Virginia Woolf in the recently released film adaptation of

Michael Cunningham's *The Hours* included information about the "loads of makeup and a dour countenance" Kidman had to wear to play Woolf. Trailers often suppress before images. The trailer for *Now, Voyager*, for example, never revealed the pre-makeover Vale, and posters for the film featured Davis post-makeover in a stylish evening gown, uttering the suggestive statement "Don't blame *me* for what happened."

Obviously, Warner Bros. understood the importance of announcing that Davis had to work hard to appear plain. In this, as in the other conventions it introduces, *Now, Voyager* offers valuable criteria for evaluating decades of makeover films that followed it. An examination of *Now, Voyager* reveals the machinery of this early makeover film at work; a comparison to *The Princess Diaries* (2001) illustrates its enduring influence. Although each of these films fits in other chapters—*Now, Voyager* describes a mid-life makeover and *The Princess Diaries* a teen makeover—we place them here to identify the before and after makeover codes and to begin the discussion of issues endemic to the genre.

Now, Voyager *(1942)*

Now, Voyager, directed by Irving Rapper, had a literary source, Olive Higgins Prouty's 1941 bestseller of the same title, and the hype for the film trumpeted its faithfulness to "the year's most sensational novel" (MGM video trailer). Film and novel pivot on the central makeover, although focus and narrative positioning of events differ. The plot remains essentially the same for both.

Change of appearance parallels change of fortune for heroine Charlotte Vale (Davis). A nervous breakdown has propelled the unhappy, dowdy Charlotte from her domineering mother's (Gladys Cooper) dreary Back Bay mansion to a cheerful clinic called Cascade where, under the treatment of psychoanalyst Dr. Jaquith (Claude Rains), she gains confidence to reenter the world. In an act of support, her sister-in-law, Lisa (Ilka Chase), whisks Charlotte off for a complete makeover. Instead of lumpen, voilà! Charlotte is lovely. Charlotte continues her transformation on a cruise ship where she assumes the identity of Renee Beauchamp, a friend of Lisa's.

On board ship, Charlotte meets her soul mate, Jerry Durrance (Paul Henreid). She tells him that her surface is entirely new, and that her interior self is fragile. Although she feels like a fraud, Charlotte gradually realizes that she *is* the charming, warm, attractive person everyone on board the ship, especially Jerry, thinks she is. Her relationship with Durrance heats up, but, because he is married, they must be satisfied with a brief, intense fling.

Charlotte returns to Boston and wages a quiet but persistent war against her mother's tyranny. Charlotte wins when she answers her mother's threat of disinheritance with the confident words "I'm not afraid." Her new aura attracts a suitable suitor, Elliot Livingston (John Loder), whom she turns away because she still loves Jerry. Her mother dies after she and Charlotte quarrel over this. Her mother's death leaves her independently wealthy, but shaken, and Charlotte returns to Cascade.

There she meets and helps Jerry's ugly duckling daughter, Tina (Janice Wilson). In the plain, miserable child, Charlotte sees herself. Under Charlotte's guidance, the child goes through a similar, self-affirming makeover. The sustained, platonic relationship that develops between Jerry and Charlotte depends on Jerry's willingness to accept Charlotte's help for his daughter. Charlotte has become a poised, powerful, and complete person.

Although there are differences, the film adaptation of *Now, Voyager* is *essentially* faithful to Prouty's work; it even advertises its adherence to the novel with an occasional dissolve to the turning pages of a book. Significantly, the film deletes a brief scene in which Jerry explains he, too, has had a breakdown much like Charlotte's. In the adaptation, Jerry and Charlotte lack this additional bond of shared experience, but the film keeps its focus, as the novel does, on Charlotte's physical and emotional transformation. Other important changes in the film adaptation affect the presentation of that process.

Before examining those differences, it's important to list here Charlotte's physical traits before and after, not only because they remain the same on the page and on the screen, but also because they form a code for decades of makeover films to follow.

BEFORE	AFTER
Orthopedic oxfords	Stylish shoes
Thick stockings	Silk stockings
Thick ankles	Shapely ankles and legs
Poorly fitting, unstylish clothing	Perfectly fitting and fashionable outfit revealing a trim figure
Dumpy figure	
Glasses (not designer!)	No glasses
No makeup	Discreet makeup
Heavy brows	Carefully shaped eyebrows
Heavy dark hair bundled into a bun	Beautiful hat
	Flattering hairdo

Now, Voyager (MGM, 1942). BEFORE: A living collection of before signifiers, Charlotte Vale (Bette Davis) stands nervously at the bottom of the elaborate stairway in the Vale mansion, anguish visible in her clasped hands and tortured gaze. Her despotic mother has ruled her life this far, and Charlotte feels that the bottom step is to be her permanent position. Soon, however, she'll shed that dreary dress, those clunky shoes, more than a few pounds, and, most notably, those glasses. Then, she'll begin her climb toward a new life, claiming the stairs, the mansion, and her *self*, as her own.

Now, Voyager (MGM, 1942). AFTER: Who is this bewitching woman, with her knowing glance and her secret smile? Charlotte Vale, transformed, has left the shadows for the light. Now, as she arranges those roses, her life blooms with possibility. Although she embodies all the qualities of an after heroine, Charlotte's not just a catalogue of signifiers; that sleek hairdo, that flattering dress, that artfully placed brooch are no longer unfamiliar borrowings. The way she looks signals the choices she has made.

While the elements of Charlotte's before and after states transfer faithfully to the screen, the film alters the focus and sequence of events. Prouty's novel opens with a transformed Charlotte already a passenger on a pleasure cruise and "keenly conscious of the clothes she was wearing, which were not her own" (1). Although Prouty uses a third person narrator, the speaker is close enough to Vale to feel the flex of her ankle (1). Through the eyes of other passengers, readers see Charlotte looking "like Katherine Cornell," with skin like "old ivory" and black hair "cut very short" (4). Charlotte's insecurities do not prevent her from reaching out to Jerry Durrance; she tells him her true identity is "proverbial spinster aunt" (11). This hopeful start frames a flashback describing Charlotte before her breakdown and before the makeover.

Prouty uses literal framing to set the scene for this flashback. Charlotte sits in her stateroom before a three-paneled dressing table mirror "[gazing] at her own reflection" (14). Charlotte's memories do not follow a linear narrative pattern or locate her collapse in a single, humiliating day. She gazes, thinking of her physical differences from her sister-in-law, and her mother's general disapproval of almost everything. The details of Charlotte's before appearance emerge during this self-exploration. She thinks of her dark heavy brows, "nearly touching in the middle," and Lisa's fairer hair and skin; her "blocky, bulky figure," and her mother's indictment against dieting; her long heavy hair in a bun "as big as a cocoanut," and her mother's disapproval of short hair (14). Her appearance becomes an indicator of her entrapment, not only a catalog of fashion mistakes.

Casey Robinson, who crafted the final screenplay, decided against Prouty's beginning, and against an alternate start by Edmund Goulding, who wrote an early treatment of the novel. Robinson believed that audiences needed to be introduced to the before Charlotte, to watch her "struggle against ... her mother" and to empathize with the after Charlotte (21). As Jean Thomas Allen puts it, Robinson "took his time in structuring the pleasure of the Cinderella story" (22). His changed sequence of events places an inciting incident first—the visit of Dr. Jaquith to the Vale home; during this scene, Charlotte Vale, pre-makeover, appears.

Weather sets the scene for Charlotte's before state of mind and body. Rain falls in Back Bay Boston, and the rain streaming down the heroine's window connects her sorrow and the weather. But Charlotte's overwhelming sadness reveals itself most clearly in her before avatar as visual synecdoche—parts suggesting the whole of her desperation. Charlotte's nervous hands appear (only her hands), carving an ivory box, snuffing out a forbidden cigarette, trashing a lipstick-smeared tissue. Then, called by her mother, who describes her as "my ugly duckling," she descends the stairway. Robinson suggested the camera work for her descent in the screenplay: "the camera lets [Charlotte] step down into the shot, in other words, [it] travels up her figure" (60).

Robinson's planned shot never made it into the film. Instead, Charlotte's shoes and ankles behind the bars of the banister become signs of her entrapment, and her body becomes visible in a long shot as she enters the drawing room, *not* as the camera travels up her figure. This changes the feel of the scene. The voyeuristic toe-to-top gaze would have introduced Charlotte as an assemblage of gawky parts. The new shot shifts the emphasis to Charlotte's interaction with her mother, her sister-in-law and Dr. Jaquith.

Davis projects Vale's character right through the beetling brows, bad hairdo and other characteristics on the before list. There's a nice hint— as there is in Prouty's text—of Charlotte's closeness with Lisa, in the smile and embrace they share, and the suggestion of an internal monologue. Although Vale remains silent, her eyes and gestures speak for her, revealing a not entirely subdued self, especially in the look she flashes at her mother (also a connection to the scene in the novel in which Vale recalls her mother's inflexibility).

In the film, Charlotte before her makeover has an affecting physical presence, and her appearance helps to explicate the tension between her and her mother. When she shows Dr. Jaquith her room, Charlotte tells him a little of her past. She describes a brief fling with a ship's radio operator and her mother's reaction. The incident helps Jaquith understand Mrs. Vale's current control of her daughter's person. "What man would want me?" Charlotte asks Jaquith. "I'm fat. Look at my shoes. Mother approves of sensible shoes."

In the novel and in the film, however, Charlotte's emotional state, much more than a desire for male attention, precipitates her makeover. Both texts reveal the terrible self-loathing and insecurity that shadow every moment of her life. It's that shadow the makeover tries to dispel.

Robinson planned to present Vale's makeover in a flashback after she had met Jerry. Prouty uses a flashback much earlier in the story. Vale recalls her makeover after she muses about her mother, herself, and her sister-in-law. Lisa has taken her for the works: haircut, massage, makeup, manicure, and so on. The narrator claims that Charlotte has "little interest" in the process, that she feels numb. But the ministrations of the beauticians release a stream of physical impressions: the pain of having one's brows plucked, the removal of "the heaviest locks" of her long hair (15), the contrast of the "steaming hot and icy cold" (15) compresses placed on her face. Reliving this experience, Charlotte realizes, while "gazing into the mirror," that "the very expression of her face had changed," even though she calls the makeover "ridiculous camouflage" (18).

Prouty invests the makeover with a not unpleasant loss of control, with physical awakening, with all those rushing sensations, and with ambiguity. Both Lisa and Charlotte are shocked at the drastic difference in Charlotte's person. The narrator reminds readers that "everyone has a style of one's own which is the result of adaptation to one's physical appearance.... It is extremely unpleasant to be stripped, suddenly, of one's ... appearance, however unattractive" (20). Prouty shows that the process of revising even a surface identity can be complex and troubling.

In the screenplay, Robinson delays the makeover, stringing out the Cinderella story with this sequence of events leading up to Charlotte's transformation:

1. Shot establishing grandeur of the Vale mansion.
2. Mrs. Vale appears.
3. Jaquith and Lisa arrive. They briefly discuss Charlotte's state with Mrs. Vale.
4. Charlotte sits alone in her room, carving an ivory box.
5. Charlotte is called and descends the staircase.
6. Charlotte flees when she discovers she is the focus of attention. Jaquith follows and gets a glimpse of her life.
7. Lisa's daughter June arrives and taunts Charlotte, who has returned to the parlor. Charlotte collapses.
8. Lisa visits Cascade where Charlotte has been recovering under Jaquith's care; he says she is well enough to leave.
9. On the cruise ship, a crowd waits for Rene Beauchamp (Charlotte's shipboard identity) to join them for an excursion.
10. Post-makeover Charlotte appears.
11. Charlotte meets Jerry and spends the day in his company.

And, here it finally comes....

12. Charlotte flashes back to the makeover.

Not only the position, much more deeply embedded in the story, but also the nature of the makeover scene changes in the screenplay. The novel includes the *process* of the makeover. The screenplay focuses on the shocking result—and places the emphasis on "shock." The scene begins when Lisa returns to find Charlotte already shorn and glamorous. Lisa is amazed, and Charlotte "starts, stares almost open mouthed" into a mirror

(92). She looks to see if the mirror is reflecting some stranger behind her. Gone are the sensations of layers being stripped away, the release of one's body to unfamiliar hands. The makeover, no longer processed by Charlotte's memory, turns into schtick.

It's not a great tragedy, then, that this scene was cut from the film, although it does, at least, involve Lisa in the transformation. Jean Thomas Allen believes it might have been deleted because no one wanted to reinforce the image of "Bette Davis as so unglamorous a character" (224). No alternate makeover scene replaced it, so the event that changes Charlotte physically is not represented. Film viewers must rely on their image of Charlotte before to imagine the process that produced her after self, and on hints in the action and the dialogue. Throughout the screenplay, Robinson diminishes the importance of Prouty's female characters, Lisa and Deb, Charlotte's first woman friend beyond her family. The absence of a makeover scene robs Charlotte—and viewers—of the physical experience and of Lisa's involvement.

Compounding this change, the film strengthens the notion that Dr. Jaquith is partly responsible for Charlotte's physical transformation as well as her emotional recovery. When Lisa comes to visit Charlotte at Cascades, Jaquith warns her, "She's lost a lot of weight." Then, he gives Charlotte's makeover process a dramatic (and scary) jumpstart when he removes her rimless glasses, claiming, "The occulist *told* you you don't need these anymore." Charlotte responds that she feels "undressed" without them. "It's good for you to feel that way," Jaquith crows as he snaps them in half. That's the last time viewers see Charlotte as frumpy spinster.

The film relies on the drama of contrast, not the explication of the planned makeover scene. Robinson details the camera shot that introduces the newly glamorous Charlotte: "[she] walks down into the scene, first her feet appearing and then her whole body. This should be sharply reminiscent of Charlotte's introduction" (86). This time Robinson's body-sweeping shot made it into the film.

At this point in the film, however, viewers know Charlotte Vale as a person, and the camera's gaze has less power to reduce her to parts. We understand how hard it must be for her to inhabit the glamorous self we see—those beautiful legs, that stylish and shape-revealing ensemble, that wide-brimmed, veiled hat tipped to offer a glimpse of a striking face.

Robinson *does* alter the narrative crucially: he visually represents Charlotte pre-makeover (introducing a set of conventions that endure); he erases the process of the makeover from the film (creating an important point of comparison for makeover films that follow); he pares down the other female characters. Yet his screenplay does not dilute Charlotte's emotional struggle to become a functioning adult.

Both the film and the novel allow Vale time to live her way into her after self, and that motion feels right in both versions. Charlotte inherits her mother's fortunes before she truly inhabits her new persona. The rest of the film details that process, including Charlotte's making over of Tina, Jerry's ugly duckling youngest child. Charlotte gives up the possibility of marriage for the role of surrogate mother to Tina, but it's hard to see the graceful, confident woman she has become as entirely self-sacrificing.

Bette Davis sought some of the credit for making over Robinson's script, insisting that she had a great deal to say about it. She claimed to have "used Miss Prouty's book" to redo "the screenplay" (Robinson 32). Irving Rapper claims he saw only the Robinson screenplay, but that Davis's changes could have been incorporated before he took the project. Unfortunately, we don't know what Davis added or changed. We do know that at the risk of being labeled a bitch, Davis fought for content and action she believed important, and often she won.

Davis's clout as a star is just one of the influences feminist critics have examined in their re-readings of *Now, Voyager*. Virginia Wright Wexman, for example, sees Charlotte's makeover as an example of dehistorization. The physical change, she claims, "diverts the spectator's attention from evolving political realities" (130). Outside the cinema in 1942, American women were undergoing a major role makeover as they entered the workplace during the war years. In the fifties, the booming male-controlled economy would push them back to their before state.

Yet, Charlotte's physical change may have symbolized political reality to the women watching the film. The exterior change parallels Charlotte's internal drama as she begins to control her own life. Her assumption of independence and power, along with her striking new look, may have been the primary draw for female viewers.

Olive Higgins Prouty was well aware of the difficulties involved in becoming a whole person. In *Pencil Shavings*, a memoir intended as a family history, Prouty quietly downplays her battle to remake herself as a writer, but the absence of any support from parents, siblings, husband or children still speaks from her pages. Even her commercial success, which was substantial, was tainted; she acknowledged that being classified as "a lady novelist" hurt (Allen 12). That bias is apparent in film reviews (written only by males) of *Now, Voyager*. Philip K. Hartung, for example, called it "tripe dished up by women's magazines" (qtd. in Allen 36), and Manny Farber, who reviewed the film for *The New Republic*, claimed that although

Davis gave the film some power, Prouty's story made it a "tragic lady movie" (577).

Prouty spent her career as a professional writer practicing self-effacement, always reassuring her husband and family that writing was her hobby, family her vocation. She must have felt less personal investment in *Stella Dallas,* a tale she spun from a cocktail party conversation, than in *Now, Voyager,* a text that came closer to her life. She, too, had a breakdown after the early deaths of two of her four children—behavior seen as weakness by her husband. She, too, had a psychoanalyst who insisted she have, for the first time, a private place to write.

Prouty read Robinson's adaptation, the first screenplay she had ever seen, with great interest. She details her pleasure in examining its "intriguing details" in *Pencil Shavings* (198). But she didn't only read and enjoy Robinson's adaptation of her work. She explains that "there wasn't a single page that escaped my comments in red type" (198). Prouty also says she added "extra pages," but doesn't describe them. One of the few specifics she mentions is her rejection of the exterior of the Vale mansion with its brass plaque; she felt it inconsistent with the Vale's status—only dentists would have such things. (The plaque appears in the film.) Her insistence on an unstereotypical portrayal of Dr. Jaquith fared better, and she noted with pleasure that Tina, played by Janice Wilson, seemed close to her "conception." She does explain that only a "few portions" of her suggestions were accepted (198).

Jean Thomas Allen credits Prouty, not Robinson, with much of the wit that enlivens the film. We would credit her and Davis, too, for guarding the novel's female perspective. Perhaps women liked, and still like, this extremely watchable film, which most contemporary critics characterized as a "weepy," not because of its melodrama, but because it attempts something larger. Lea Jacobs argues that it is, after all, Charlotte's vision and revision that draw us into the text. Even though Dr. Jaquith orchestrates Charlotte's transformation, female viewers take pleasure in "Charlotte's desire, like our own, to *experience* narrative" (qtd. in Mayne 55).

Besides the many characteristics that became conventions, and besides the strengths of this story, *Now, Voyager* includes more than enough complexity and contradiction to begin our discussion. If, as we believe, *Now, Voyager* is the mother of Hollywood makeover films, and if makeover films are indeed an identifiable genre, subsequent films should bear discernible traces of their progenitor. Although 59 years and the feminist revolution separate it from *Now, Voyager, The Princess Diaries* (2001) offers a valuable test case.

The Princess Diaries *(2001)*

Reviewer Michael O'Sullivan calls the newer film "squeaky clean" (WE37), and, certainly, it's lighter in tone and content and directed at a younger female audience. But a makeover film is a makeover film, and even one as different from *Now, Voyager* as *The Princess Diaries* shows connections to its 1942 predecessor. A thinner story, billed as a comedy (not a "weepy"), *The Princess Diaries* demonstrates the persistence of type over time.

First of all, there's the shielding of the young star, Anne Hathaway, from any potential fallout that playing a plain person might provoke. The contrast between the female leads of these films is obvious. Hathaway, who plays Mia Thermopolis, is no Bette Davis. She's a neophyte with just one film and a television series under her belt. Hathaway's name calls no particular image to mind, as Davis's did, but pre-release publicity for *The Princess Diaries* makes it clear that she is being groomed for mega-beauty status. Garry Marshall, who directed *The Princess Diaries* (and *Pretty Woman*, another giant makeover film), described Hathaway for Army Archerd's column in *Variety* as "a combination Julia Roberts, Audrey Hepburn and Judy Garland" ("For Variety"). No mean comparisons!

Reviewer Jeffrey M. Anderson was surprised that "Disney does not provide any pictures of the 'before' Mia in the movie's press kit" ("Glasses"). Considering the genre, the omission makes perfect sense. The posters for *Now, Voyager* featured a svelte Davis, and the posters for *The Princess Diaries* feature a glam Hathaway in an evening gown, a tiara, earphones and sunglasses, obviously a cool princess. As the tagline says, "She rocks. She rules. She reigns." Behind Hathaway, also in full royal regalia, stands Julie Andrews, who plays her grandmother.

In his review of *The Princess Diaries,* Anderson claims to recognize "the standard makeover plot line" ("Glasses"), voicing an underlying assumption that makeover films *are* a genre, with repeating narrative devices as well as repeating before and after criteria. As does *Now, Voyager, The Princess Diaries* has a literary source, Meg Cabot's novel of the same name. As does *Now, Voyager, The Princess Diaries* links transformation and inheritance, but Mia Thermoplis, the fourteen-year-old protagonist, inherits a literal kingdom, not just a family fortune. The screenplay by Gina Wendkos follows this storyline, which reveals similarities to its "mother," *Now, Voyager.*

Mia (Anne Hathaway) lives in San Francisco with her mother (Caroline Goodall), a self-supporting artist, in a restored firehouse. At fifteen, she's klutzy and unrefined, an insignificant outsider at Grove High School.

She has a best friend, Lily (Heather Matarazzo), and an admirer, Michael (Robert Schwartzman), who is also Lily's brother, but she daydreams about Josh (Erik Von Detten), the coolest guy in school.

As the story begins, Mia nervously sets out to present an argument in a class debate. Her mother and Lily try to bolster her confidence, but Mia gets more than nervous, especially when the with-it chicks, led by Lana (Mandy Moore), laugh at her bushy hair and clumpy shoes. She leaves the room at a run, apparently to be sick.

Soon afterward, Mia's mother announces that Clarisse Renaldi, Mia's fraternal grandmother, has come to town and has invited her for tea. (Mia never met her father, who died two months earlier, nor his mother.) Mia finds her grandmother (Julie Andrews) occupying an elaborate embassy, and Mia's amazement compounds when she discovers her grandmother is Queen of Genovia (a tiny country famous for its monarchy and its pears). Mia's father was the heir apparent, which makes Mia a princess and next in succession, a position her grandmother would like her to accept at the upcoming Genovian ball.

Mia panics and runs. Later, with her mother's help, Queen Clarisse gets Mia to begin "princess lessons." The Queen teaches Mia how to "walk, talk, sit, stand, eat, dress" like a princess, and gives her a bodyguard and confidant (Hector Elizondo). Queen Clarisse provides Mia with wardrobe tips, and she enlists a stylist to make Mia into a princess.

When the media learns Mia is a princess, she becomes popular. Her dream date, Josh, invites her to a dance, and she accepts, although it means she must break promises to Lily and Michael. Mia discovers Josh's interest is a ploy for media attention; he and his friends make Mia a target for the paparazzi. After Queen Clarisse speaks some harsh words about Mia's appearance in the tabloids, Mia renounces the crown. Even so, Queen Clarisse gives Mia a beautiful diary as a gift for her sixteenth birthday, explaining that it is from her father. She also insists that Mia attend the ball, where she must formally refuse the title of princess.

Mia prepares to run away rather than face the Genovian Ball. As she packs, she finds a letter from her father in the diary. His loving words help her accept her role. She appears at the ball and makes a speech that shows her new poise. Both Lily and Michael forgive her, and her mother promises to move with her to Genovia.

As you can see, this plot summary of the film contains the central makeover motif—the change in the heroine as she becomes more attractive, more confident and more independent. *The Princess Diaries* also has specific parallels to *Now, Voyager*: Mia and her mother live together, as Charlotte and her mother did, in a distinctive home in a distinctive neighborhood; Mia's mother, like Charlotte's, has confidence and presence; Mia, like Charlotte, has no confidence and feels unattractive; and Mia and Charlotte each have female champions in Lily and Lisa, while meaner, more soignée females tease them. Lana and her posse tease Mia the way that June "rags" Aunt Charlotte. Unavoidable situations force both women to shed their before skins, and both put themselves in the hands of others for their makeovers. In her after persona, Charlotte attracts desirable, wealthy, blonde Elliot Livingstone, who seems perfect, but who can't return her passion. Mia, similarly, attracts popular, wealthy, blonde Josh Richter who wants her only for her star quotient. Each woman finds a true lover, but neither relationship reaches traditional closure: Charlotte and Jerry will create a union built around Tina, while Mia and Michael are separated by Mia's royal rank. Charlotte and Mia each have a talisman: Jerry's camellias give Charlotte courage, and her father's note does the same for Mia. Both women accept their inheritances and plan to use them to benefit others.

Casey Robinson stayed close to Olive Higgins Prouty's novel, and *Now, Voyager* even incorporated those dissolves to turning pages to signal its authenticity. In contrast, the film adaptation of *The Princess Diaries* rings many changes on Meg Cabot's novel. The screenplay does not reflect the intimacy of Cabot's diary format; the location shifts from New York to San Francisco; and some supporting characters are deleted and one is added—the security chief (Elizondo) who becomes a romantic interest for Andrews.

A major change in situation ups the emotional ante in the film. While Cabot gives Mia a *living* father who cannot produce another heir and a grandmother she knows but does not like, Wendkos has Mia's father die before the action begins and she sets the first meeting between grandmother and granddaughter after his death.

The screenplay alters its source material most significantly, though, in its presentation of Mia's appearance, behavior, and makeover. In Cabot's novel, fifteen-year-old Mia describes herself as a "dishwater blonde" with "a really big mouth, and no breasts and feet that look like skis" (45). Lily has told her that her gray eyes are her "one attractive feature" (45). Mia is sure she is "the biggest freak in the entire school" (1). Her daily anxieties about passing math, negotiating her friendship with Lily, getting used to her mother's romance with her algebra teacher, and wishing for some male attention sound like fairly common concerns of young teen girls. Mia's diary contains engaging "Things to Do" lists (à la *Bridget Jones*) with groceries Mia must remember to get (cat litter is a recurring item), and suggestions for self-improvement such as "be more assertive" (6).

Director Garry Marshall briefly nods to Mia's anxieties about her appearance as the film opens. Viewers see her examining herself in a full-length mirror and sighing "As always, that's as good as it's going to get," but the film offers a lot less information about Mia's personality, and perhaps there's a reason for that. As Elvis Mitchell notes, "this is *Pretty Woman* for children" ("Pygmalion for Another Fair Lady"). Sketching surfaces instead of suggesting depths, Marshall hauls out the before makeover code, using the most rudimentary signs to indicate that Hathaway is *playing* plain.

Hathaway's Mia enters the film as Vale does, first alone in her room, then descending the staircase at her mother's summons. Time warp! Mia wears clunky shoes and messy socks, and her sloppy school uniform masks her figure. Hollywood hangs on to a formula that works, and shades of Charlotte Vale are particularly prominent in Mia's before persona from the neck up: she wears glasses; she has heavy, dark brows; she has dark, frizzy, uncontrollable hair.

Wait a minute, though. The modern context *should* render this formula anachronistic. Don't all women wear clunky shoes? Aren't glasses newly cool? Isn't big hair perfectly fine? Aren't natural brows, à la Penelope Crux, sexy?

But it's apparent we are never meant to see the before Hathaway as real. The sound track cheerfully asserts that Mia is "supergirl" as she descends the staircase, suggesting the plot's trajectory. While Davis created a character around and through Charlotte Vale's before persona, Hathaway wears the signifiers of ugliness the way one would wear Groucho glasses, eyebrows and moustache—for fun. As Anderson points out, "[Hathaway's] so gorgeous in this [before] state that any red-blooded American boy would chew off his own arm for the chance to speak to her" ("Glasses").

Mia's friend, Lily, shades Hathaway's before portrait. Matarazzo, a more experienced actress than Hathaway, starred as Dawn Wiener in *Welcome to the Dollhouse* (1996), a film exploring the reality of a plain preteen ostracized by her classmates. (There's no makeover in that story.) In *The Princess Diaries*, Matarazzo is, in effect, still cast as Dawn Wiener. Hathaway is *playing* at being an oddball; Matarazzo is relentlessly portrayed as a real one. Insane hairdos overpower her expressive face, and the camera shoots her in the least flattering ways until the final scene, when she, too, appears as a glamorous guest (recipient of a makeover?) at Mia's big party.

In the novel, both Mia and Lily champion environmental causes. In fact, Mia's father pays her for taking "princess lessons" by contributing to

Greenpeace. In the film, most of the activism belongs to Lily. Perhaps we are to read Mia's individuality in her willingness to choose an eccentric, politically-charged person for a friend instead of being one herself. Although it's reassuring that Mia is less alone than Charlotte Vale, it's upsetting that her best friend acts as a label, not a person, and that Mia's character loses the hipper sensibility Cabot gives her.

In her emotional, pre-makeover state, Charlotte Vale's anger and self-loathing reveal themselves in her nervous hands and halting step. In Cabot's novel, Mia mentions her awkwardness, which she sees as klutzi-ness of epic proportions. On the screen, her clumsiness translates into slapstick. We are supposed to chuckle when Mia bashes trash cans with her scooter, giggle as she wrestles into pantyhose in the backseat of a limo, and laugh out loud when she brains her gym teacher with a soft-ball. Watching her start a fire at a Genovian Embassy dinner? A real scream. On the day we saw this film, however, we could hear only the munching of popcorn as the audience sat, unamused, through the "funny" stuff. Hathaway has less than great timing, and the script fogs, instead of clarifies, what's going on. The slapstick continues after Mia's makeover, so it may be meant to show she has not become a perfect person. At least the gags do not cement the mean idea that only ugly girls are klutzy. There's plenty of meanness in *The Princess Diaries* to go around, though, without that implication.

Mia's clumsiness appalls her grandmother, who acts as the catalyst for her makeover. As Clarisse Renaldi, Julie Andrews adds a bit of zest to an otherwise bland film. Her casting should pack a makeover wallop. If Andrews, stage star of *My Fair Lady*, does not know how to turn a "cab-bage leaf" into a lady, who does? In the novel, Cabot makes Mia's grand-mother an arrogant, vain woman with tattooed-on eyeliner and lots of purple clothes. Her erratic princess lessons contain information about manners and marriage proposals. She's intriguing, but not an appealing person, and she's not above alerting the press to Mia's status. A cuddly, protective grandma? No way.

For the most part, Wendkos keeps Grandma Clarisse's regal cold-ness, but loses her intriguing eccentricity. An added scene attempts to create a touch of intimacy between the Queen and her granddaughter, but it falls flat. Mia convinces Clarisse to spend a day seeing the city instead of practicing princess posture—fun instead of torture. This starts out well, and Julie Andrews's character looks as if she enjoys eating a corndog and playing penny arcade games. Because they are alone and in neutral territory, one might expect the two women to use this time for meaningful conversation. They seem on the brink of doing so when the scene collapses into more meaningless slapstick, scuttling the suggestion of developing closeness. Leah Rosen thinks this section of the film adds up to "exuberant fun" (33), but we found it dreadful.

Queen Clarisse's defining moment remains an earlier scene in which she casts a derisive eye on her granddaughter as she estimates the work that must be done to turn Mia into a princess. Clarisse demonstrates distress as she eyes her granddaughter from head to toe, making comments to her glamorous, note-taking assistant—well within Mia's hearing—as she enumerates targets for improvement: "Bad posture, hair style, complexion, bushman eyebrows, nails, clothing." Only Mia's eyes, neck and ears meet with her approval. The business-like nature of her appraisal turns Mia into a commodity desperately in need of better packaging. All the Queen's princess-producing techniques have a mean aftertaste. For example, Clarisse teaches Mia to sit properly at the table by tying her to her chair with Hermes scarves. After she works on Mia's deportment, she calls in an expert for Mia's makeover, and this scene differs significantly from Cabot's text.

The makeover occupies two-and-a-half pages of Cabot's almost 300-page novel, and it recalls Prouty's scene in *Now, Voyager*. Remember, the book is written as a *diary*, so Mia's voice relates the process, as Charlotte's memory did in Prouty's novel. Mia's grandmother takes her to a trendy New York salon where everyone "is dressed all in black." The stylist, Paolo (Larry Miller), Mia tells her diary, "takes unfashionable, frumpy people, like me, and makes them stylish" (128). Mia gets the works: haircut, color, makeup, fake fingernails.

As Charlotte does, Mia complains that the makeover hurts. As Charlotte does, Mia complains of loss of control. She, too, is shorn. Mia describes Paolo lifting her hair and saying, "It must go. It must *all* go." Mia tries to explain why she let the makeover happen: "It's sort of hard when all these beautiful, fashionable people are telling you how good you'd look in this, and how much that would bring out your cheekbones, to remember you're a feminist and an environmentalist" (128). As Charlotte does, Mia expresses discomfort about losing her identity when she complains about her grandmother: "She's turning me into someone else" (129).

Casey Robinson's makeover scene that turned Charlotte's makeover into comedy didn't make the final cut. Wendkos's burlesque version of Mia's makeover, however, centers *The Princess Diaries*. The stylist's name is the same, but the film makeover has a nastier tone.

The audience sees Paolo arrive at Queen Clarisse's mansion armed with a blow dryer and a curling iron, accompanied by two hard-looking female assistants. He asks for the "beautiful young lady," and when he sees Mia, he screams in horror. He tells her she has "hair like a wolf," and when he tries to brush her thick, curly mane, his hairbrush snaps in two. As he plucks her eyebrows, Paolo wisecracks that they should have the names, "Frida and Kahlo" (a direct reference to the unibrowed Mexican artist, Frida Kahlo). He also tells Mia that "if Brooke Shields married Groucho Marx, their child would have these eyebrows." Paolo makes it clear that he finds Mia in her before state an acceptable target for ridicule.

In what has to be an allusion to *Now, Voyager,* Paolo removes Mia's dark-rimmed glasses and asks her if she has contacts. Mia says she does, but doesn't like to wear them.

"You do now," Paolo replies, snapping the glasses in two, à la Dr. Jaquith.

The camera shoots Mia's makeover in a series of close-ups and extreme close-ups, focusing on nails, brows, and other aspects of her appearance. Never are we privy to Mia's thoughts. She drifts through the process, plugged into her headphones instead of worrying about the changes, as she did in Cabot's novel. Finally, we watch from behind her chair as she examines her new self in the mirror. Still, she says nothing.

Cabot's incipient princess has some post-makeover funkiness—a short, short do reminiscent of Charlotte's and of Mia Farrow's sensation-causing *Rosemary's Baby* Sassoon haircut. In the film, Mia emerges from her treatment ironed flat of anything unique, processed into a human Barbie doll. Her after appearance includes the mandatory smooth, straight mane, arched brows, and full make-up. Wendkos does not let Mia comment on her transformation, but we get a hint that she isn't entirely thrilled about it when she wears a hat to school to cover her newly smooth tresses. Queen Clarisse has already been working on her wardrobe, insisting on tan hose (ugh) and dark pumps that resemble Naturalizers, leg and footwear that look way too frumpy for Mia, but a trimmer leg and foot do fit the after code.

Two later scenes show Mia wearing glamorous, form-fitting garb, another after requirement. At a state dinner, Mia sports a retro, clingy knit cocktail dress that Charlotte Vale could have worn in the forties, and, at the Genovian ball, she floats in a strapless tulle gown and a sparkling Cinderella-like tiara. Part of the spin-off merchandising for this film offered copies of that tiara shrink-wrapped to VHS tapes of the film so that little girls could imagine themselves undergoing princess makeovers while they watched. Charlotte Vale has time to live her way into her remade self. In the *Princess Diaries,* however, Mia's makeover parallels her "outing" as a princess, and she is thrust into the public eye without much time to look herself over.

In Cabot's novel, Mia's new appearance and position trigger a break with Lily and virtual exile at school. During her isolation, Mia makes friends with Tina Hakim Baba, the only other girl in school who has a bodyguard. The other students have ostracized Tina, but Mia comes to know and like her and her family.

Mia's isolation ends when the popular kids begin to seek her out. Through her experience with them, Mia learns that wealth, position, and beauty attract false followers. Josh Richter invites her to a school dance only to grab media attention for himself. Cabot ends her novel shortly after this dance, when Mia reconnects with Lily and realizes that it's Michael she truly likes. Mia's comfortable again in her own environment, and she has Tina, one more friend than she had before. Prouty's novel ends similarly, with Charlotte at last comfortable in her home and with a Tina of her own. The film adaptation of *The Princess Diaries* deletes Tina, diminishing the importance of female friendship, as Casey Robinson's screenplay did to Prouty's novel.

The film adaptation does show the temporary rift Mia's makeover creates between Mia and Lily. Mia's new look and expensive new backpack convince Lily that Mia wants to join Lana and her posse—the popular girls. In self-defense, Mia tells Lily about the whole princess thing as a way of explaining her physical change. The implication is that everyone understands princesses should look a certain way. Lily accepts the explanation, and the girls work at re-establishing their friendship.

The film also features nasty Josh's grab for fifteen minutes of princess-dating fame, but it replaces the low-key school dance with a wilder beach party and a vile example of female insensitivity reminiscent of June's thoughtless treatment of her Aunt Charlotte. Lana, the leader of the in-chicks, cooks up a trick to embarrass Mia. At the beach party, she and her clone girlfriends lead the media, helicopters and all, to the cabana where Mia is changing. Smirking as they pull, they yank down the tent walls down to reveal a partly nude princess. Casting throws a curve here. Mandy Moore plays the evil Lana, but she also gets to do a snappy rendition of "Stupid Cupid," a concession to her pop-star status that pops her out of the film's fiction. Is she still a bad girl when she's singing? Moore presents an image of teen perfection—a reason for young viewers to long to make themselves over. She's glossily groomed, trendily dressed, sexually knowing à la Britney Spears. Charlotte gets to silence June, and then to enlist her as a friend. Mia pushes an ice cream cone into Lana's chest—a more Freudian, but less satisfying, resolution.

In contrast to Cabot's novel, which concludes quietly, the film lifts Mia out of her environment by adding a grand ball, at which Mia must accept or decline princess status. When she finally decides to become Genovia's princess, Mia arrives late, wet, and clad in a sweatshirt. Instead of being embarrassed, Mia's able to use her newly acquired princess poise to speak to the audience; she doesn't need the princess attire to perform. Paolo the hairdresser appears in a minute to undercut the idea that a princess can look like a person. He whisks her away to render her perfect, and it isn't the last whisking off. After the ball, Mia travels to Genovia, which looks suspiciously like Disney World, where she will assume her duties.

In *Now, Voyager*, the audience gets to see Charlotte's trip and its aftermath. In *The Princess Diaries*, we leave Mia as she reaches Genovia. The earlier film uses its central makeover as a starting point for the regeneration of Charlotte's soul. Little more than Mia's speech at the Genovian Ball suggests the depth of her transformation. It would be asking too much for this fluffy teen comedy to parallel the depth of *Now, Voyager*. Still, both films, so far apart in time and tone, reveal makeover issues we will use as touchstones for the genre.

The Princess Diaries continues the assumption (with few exceptions) that the star of a makeover film must first be perceived as beautiful, or at least glamorous. Surely this external convention subverts any truth about internal beauty the story tries to deliver.

These films, 59 years apart, both present female unattractiveness and its reverse as an apparently unchanging list of quantifiable physical qualities. Only Davis's considerable ability makes her appearance creditable, more than a mawkish representation of ugliness, while Hathaway wears her "ugly" signifiers like a mask.

In each of these films, the heroine is invisible before her makeover. Handsome Elliot Livingston wonders why he has never "seen" Charlotte before; Charlotte points out that he has seen but not noticed her. In *The Princess Diaries,* a male student almost sits on Mia because he simply doesn't see her. Years of makeover films repeat this premise: only *beautiful* women are visible.

Although they seem to be "invisible," the heroines are bright, interesting people before their makeovers. Charlotte reads widely and carves exquisite ivory boxes. Mia does yoga, climbs rocks, holds down a job, supports her friend, and helps her mother.

The subtext of tense female-female relationships troubles both plots. Women cause problems. It's Charlotte's mother who calls her child an "ugly duckling," and she who works to keep Charlotte exactly that. It's

Jerry's wife who drives their youngest child to Cascade. *The Princess Diaries* provides Mia with a supportive mother and a good friend, and that's a big step forward. Unfortunately, it parallels the stereotypical sub-plot of its predecessor. Most women dismiss Charlotte before her makeover, just as those super-mean chicks in *The Princess Diaries* see pre-makeover Mia as part of a species different from theirs. Both makeover films show that plain women are fair game; both films show the fright-ening power of women who have internalized (and externalized) the beauty codes.

Within the story, Vale herself raises the issue of beauty as the most powerful enabler. Charlotte tells Tina (Jerry's child) that instead of pret-tiness, she should seek "a light that shines from inside you because you're a nice person." Yet, Vale doesn't settle for fostering that light. Tina's glasses disappear. (Has Vale snapped them?) Tina gets a new mini–Charlotte hairdo and a frilly party dress as well. When Queen Clarisse goes to work on Mia, she waves some classic novels at her, but the Queen concentrates on her granddaughter's external changes.

Other people control the makeovers. In the novel and in the film, Charlotte has little to say about what is done to her. The chopping of hair and that cavalier snapping of the glasses are controlling acts. Does *Now, Voyager* encourage women to let others decide what is best for them? This notion is more dangerous for a young audience. Mia has no control over the physical changes that process her into a princess.

Then there's the romance question. Although Charlotte's makeover is not initiated as a means of attracting men, it certainly has that effect, reinforcing the belief that beauty alone feeds desirability. In *The Princess Diaries*, Michael likes Mia before the makeover, so we have to assume it's her real self he sees. How common is such vision? Without it, makeover films could be read as injunctions to women to fix themselves up or to prepare for celibacy.

Besides raising these issues, *Now, Voyager* and *The Princess Diaries* cement their membership in the makeover genre by revealing traces of a shared literary source. It's a story we all know, a story in which the makeover *is* the story, and it begins like this: *Once upon a time, there was a girl whose dear mother died. Soon her father married a stepmother, who proved to be hard-hearted and wicked.*

So Many Cinderellas

Both *Now, Voyager* and *The Princess Diaries* allude to an important, ancient origin for all makeover plots: Cinderella and Cinderella stories. When Casey Robinson rewrote the screenplay of *Now, Voyager,* he consciously tried to fashion a Cinderella story, and Gina Wendkos's screenplay for *The Princess Diaries* elaborates on the idea of the Cinderella moment—she creates a special ball at which Mia has to appear as a possible heiress to the throne. Wendkos also ends her screenplay with a long shot of a palace fit for Prince and Princess Charming, certainly a Cinderella finish. Centuries of Cinderella tales have prepared audiences for transformation as an integral part of a central female character's quest. After all, Cinderella's power stems from a magical change in appearance, which, in one focused moment, reveals her beauty to the world.

Cinderella tales have conditioned us to expect certain after components as part of that moment: slippers, delicious gown, special hair and jewels. (Remember the focus on Charlotte Vale's feet—first the laced oxfords, then the perfect pumps.) Part of the pull of Annie Leibowitz's photo of Susan McNamara lies in its confirmation of the Cinderella thesis: the right collection of accessories will transform a woman into a beauty icon.

Such a transformation is found in the ancient "Yeh-hsien," recorded in China in the ninth century and thought by many folklorists to be the oldest Cinderella story. Some of the narrative feels unfamiliar to modern Western readers: lonely Yeh-hsien befriends a fish, and the fish comes to love her. When her jealous stepmother kills and cooks the fish, magic stems from its bones. A man, a god come down to earth, instead of a fairy godmother, heralds the magic.

This tale also contains many familiar elements: a wicked stepmother and sisters who treat Yeh-hsien like a servant, a festival (similar to a ball), and Yeh-hsien's transformation into a beauty who wears special clothing: "a cloak of stuff spun from Kingfisher feathers and shoes of gold" that make her as lovely "as a heavenly being" (Tatar 108).

Yeh-hsien runs from the festival and is identified by her lost slipper, which is "an inch too small" (Tatar 108) for every other woman who tries it. In the context of early Chinese culture, which valued tiny female feet enough to make foot binding an accepted practice, this detail, repeated in Cinderella tales that followed, fits.

As does the teller of "Yeh-Sien," each subsequent teller inflects the tale for his or her culture. Most tellers elaborate on the makeover—the assumption of the regal garments—and the moment when Cinderella, so altered, appears before the fashionable world and the Prince. Some Cinderella tales present feisty and active heroines, but the version our culture most often retells—Charles Perrault's—does not.

Because almost all film adaptations of "Cinderella" stem from Perrault and are embellished with details from a later version told by Jacob and Wilhelm Grimm, it helps to remember those famous Cinderellas, each a tale that fits its time, before we consider the debt that the following Cinderella films owe to their sources: Walt Disney's *Cinderella* (1950), Rodgers and Hammerstein's *Cinderella* (1965), Disney's remake of Rodgers and Hammerstein's *Cinderella* (1997), Bryan Forbes's *The Slipper and the Rose* (1976), Andy Tennant's *Ever After* (1998), and Disney's *The Confessions of an Ugly Stepsister* (2002). Perrault's French version, "Cendrillon ou la petite pantoufle de verre," "Cinderella; or, The Little Glass Slipper" (1967), perfect for conditioning seventeenth-century maidens for the hardships of arranged marriages and blended families, places the emphasis on Cinderella's sweetness, taste, and placid obedience. Cinderella's mother has died before the start of the tale, but in this version her father remarries and listens only to his new wife. (Twentieth-century retellings of the story generally kill off her father. It's too upsetting for modern viewers to see a living father so in thrall to his new wife that he neglects his only biological child.) The stepmother dominates the household, privileging her own daughters and relegating Cinderella to the status of servant. One of her new stepsisters christens her "Cinderbritches" because she spends so much time sitting on the hearth. The other, who is kinder, changes it to Cinderella, which sounds better, though it's still demeaning (Hallett and Karasek 55).

When the invitation to a ball comes from the palace, the stepmother says it would be inappropriate for Cinderella to go. She is, after all, a servant, with no finery. Still, Cinderella cheerfully helps the stepsisters select their ball gowns and dress their hair. Only when they leave does Cinderella acknowledge her sadness.

Her chance comes when her godmother, a fairy, appears to transform her. Perrault's version gives us the pumpkin-turned-carriage, the mice and rats turned into horses and footmen, and the injunction to leave at twelve when the spell dissolves. Most importantly, Cinderella gets the perfect ball gown, jewels, and those glass slippers.

At the ball, she charms everyone, including the Prince and her stepsisters, who do not recognize her. Each night of the balls (there are three) she appears in a grander gown, and each night she runs from the palace at the stroke of twelve. On the last night, she loses her glass slipper. The search for the foot that fits the slipper culminates in Cinderella's triumph. The Prince marries her and takes her to the castle. Even then, despite their behavior toward her, she shares her good fortune with her stepsisters, finding them husbands of note. To the end, her charm and good humor dominate. Perrault obviously uses his Cinderella tale to reinforce the importance of correct social behavior.

The Brothers Grimm, however, who aimed at elevating what they saw as crucial German virtues, emphasize the idea that Cinderella is unfailingly loyal to the memory of her dead mother and that all the magic stems from her mother's love, which has not died. Nature plays an important role in their version, for Cinderella's empathy with the natural world leads to her rewards. In the Grimms' "Cinderella," "Aschenputtel," the stepsisters do not get away with their bad behavior; the Grimms make it clear that evil reaps unpleasant consequences. First published in 1857, this tale features an unselfish and compliant Cinderella who asks for a simple tree branch as a souvenir when her father takes a trip. (Her greedy stepsisters ask for jewels and gowns.) Cinderella plants the twig upon her mother's grave and waters it with her tears. Two doves come to live in the tree and befriend Cinderella.

The stepmother makes Cinderella into a servant who sleeps on the hearth, and the stepsisters, "whose features were beautiful and white, but whose hearts were foul and black," mistreat her terribly (Tatar 117). When the palace announces a ball to find a bride for the Prince, the stepmother tells Cinderella she can go if she completes her tasks and finds something to wear. Then, she gives Cinderella some awful tasks. She throws a basket of lentils into the ashes in the hearth and tells Cinderella she must pick them out. This would be impossible, but Cinderella gets help from her doves. The stepmother doubles the task, and Cinderella still completes it, but the stepmother refuses to let Cinderella go because she has nothing to wear.

Cinderella knows where to turn. She runs to the tree growing from her mother's grave. The doves throw down a beautiful dress, and Cinderella is so transformed that her stepmother and sisters do not recognize her, believing her to be the daughter of some "foreign king" (Tatar 119).

The balls repeat and each night Cinderella's gowns are grander. Each night, the Prince tries to escort Cinderella. (Male characters in the Brothers Grimm version are more active than in Perrault's telling, but they couldn't be called intellects.) The Prince himself comes looking for Cinderella each night, and her *father* helps him; of course neither recognizes the girl dressed in rags, lying in the ashes as the beautiful Princess. In this version, no stroke of midnight governs the spell. "She wanted to leave," we are told, probably because she does not want the Prince to discover her humble status.

On the final night of the ball, Cinderella loses her slipper (a golden shoe), and the Prince initiates the search. When their turn comes, both stepsisters mutilate themselves at the urging of their mother. To try to make the shoe fit, one cuts off her toe and the other her heel. Their mother's reasoning is that a princess does not have to walk. (This remark echoes early Chinese culture in which a lady with bound feet was taught to see her immobility as proof of her status.)

Inexplicably, the Prince accepts the first sister, then the second, recognizing their fraud only when Cinderella's dove tells him "blood's in the shoe" (Tatar 121). Finally, he gets it right, and the doves confirm his choice.

Unlike Perrault's tale, which emphasizes compliance, this version stresses maternal love and a connection to nature. Unlike Perrault's heroine, who accepts her place until the fairy godmother appears, Cinderella acts in her own behalf. Although she mourns, she also plants, waters and visits the tree. She must seek and nurture the magic force that will save her. Also unlike Perrault's, this tale takes a violent revenge on the stepsisters, and is, therefore, a cautionary tale; if you mistreat your stepsiblings, you, too, might suffer thus. As Cinderella becomes the princess, the doves peck out the eyes of the wicked stepsisters as punishment for their cruelty.

Both Perrault's and Grimms' *Cinderellas* provide fascinating material for modern retellings because they grate against modern sensibilities. Why does Cinderella obey her mean stepmother and sisters with such docility? Why do the stepmother and sisters hate her so? Why does the *Prince* get to choose? For anyone interested in the makeover genre, the issue of recognition provokes specific questions: Why doesn't the Prince recognize Cinderella without her finery? Why does he need that slipper or foot confirmation that he has the right one? What do the makeovers in these tales tell us? Shouldn't modern film retellings consider these questions?

Walt Disney's Cinderella *(1950)*

Fifty-one years before *The Princess Diaries,* Walt Disney combined elements from the Grimm and Perrault's stories in his version of *Cinderella* (1950). Audiences liked Disney's musical, animated retelling, still the most familiar film Cinderella, more than critics, who found it less compelling than Disney's first full-length animated feature, *Snow White* (1937) (Eliot 208). *Cinderella* grossed $5 million, a small figure by today's standards, but enough to make Disney flush again after some lean years, "prompting *Variety* to compare the studio's good fortune to that of its heroine" (Eliot 208–209).

Disney claims to have based his version on "Charles Perrault's 'Cinderella,'" but Jack Zipes notes that when Disney adapted fairy tales, he neglected to identify sources fully, and he tended to turn tales into something particularly American (Tatar 347). In the case of *Cinderella,* Zipes has a point. (Disney's current retelling of *Rapunzel* (2002) almost does away with the traditional sources and warps the tale out of recognition.) Generally, Disney's *Cinderella* follows Perrault, but he elaborates on Cinderella's connection with nature, as do the Grimms, and he uses subplots to create a democratic flavor. The title frame shows the pumpkin carriage, suggesting Perrault, while another frame concluding the credits features the glass slipper flanked by two birds (those doves from the mother's grave), demonstrating the importance of animals to story.

In this telling, Cinderella's father dies and leaves her with her evil stepmother and two mean, ugly stepsisters. Cinderella performs household tasks and befriends the mice and other animals around the chateau. Meanwhile, in the castle, which looms over the village, the king hounds the Prince to marry and plans a ball as a marriage mart. When the ball is announced, Cinderella longs to go, and is told she can *if* she finishes her tasks and finds something to wear (shades of the Brothers Grimm). The birds and mice remake one of her mother's old dresses for her while she works, but the stepsisters rip it from Cinderella's body. That's when the fairy godmother enters and does her Perrault-inspired magic.

Cinderella goes to the ball and enchants the Prince, leaving a little too late. The Prince finds her slipper and sends out emissaries to locate the young maiden who can slip it on. Although Cinderella's stepmother doesn't recognize her at the ball, she finally does figure things out. She locks Cinderella away, but the mice release her, the slipper fits, and you know the rest.

This plot summary shows Disney's debts to Perrault and the Brothers Grimm, but it doesn't quite make clear the importance of the mice and the other animal characters. In the Grimm version, the birds change Cinderella's fate; Disney's mice do that, but they also add humor, and their fortunes become an important subplot, occupying as much film time as the main story. Their plotline details several comic attempts to thwart the evil cat, Lucifer. Cinderella champions the mice and protects them. The very American subtext here focuses on the rights of the small and underprivileged versus the absolute rule of Lucifer, a lazy, mean despot and the special pet of Cinderella's stepmother. Of course, the mice triumph and help Cinderella to do the same.

Disney's other subplot gives the king a comic counselor (an effete, vaguely Russian aristocrat) and a burning wish for grandchildren. There's no queen in this tale, so the subject of heirs becomes a male preserve. This subplot, besides adding comedy, also exposes the foolishness of monarchs. The king is an often bad tempered, silly old autocrat, obsessed by his single vision. These subplots put a "Made-in-the-USA" stamp on the tale, and the image of Cinderella especially gives the film a timely, American slant.

The title song proclaims Cinderalla's beauty, and in this version, Cinderella is lovely in a very fifties way. Since this song opens the film, her loveliness is never in question, even though the name *Cinderella*, according to the Grimms and Perrault, is a mocking insult used by the stepmother and stepsisters. From the first line of music, this *Cinderella* follows the movie makeover rule that the audience should know the heroine never could *be* plain or, apparently, even disheveled. Many critics have pointed out "all [Disney's] animators were male" (*Happily* 51). Disney's Cinderella certainly fits the general idea of a dream girl a group of fifties males might create.

Charlotte Vale, as she was before, illustrates Hollywood's criteria for plain women, but Cinderella tales have their own special set of before signifiers, the tokens of poverty: filth and ragged clothing. Most film versions downplay these, refusing to let their heroines, even temporarily, look so downtrodden. Disney's Cinderella has to do a servant's tasks, but she remains clean and fetching. Never does she sleep on the hearth, and never does she wear even a cute smear of ashes. If you didn't know why she was called Cinderella, this film would hardly help you figure it out. Then, there's her physical image. Disney's Cinderella is quite perfect. Disney and his crew had had practice creating a nubile heroine in Snow *White (1937)*. She has an oval face, arched, plucked brows, and honey-colored hair worn simply down in waves or pulled back with a ribbon or kerchief.

She's thin and lithe and graceful, in her slightly full knee-length skirt, apron and jumper top (similar outfits are a staple before look in live action makeover films as well). No rags for her. Her apron has one tiny rip—a sop to poverty. She moves with grace, her little feet in ballet slippers gliding along and her apron strings floating behind her. Her voice is musical and cultured (like a young Jackie Kennedy's). Every task she accomplishes—washing the floor, feeding the chickens, fixing breakfast—is done with good humor and flair. With the resident mice, she's loving and maternal, dressing them in tiny, adorable clothes.

Disney uses Cinderella's floor scrubbing task as one opportunity to showcase her beauty and show off some animation special effects. As she labors over an enormous marble entry hall, Cinderella sees her reflection in a soap bubble that floats from the bucket. She primps, using the bubble as a mirror. Then a screen full of colored bubbles, each carrying her reflection, shows us the joys of Technicolor. Such special effects demonstrate the sophistication animators had achieved. The bubble scene *is* pretty, but its beauty diminishes the drudgery of Cinderella's task.

Watching her work is like watching Martha Stewart garden or make pasta; she exudes charm and capability. This Cinderella is a fantasy housewife: girlish, playful and efficient, a type that fits the time period. Cinderella matches the image 1950s women's magazines tried to promote, an image Betty Friedan describes in *The Feminine Mystique*: "young and frivolous, almost childlike, fluffy and feminine, passive, gaily content in a world of bedroom and kitchen" (36). Of course, Cinderella *isn't* content; this is not *her* house. American women had left factories and returned to housework after the war, and they were being told that in their homes, they could excel, making cooking, childcare and husband tending an art. If they did this, they could create perfect palaces of comfort for their husbands.

Disney's Cinderella drifts through the tale dreaming of the palace, and it is the first image viewers see. In her opening song, "A Dream is a Wish Your Heart Makes," Cinderella never states a specific dream or wish but keeps the palace, floating in the distance, in view. In fact, that piece of real estate gets much more screen time than the Prince, an almost silent Ken doll. The emphasis is on transporting Cinderella from her current location to the palace, where she can breed those perfect grandchildren for the King via the Prince.

Cinderella stands for female perfection, but her stepsisters provide us with the opposite recipe. Neither Perrault nor the Grimms dwell on the physical unattractiveness of the stepsisters, but Disney cannot resist a heavy-handed treatment of the two. The first thing viewers notice about Drucilla and Anastasia is their big feet. (Their too-short nightgowns highlight this characteristic.) Both ungainly girls have harsh, loud voices, unattractive hairdos, ugly noses, no taste, and no talent. Neither can sing nor play an instrument without torturing her listeners, while Cinderella can sing like a bird. Both have bad tempers, bickering and attacking Cinderella. They are grotesque in contrast to Cinderella's charm. They are *not* at one with nature; no little animals sidle up to them. A cautionary tale for young female viewers is evident in these portraits: if you don't try hard to fit the Cinderella mold, you, too, could be subject to ridicule.

In Cinderella's stepmother, Disney replays an earlier, evil stepmother. She's a polished rendition of the horrendously evil queen Disney presents in *Snow White*. A clear descendant of the queen in *Snow White*, Cinderella's stepmother is tall, dark, and strong featured, like Joan Crawford gone psycho. Her upswept hair bears dramatic gray streaks, a detail that links her to later female baddies like Malificent in *Sleeping Beauty* (1957) and Cruella Deville in *101 Dalmatians* (1961).

The shots of Cinderella's stepmother fit the times. As Giannetti and Eyman point out, Alfred Hitchcock was at his zenith in the fifties (*Flashback* 313), and this film for kids includes elements of the suspense genre. Often shot from below, she casts long, black shadows. The stepsisters are ugly and ridiculous, but Cinderella's stepmother is scary.

It's she who spoils Cinderella's first makeover—yes, there are two. Disney reduces the three-ball sequence as it is presented in Perraults and the Brothers Grimms tales to one night (a convention other Cinderella films follow), but he creates an initial failed makeover for Cinderella before he shows viewers the one that "takes." The mice engineer Cinderella's first makeover by remaking her mother's dress for her. They cleverly change the neckline and add a sash and string of beads, while they sing the catchy "Cinderelly, Cinderelly." The end result is impressive, and when the stepsisters see lovely Cinderella running down the staircase, they whine. How does a makeover that turns the heroine into a beauty affect the women close to her? In this film, the answer could make one avoid makeovers forever. The wicked stepmother points out that the sash and beads now decorating Cinderella's dress used to belong to Drucilla and Anastasia, thus sanctioning their attack.

This added scene demonstrates the epic viciousness of the stepsisters. Like harpies, they rush Cindrella, destroying her dress and leaving her in rags before they flounce off to the ball. If any viewers doubt the

stereotype of female jealousy and the damage it can cause, they have only
to watch the "funny" stepsisters set upon Cinderella. This first makeover
sequence allows Disney to accomplish several objectives: the mice get a
terrific central scene; the contrast between pretty, good Cinderella and
the plain, bad stepsisters (those ravening beasts) is hammered home; and
most importantly, Disney gets double mileage out of the makeover.

There's another reason that the mouse-makeover and subsequent
"rape" by the harpies matters. In her ripped gown, which hangs from one
shoulder, Cinderella looks charming and a little sexy. A battle scene in
George Lucas's *Attack of the Clones* (2002) has a similar result. In the heat
of the fray, a villain conveniently shreds Padme Amidullah's (Natalie Port-
man) jumpsuit to leave her with a bare, beautifully-toned midriff. The teen
boys in the audience get their chance to salivate, but Lucas has done nothing salacious—it was an *accident*. Similarly, in *Cinderella*'s violent scene,
the stepsisters (with a little help from those male animators) rudely rip
Cinderella bare (well, *barer*) and push her towards her second makeover
and a more adult, more magical glamour.

In her mouse-made dress, with a little blue bow tied on top of her
head, Cinderella looks almost as girlish as Walt Disney's Snow White.
The heroine in that earlier film looks about eight or ten when the film
begins, and she looks about eight or ten after the Prince rescues her. In
contrast, Cinderella's "real" makeover completes her transformation into
a woman. To do that, as both the Perrault and Brothers Grimm versions
confirm, you need some powerful, beneficent female magical agent: a fairy
godmother or a dead mother's love.

Lightning bugs blink; their glimmering coalesces in an entrancing
animation touch that introduces the fairy godmother. Disney doesn't try
to keep that level of visual magic going. Instead, he gives her a clever
song—"Bibbidi Bobiddi Boo"—and turns her into a plump bumbler who
can't find her wand and has to be reminded that Cinderella could use a
gown. (You can see her again, times three, in the good fairies in *Sleeping
Beauty*.) Perrault's Cinderella has to help a little in her transformation;
her godmother makes her fetch the pumpkin (Hallett 54). Disney's Cinderella is pretty much a passive bystander, eagerly waiting her turn to be
touched by magic.

The fairy godmother transforms the pumpkin, the mice, and the dog,
saving Cinderella for last, prolonging our anticipation. Finally, she gets
down to makeover business, measuring Cinderella with her wand, examining "[her] size and the shade of [her] eyes," and deciding on something
"simple," but "daring," her remarks emphasizing the nature of the makeover.
The after state must signify Cinderella's return to her rightful role as

respected daughter in the household, with the cleanliness and stylish clothing that position entails, but it must go farther than that to suggest her
maturity and potential; Cinderella must look like a princess. Magic shoots
from her wand, swirls up and around Cinderella, while voices swell in the
background, making it clear that this is *serious* magic. Cinderella looks
down, then pirouettes in a frothy, sparkly champagne-colored gown with
a low, fitted bodice that accentuates her bust. A sleek headband holds back
her upswept hair, and a black ribbon encircles her throat, another sexy
touch. She's thrilled by her after appearance; as she used the soap bubbles
for a mirror, she uses a pond for primping while two of her little bird
friends watch. Her makeover fits the tenor of the times. Alison Lurie points
out that in the fifties there was a "curious split in fashion. Suddenly it
appeared that there were two kinds of women" (78). Fifties designers used
two distinct types of models. Ballet slippers, trousers, full skirts and
jumpers were usually shown on younger models, while pencil slim skirts
and dazzling evening wear called for sophisticated, "super-adult" women.
The truth was, Lurie notes, that most women had both kinds of clothing
(79). Cinderella's "real" makeover takes her from one side of the "curious
split" to the other.

This makeover is certainly potent: one ball, one dance, and the Prince
is hers. In all the film versions of Cinderella, her entrance has to be powerful. After all, in that moment, she tests her makeover appeal. Disney's
version gives Cinderella a significant cue. The Prince has been dismiss-
ing one damsel after another when the king says, "I can't understand it.
There must be at least *one* who'd make a suitable *mother*, a suitable *wife*"
(emphasis ours).

Enter Cinderella, alone, silhouetted against a midnight blue sky. Even
the line of palace guards knows she is the one. Their eyes follow her as
she drifts down the passage to the ballroom. Drucilla and Anastasia have
just been introduced, and they stand closest to the Prince, their plumes
framing Cinderella as she appears in the background. Their clumsiness
again provides the contrast for her grace.

The Prince, instantly struck by her beauty, goes to her and leads her
from the dance floor to the terrace. A silhouette sequence follows, and
then the Prince waltzes Cinderella around in the moonlight, a scene the
animators crafted as a supreme Technicolor moment. From the vantage
point of the carcinogen-wise twenty-first century, their moonlight whirl
reads like an ad for sunscreen. Both the Prince and Cinderella look as if
they have spent way too much time soaking up UV rays. Against their
dark skin, their eyes gleam and their teeth glisten a dazzling, frightening
white.

The dated look of this scene is less important than the result of Cinderella's makeover. After one glance, the King perceives her as the prime breeder for his grandchildren, and he feels so confident that he goes to bed. The Prince and Cinderella sing "So This is Love," the only dialogue until they kiss and the clock strikes twelve. The Prince has one or two lines like, "Why are you leaving?" besides his song, but it's clear that he's smitten. As far as he's concerned, the film is almost over. Cinderella finds out exactly who he is *after* the ball (a conceit that's hard to believe), and falls even more in love (there's the matter of the *palace*). In this film, the Prince does not bother to search for Cinderella. He sends the counselor to do the slipper seeking.

This version keeps the detail that appears in that early Chinese folk-tale—the small size of Cinderella's foot as the determiner of identity. (There's some foreshadowing at the beginning of the film when one of Cinderella's tiny ballet slippers slips off on her way up the staircase; she can't even keep *those* shoes on.) Fruitlessly, those clunky, graceless step-sisters try to squash their feet into the slipper, and before Cinderella gets to try it, the slipper is broken. But she has the mate in her pocket, and it slides onto her mini-foot. The Prince doesn't *have* to be there; her dainty foot stamps her a Princess.

Walt Disney's Cinderella II *(2002)*

A recent addition, *Cinderella II* (2002), a direct-to-video production, speculates about what life in the palace might be like for Cinderella. This weak attempt to capitalize on the characters from the original *Cinderella* relies upon the makeover theme again. A misguided, vaguely threatening palace housekeeper, yet another tall, dark-haired, evil woman, tries to "help" the unprepared Princess find the right way to rule. At first this seems as if it might be interesting, a combination of *Rebecca* (1940) and *Cinderella*, but the tale finds a quick and bland resolution. Cinderella resists the makeover forced upon her—a heavy dress and stiff hairdo. She adds dishes she likes to the menu (chocolate pudding instead of stewed prunes), and she invites her village friends to the ball. Voilà—problem solved. In 2002, Cinderella's character as the perfect fifties housewife links *Cinderella II* to the original, but this stunted sequel hasn't a spark of life.

In the 1950 *Cinderella*, Disney, like Perrault, emphasizes Cinderella's grace and her reward, not her trials. Even more than Perrault, Disney works hard to showcase Cinderella's physical beauty, to diminish her hardship, to illuminate her makeover transition from childish grace to adult glamour, and to escalate the stepmother's darkness and the stepsister's ugliness. Disney exaggerates the conflict between the women, a tendency familiar in makeover films: think of *Now, Voyager.* Charlotte's makeover gives her an entre into the fashionable female community, but it enrages her mother to the point of hysteria.

Why do Cinderella's stepsisters and stepmother hate her? The attack scene tells us they harbor intense jealousy. Why does she obey them? Her demeanor throughout the film suggests that she understands her superiority and is simply waiting for her moment to move to the palace, where she will cheerfully accept new tasks. If you delete the animal fun, and look past the Technicolor extravagance, Disney's *Cinderella* fits the climate of gender politics in the fifties perfectly.

Rodgers and Hammerstein's Cinderella *(1965)*

In 1965, however, in the heat of the civil rights movement, on the edge of the sexual revolution, one might expect a very different retelling. Although both of us remember watching (and liking) Rodgers and Hammerstein's *Cinderella* on *The Hallmark Hall of Fame,* our reviewing left different impressions. This bland Cinderella attempts a little interpretation, but essentially it traces Perrault, channels Disney, and adds some lovely music.

The Hallmark Hall of Fame production starring Leslie Anne Warren as Cinderella and Stuart Damon as the Prince revived an earlier black and white production. (As teens, we thought Damon was hot, and his current *General Hospital* soap-star status proves some still do.) In 1957, Rodgers and Hammerstein received $300,000 from CBS for *Cinderella,* their first television venture (Hyland 257). Initially, this musical was to provide a vehicle for the young British star Julie Andrews, who played Cinderella when the special aired on March 31, 1957 (*Fact Book* 415). Generally, reviewers complained that the music "lacked surges of inspiration," but one can sense, and understand, a reluctance to dismiss a major project by collaborators who had written classics like *Carousel* and *Oklahoma!* (*Fact Book* 415). The broadcast garnered a huge audience, which led the network to reprise *Cinderella* seven years later, in color, with a new cast. Several songs were added, but the book and action remained substantially the same, although the times had changed dramatically. Samuel Goldwyn Home Entertainment and Hallmark Home Entertainment still market the color production, marked with a sticker that declares "A Rodgers and Hammerstein Video Tape."

The first shot, a painted backdrop of a castle, places the focus on that desired property and makes Disney's influence clear. It looks amazingly like the castle that opens Disney's *Cinderella*. Although director Charles S. Dubin was familiar with television, this static opening—held for seven minutes of the overture—signals Rodgers and Hammerstein's Broadway orientation. Television had proven itself worthy of experimental work, like *Marty* (1955), but these collaborators treat *Cinderella* as if it were a stage piece, an approach that mandates visual limitation and stiffness.

The Disney parallels continue, as Cinderella appears wearing a familiar before outfit: ballet slippers, an ankle-length semi-full skirt with a jumper top and a kerchief around her long, dark hair. She's lithe and adorable, and the bodice of her dress shows off her figure. Only her long, straight hair suggests the time—Joan Baez look–alikes were beginning to appear by 1965. Disney's Cinderella had that one little rip to signify her status as servant, but Lesley Ann Warren has two strategically placed smears of soot, one on each high cheekbone, like exaggerated blush.

She's a waif, reminiscent of a makeover doll manufactured by Horseman, available in toy stores around this time. Poor Pitiful Pearl also had the smudges and a homespun dress, but she came with the materials necessary to turn her into a bright-faced, gleaming girl in a party dress and pretty slippers. (You can still find Pearl on eBay, if you are willing to pay $60 or $70.) Like Pearl's, Warren's sooty state is clearly temporary. Cinderella is glowingly lovely from the start, which fits the makeover pattern, of course.

A scene at the beginning of this version gives the Prince some depth and introduces the issue of recognition. He is returning home from a dragon-slaying mission, which is treated quite seriously—not much humor here—and bemoaning the fact that he hasn't yet found his true love. In this mood, he encounters Cinderella, who gives him a dipper of water, even though her stepmother has ordered her to stay inside the house. They meet before the ball, and for Cinderella, at least, it's a significant meeting that plants the Prince's image in her mind. A nice costuming touch hints that they are meant for each other. Both wear the same brown with a splash of orange. After they meet, however, the Prince sings that he would know his true love, *if* he saw her. The positioning of this song throws viewers back to question the meeting between the two. Why can't the Prince *see* her in the before state? This must be another case of plain equals invisible (though she's not *really* plain).

The Prince has a sympathetic family: the Queen (Ginger Rogers) and the King (Walter Pidgeon). Unfortunately, there's little for them to say and less for them to do. When the King leads the Queen to the floor during the ball, expectations rise. Will we get to see Ginger whirl? Inexplicably, they dance for a few seconds only, then the others dancers take over.

The rest of the production disappoints as well. Character development has to depend on lyrics because there's almost no dialogue. The songs are sweet and catchy. Over thirty years have passed, but we could remember the tune of "In My Own Little Corner." Unfortunately, sweet and catchy is not enough to carry the whole production.

Cinderella's tepid, barely interesting interactions with her stepmother (Jo Van Fleet) and stepsisters (Pat Carroll and Barbara Ruick) don't create much conflict. The women hardly address each other, and their body language doesn't suggest tension or any strong emotion. The stepsisters briefly come to life during the ball. There, they sing the song "Merely Lovely," in which they bemoan the eternal male preference for girls who are just attractive. Like Disney's stepsisters they are supposed to be funny. Instead of ripping Cinderella to shreds, they fantasize and sing about it. Disney let hostility become physical while Rodgers and Hammerstein set it to music, but the implication remains the same: beautiful women provoke jealousy.

Not that Cinderella looks plain, or even fatigued *before* her makeover. Even Disney's Cinderella works harder than this one, who seems only to carry cloaks and set dinner tables. Reviewer Jack Gould complained: "Cinderella was lovely to look at, but that's not the same thing as sharing the enchanting transition from a drab kitchen maid to the radiant princess" (*Fact* 415). This version leaves you longing for Disney's mice, or even a few doves.

As Gould points out, placid Cinderella doesn't much need her makeover, and that diminishes the excitement of the moment when it happens. On the night of the ball, she hardly has time to squeeze out a tear before dots of light begin to coalesce into her fairy godmother, à la Disney. Much more elegant than her bibbidi-bobbiding counterpart, Rodgers and Hammerstein's godmother (Celeste Holm) looks like Glinda, the good witch from *The Wizard of Oz* (1939), but her magic comes in glistening spurts from her wand, as it does for the Disney godmother, and she, too, almost forgets to dress Cinderella in a new gown. Her more sophisticated song, "Impossible," makes her seem skeptical of those who believe in magic at first, but then acknowledges the power of magic in everyday life. The catchy tune sounds a bit like "Cockeyed Optimist" played backwards, and it has a similar point, but it's better not to begin that game with Rodgers's and Hammerstein's tunes and lyrics and to concentrate on the makeover.

Cinderella spins around and appears in her frothy, sparkly, champagne-colored dress, the same color as the gown in the Disney version. Lesley Ann Warren's gown has the regal detail of an ermine-bordered neckline, which makes her match the Prince, Queen and King, and her upswept hair is held in place by a sparkling tiara. She belongs with them, as the costuming makes clear. Essentially, though, Warren looks exactly the same after as she did before her makeover. She's got a lovely mature figure, visible in both costumes, but her girlishness is not diminished by her regal garb. She remains an ingénue, without any Bridgette Bardot edge, a truth that may have led Jack Gould to note that he found the production "wholesomely pleasant in spots" (*Fact* 415). To guard against any glimpse of cleavage—horrors!—her gown has a lace insert, like a pilgrim woman's tucker. Her fluffy bangs make her French twist look more like a do a little girl would try for dress-up fun than an adult coiffure.

There's an appropriate cue for this ingénue Cinderella's appearance at the ball as well. The Prince claims "fatigue," and when his father questions him, he says that he's tired of feeling as if all the maidens are seeking a prize, "and," he smiles, "I am the prize." As he says the word "prize," trumpets blare and Cinderella enters, poised, at the top of the steps. Then all sound stops. Her entrance recalls a Miss America contestant's descent to the stage for the evening gown competition. Led by a courtier, Cinderella glides silently down two flights of steps, holding her head high. Obviously, the real prize, a bona fide virgin, has just appeared. The Prince kisses her hand, and the camera moves in for a close-up of her already adoring face; she's in love. As they whirl into a waltz, we have another moment to notice that they match. Both have small crowns circling their dark hair, and both wear ermine and champagne-colored clothing.

There's more dialogue in this scene than in the equivalent scene in Disney's *Cinderella*, but it rings strange when one places it in the context of the musical numbers. The Prince and Cinderella wonder if they have met before. The Prince asks if it's "possible" that they have spoken. (He recognizes a phrase she used when she gave him the water: "You are most kindly welcome.") Cinderella agrees it's "possible."

But as the light of recognition begins to dawn, the lyrics of their next lovely song make it unclear if they *do* remember meeting. The prince sings that he met her only ten minutes before, when she walked in, and Cinderella repeats the verse. This is the second time the position of a song clouds meaning.

But Rodgers and Hammerstein's retelling of Cinderella lacks much meaning anyway. There is an appealing moment when the Prince recognizes Cinderella. The slipper search has found no foot small enough for the slipper. Cinderella hides herself at her stepmother's request when the search finally reaches their dwelling. After the stepsisters and stepmother fail to mash their feet into the shoe, Cinderella comes out to watch the Prince leave. She is *so* passive that her fairy godmother has to goad her into action. At her urging, Cinderella hands the Prince a dipper of water and repeats the phrase, "You are most kindly welcome." Finally, the clouds part, and Prince *knows* who she is. The slipper test that follows is a formality, but this nice touch is too little too late.

Ultimately, Rodgers and Hammerstein's Cinderella provides a vehicle for their pleasant tunes, a summary of Perrault's version of the story, and a minimum of interpretation. Perhaps this version is less anachronistic than it seems. In 1965, two years after our political Camelot had been extinguished, during a time of great change and civil unrest, a clean, uncomplicated, catchy, very fifties *Cinderella,* with its passive heroine, regal makeover and moonlight romance, soothed a stressed audience.

Rodgers and Hammerstein's Cinderella *Redux (1997)*

The most current remake of Rodgers and Hammerstein's *Cinderella* could never be called soothing. Produced by Whitney Houston, the lavish Disney (ubiquitous, no?) remake, also for television, compensates for anything the earlier production lacked in glitz or political correctness. From the first moment, it announces its agenda. The film opens with a camera shot of frantic feet in motion. As the camera tilts up to show the busy owners of those feet, viewers realize that this is a multi-cultural village—so multi-cultural that it's dizzying

Every family is a racially blended family. Cinderella (Brandy, who is African-American) has a white stepmother (Bernadette Peters), a white stepsister (Natalie Desselle), and a African-American stepsister (Veanne Cox). The Prince (Paolo Montalban, who is Asian-Hispanic, has an African-American mother (Whoopi Goldberg) and a Caucasian father (Victor Garber). This concept seems intrusive at first, but you stop noticing as you watch, which is the point.

Besides making the production aggressively multi-cultural, the creators have tried to add some humor by casting Jason Alexander as Lionel, a busybody courtier for the royals. For the most part, this does *not* work, although Alexander gives it what looks like an exhausting go. Goldberg, too, tries to be funny, but you can feel her effort. Her recurring piece of business—a high-pitched whine—irritates instead of amuses. Bernadette

Peters fares a bit better. They've added a song for her, "Falling in Love with Love," which doesn't fit, but at least gives her a chance to perform. She's bitchier than Jo Van Fleet, and she gets to flirt with Jason Alexander, a scene that almost justifies his presence.

Robert Freedman worked on the screenplay, and the changes are especially noticeable in the scenes between Cinderella and the Prince. They have an extended meeting before the ball, and share some obvious similarities. An added shopping sequence introduces Cinderella, who is trailing along after her stepmother and stepsisters. While they squabble, she drifts through the square looking for a friend, or maybe the "Dearest Love in All the World," another added song that's a better fit. Brandy portrays this Cinderella as a sensitive outsider. The Prince, who leaves the palace to mix with the commoners, is clearly the same sort of person. In a nicely choreographed duet, they wander through the square, just missing each other. When they finally meet, their "Dearest Love" duet has established a connection between them. Their dialogue screams political correctness. When the Prince asks Cinderella if she'd like to be treated like a Princess, she answers, "No, like a person."

Such revising could have interesting consequences if it were extended to the whole tale. It's not. Cinderella still moons around, waiting for something to happen. She tells her fairy godmother that she promised to "keep the family together," but that doesn't explain her inertia. Whitney Houston, a much crankier and incredibly frenetic fairy godmother, does tell Cinderella to believe in herself, but her words carry less weight than the makeover that comes next. In 1997 you might expect a funkier makeover to match the rest of the over-the-top costumes and sets. After all, Brandy's before look includes a stylish head wrap and braids. Instead, Brandy's Cinderella gets the same little-girl-dressed-up treatment Lesley Ann Warren received, but, this time, her filmy gown is pale blue to match her eye shadow.

At the ball, the two stepsisters still sing their venal lament, and, after all their conversation, Cinderella and the Prince still don't recognize each other. The Prince oversees the slipper search, and this part of the tale gets an interesting "footlift." It's not the size of the slipper that matters, apparently. As the earlier version did, this production shows close-ups of feet trying and failing to fit the slipper, but it isn't a petite foot that matters here. Some of the feet that don't fit the slipper are too big, and some are too small. So what is it that makes this Cinderella's slipper? Does she have the only size seven foot in the kingdom? We guess viewers are to believe that the slipper, a magic shoe, after all, knows its owner's foot, and be content.

There is a final attempt to make this Cinderella more active. When her stepmother denies Cinderella the chance to try the slipper, Cinderella packs her things and gets ready to leave. But why would she do this, when the thing she wants most—the Prince—stands right behind her in the house? The Prince intercepts her, and all is well. The reworking of the slipper sequence isn't enough to save this *Cinderella*. For all its good intention and obsessive political correctness, the remake ignores larger issues of the tale.

Disney and Rodgers and Hammerstein shape and change *Cinderella*, with music, with humor, and with political correctness, but, generally, they do little to alter the central makeover and its subsequent magic. It's as if imagination weakens at the threshold of transformation, as if that part of the tale can only follow one order: the appearance of the fairy god-mother, the magic change of pumpkin into carriage, the whirl that turns rags into glamour, the arrival at the ball, the arrow of love, the leave-tak-ing, the slipper-confirmed recognition, the ascension to the palace. No matter how it tugs the tale in other places, each of these film versions returns to Perrault's vision of Cinderella's change and the Prince's subse-quent reaction. Can't our time inflect that part of the story as well? A made-for-television British production adds a note on the difficulty of revision.

Written by Nick Drear and directed by Beeban Kidron, this visually exciting *Cinderella* (2000) attempts a new-age retelling of the Brothers Grimm version of the story. Natural images dominate the tale, and Drear keeps Cinderella's father (David Warner) alive (a prisoner of lust). The expressionistic use of fantastic color, light and plenty of watery distor-tion create a magical mood. Its setting suggests a cross between Finland and Disney-world; Kidron shot the film on location on the Isle of Man. The stepmother, Claudette (Kathleen Turner), and her two daughters, Goneril (Katrin Cartlidge) and Regan (Lucy Punch), are costumed like escapees from some soft-porn 1930s Berlin nightclub. (Their names, the same as the bad sisters in *King Lear*, foreshadow their treachery.) The hip, bored Prince Valiant (Gideon Turner) wears black and plays in his own rock band. Those updates sound like enough to reshuffle the traditional tale, but when Cinderella (Marcella Plunkett) needs a dress, the storyline loses its humor, abandons Grimm, and turns to Perrault. Cinderella finds a fairy godmother in the person of a watery nymph (Jane Birkin), and just before she enters the ball, she gets a pair of tiny shoes made of flower petals. The Prince, apparently obsessed with fashion, falls for Cinderella's dress and does not recognize her when she's not wearing it, although she looks exactly the same. Even this odd mélange, as if caught in a lockstep,

abandons its appealing zonkiness and returns to the convention of the slipper search.

Less self-conscious about making the story new than Drear and
Kidron, their attempts to reimagine the whole Cinderella tale characterize Bryan Forbes's *The Slipper and the Rose* (1976), Disney Studios' *Confessions of an Ugly Stepsister* (2002), and Andy Tennant's *Ever After* (1998).
With varying degrees of success, these revisionist adaptations tackle perspective, magic, and makeovers to create new originals of the classic story.

The Slipper and the Rose: The Story of Cinderella *(1976)*

Lush and beautifully filmed in Austria and England, this musical version of Cinderella, starring Richard Chamberlain as the Prince and
Gemma Craven as Cinderella, makes crucial changes in Perrault, altering the focus of the tale.

Most other film versions of *Cinderella* take some pains to define the
roles of stepmother and stepsisters more completely than a folktale could,
and through Cinderella's interactions with these "evil" characters, we can
better measure her good. Instead, *The Slipper and the Rose* opts for sketches
of the stepmother (Margaret Lockwood) and step sisters (Sherri Hew-
son, Rosalind Ayres); they have no musical number and little screen time.
While it ignores them, this version creates a new emphasis. In Perrault's
telling and in most films, the fairy godmother plays an important, if flat,
role, appearing only in time to affect the makeover and to shepherd Cinderella to her position as princess. Little concern is given to her feelings
or her occupation. *The Slipper and the Rose* changes and expands her role
dramatically. Since the Sherman brothers, who wrote the music for *Mary
Poppins (1964)*, also created the music and lyrics for this production, it's
not so surprising that the fairy godmother (Annette Crosbie) has a Pop-
pinsesque flavor. She's a piquant, perky character, who wears a mobcap or
a flat, flower-decorated straw hat and a cloak. She arrives out of nowhere
to help Cinderella prepare an enormous table of vegetables (shades of the
Grimms) and to create beautiful new ball gowns for her stepmother and
sisters, another task she is given. A small dog who appears when she does
befriends Cinderella and fetches the fairy godmother when she's needed,
as would a witch's familiar.

Crosbie's fairy godmother complains bitterly about the volume of
work she must do, and she makes it clear she has other clients besides
Cinderella. A scene set in her home showcases the cackling storybook

chicken, Henrietta, a thank you letter from Robin Hood and Maid Marian, and a manuscript for Scherazade. The fairy godmother also complains that Cinderella is at fault for not managing things better. It's the "young girls," like Snow White, who give her trouble, she claims. Entertaining and clever as it is, all this business distracts attention from Cinderella.

Even Cinderella's makeover provides a showcase for the fairy godmother's magical *method* instead of its result. The whole event has an impromptu feel. In the other film versions, Cinderella's wish to go to the ball draws the fairy godmother to her, but the fairy godmother precipitates events in *The Slipper and the Rose*. On the night of the ball, as the fairy godmother walks through the town, she sees the entrance to the stepmother's home. She walks past, then turns and says to herself, "Oh, why not? I'll just make time." Apparently, Cinderella's makeover and appearance at the ball had not made her to-do list.

Other film fairy godmothers point their wands right at their Cinderellas while they turn them into potential princesses. This fairy godmother does not look at Cinderella as she does her magic. We don't, either. For most of the transformation scene, the camera follows the fairy godmother, who explains she'll have to "borrow" magic till midnight because she's tapped out. First she approaches a dress form, suggesting that Cinderella's ball gown will appear there. What does appear? Regalia for a knight. "You'll have to go as you are," the godmother tells Cinderella.

As she speaks, the camera shifts to Cinderella, whose dress has been transformed into a stiff, shell pink, low-cut gown covered with frills. The fairy godmother whirls a dust mop to create Cinderella's powered wig and fires up some magic powder in an aspic mold to create the glittering glass slippers. More than the other magic makeovers, this transformation has a period costume feel. Dressed in her ball gown and elaborate wig, Cinderella looks like any eighteenth-century lady of fashion. It's difficult to see what sets her apart from the other potential princesses at the ball, who also have stiff dresses and powdered wigs and who are also beautiful.

Most film fairy godmothers oversee Cinderella's trip to the ball and then return to re-transform her happily at the end of the slipper search, but this one must act more aggressively because *The Slipper and the Rose* goes on beyond the slipper search, which fails. When the Prince finally finds Cinderella, his family will not acknowledge her. She is taken off to hide forever in some pleasant, remote place (virtually a prison). Meanwhile, like a hero from an opera, the Prince agrees to marry a princess who will bring his small country political stability, and the wedding begins. It's the fairy godmother who, at the last minute, engineers the marriage between the Prince and Cinderella. Again, the focus is on her as she blows a glass trumpet, announcing Cinderella's march down the center aisle of the cathedral. The fairy godmother's increased importance renders Cinderella *less* so because there's less time spent on her.

The failure of the slipper search, another major change, also leads the tale away from Cinderella. When the search fails, the Prince has the slipper placed in a glass case, on a pedestal in the town square. Seasons pass. Disgusted at his inability to find his true love, he opens the case and tosses the slipper out. The fairy godmother's dog fetches Cinderella and brings her to the slipper. Holding it aloft, she dances with it until the Prince's man sees her and runs to tell the Prince, who arrives on a white charger to carry her off. Again, the focus is on the machinery of the event, not Cinderella.

The Slipper and the Rose should be subtitled *The Story of the Prince*. Although the opening scenes nicely parallel two homecomings—the Prince's from a trip to find a bride, and Cinderella's after her father's funeral—the balance of the film concentrates on the Prince and his problems. The screenwriters, Bryan Forbes and the Sherman brothers, signal their repositioning of the tale by giving the Prince the first scene, the first important song, an officious high chancellor to worry about, a snobbish cousin to plague him, and a man servant, John, who is also his best friend. Cinderella's story seems a counterpoint to the explication of the Prince's position.

Richard Chamberlain, still a powerful draw in the mid-seventies, does a credible job of delivering his musical numbers—often he speaks the lyrics as Rex Harrison did in *My Fair Lady*. It's his body, dressed in magnificent costumes, dancing, posturing, we most often see. It's his face the camera loves, and it's the Prince's mind we come to know. Like the Prince in the updated Rodgers and Hammerstein version, this Prince, Edward, longs to have the freedom of the common folk. This Prince dreams of a "private kingdom" where political necessity and class would not be issues. Although "The Slipper and the Rose Waltz" got an Oscar nomination for Best Song in 1978, the political numbers have more humor and zest, and the Prince, the King, and the other palace officials—all men—sing those songs.

This endless discussion of policy makes *The Slipper and the Rose* a male drama. At the beginning of the film, the Prince sings that he would like to be "two people": one the public monarch and one the private man. It's hard not to see such a twist on character as a *male* makeover—the bland, not-so-bright Princes of Perrault and Grimm are reimagined into this democratic, self-confident man, who steals the show. *The Slipper and the Rose* focuses on its anti-establishment discussion and subordinates Cinderella's makeover to the Prince's.

The film fits its mid-seventies post–Vietnam, post-demonstration context, but the fairy godmother's expanded role is the only hint that a feminist revolution had taken place as well. Very little of the spotlight goes to Gemma Craven's Cinderella, who floats adorably through the film. Like the Disney and the Rodgers and Hammerstein Cinderellas, she's rarely disheveled and always lovely, with a tiny, well-modulated voice. Her details of character, though, don't quite add up. She has the grit to say "I hate you" to her stepmother and sisters, but not to ask to go to the ball. Shots placing her in the Austrian countryside suggest her connection to nature—a Grimm influence—and demonstrate her loyalty to memories when she's shown honoring her parents' grave. She's daring enough to spy on the prince and his man, but she hides after the ball and doesn't appear during the slipper search. Obedience and patriotism triumph over love when she allows herself to be whisked away into exile, complaining meekly only once. She making it clear in her song that she wants the Prince to forget her, to have a politically viable and happy marriage. Finally, exiled, she sits in a flower-bedecked swing, blandly wondering who the Prince will marry when she hears it's his wedding day. The fairy godmother must prod her into action.

These glimpses can't make Cinderella real. Like her stiff ball gown and wig, she remains a shell, an unknown quantity. Linda Seger claims that a film adaptation should retain the heart of the source material (76). *The Slipper and the Rose: The Story of Cinderella*, glistens with clever shots and beautiful scenery. Lively musical numbers and an attractive, competent cast should bring it to life. They can't because this production has a big hole instead of a heart. The heart of Cinderella *is* Cinderella. This version buries her in a flurry of political discussion.

The Confessions of an Ugly Stepsister *(2002)*

Walt Disney's made for television movie, *The Confessions of an Ugly Stepsister* (2002), also shifts perspective, using its vision to reimagine a Cinderella plagued by her own beauty. This film, with its prestigious cast members Johnathan Pryce and Stockard Channing, appeared as part of the "Month of Princesses," a promotional device to tout *Cinderella II* and the latest version of *Snow White*, on ABC's *The Wonderful World of Disney*. Based on a novel by Gregory Maguire, the teleplay, by Gene Quintano, has a derivative feel because it echoes other current popular books and films. For example, it is set in Harlem in the Netherlands, and the pre-commercial break freeze frames, that look like Vermeers, recall the recent bestseller *The Girl with the Pearl Earring*. Like the girl who tells that story, the main character in this "Cinderella," Iris, has artistic leanings.

Then there's the plot machinery of a mother who knows herb lore and must flee from her village because townspeople label her a witch. She and her cloaked daughters escape to a new place, bringing all their belongings. That's a taste of *Chocolat* (2000), isn't it?

The plot of the television production is a strange amalgam, although the opening voiceover assures us that this will be "the complete truth." Margarethe (Channing) and her daughters, Iris (Azura Skye) and Ruth (Emma Poole) settle in Haarlem, where they first take shelter in the home of a master painter (Pryce). Iris catches his eye. Although her mother has convinced her that she's not pretty enough to win any man's eye or hand, Iris finds an admirer in the artist's apprentice, Casper (Matthew Goode). The master insists on painting Iris, and the painting leads to a big commission. As they get to know Haarlem, Iris guides and protects her larger, slower sister, Ruth.

Eventually, Margarethe finds her way into the home of the wealthy Piter Van Den Meer (David Westhead), where she uses her herbs and her wiles to move from housekeeper to wife. Van Den Meer has all his guilders invested in fancy tulips and all his love invested in his beautiful daughter Clara (Jenna Harrison). Gypsies kidnapped Clara in her early years, and now she rarely goes out. Every time she does venture beyond the door, a mysterious fortuneteller (Trudie Styler) accosts her. Clara mourns her dead mother and hates her own spectacular beauty. When the family fortunes are reversed—the value of tulips drops—it's she who takes on the duties of the scullery as Iris practices painting. "From now on, you can call me ... Cinderella," Clara says.

Margarethe drugs her husband so that she can handle family finances. She decides that the only solution is for Iris to attend the upcoming royal ball and to win the Prince's eye and hand, and for Clara to wed a lecherous old man who has been lusting over her. Iris wants Clara to have a shot at the Prince and helps her prepare for the ball. On the night of the event, Ruth drugs their mother and helps Clara begin to dress. Before she can finish, Margarethe awakens and foils their plans. Iris and Ruth end up at the ball and Clara is left at home.

To Clara's surprise, the dreaded fortune-teller enters the house to tell her a valuable secret. She has always been a friend, never a threat. She leads Clara to a beautiful gown and slippers laid away by her mother and she whisks Clara to the ball in a golden coach.

After a series of complicated events, created, apparently, to give Pryce and Channing more to do, the Prince (Mark Dexter) calls at the Van Den Meers the next morning to find Clara, and Casper comes to claim Iris. Clara and Iris have become friends, and Clara gets the Prince's promise that he will care for *all* her family before she accepts him. Unfortunately, Quintano's complex teleplay defuses the essence of Maguire's novel.

The teleplay lets us see the financial necessity driving Margarethe and the fragility of her daughters' position, so it attempts to illuminate her character. It doesn't, however, offer any explanation for Margarethe's cold insensitivity to her own daughters. Only once, does she tell Iris something that sounds admiring of her daughter's "strength." How are we supposed to feel about this stepmother? Maguire's novel provides answers. Its gawky but more introspective Margarethe understands she has blinded herself by keeping her focus always on the expedient. She asks Iris, "Can it be that my eyes have become so crusty with the ugliness they have been exposed to that I don't know how to appreciate the beauty that everyone tells me is here?" (331). It's hard not to feel empathy for her character when she identifies and recognizes her own shortcomings.

In the teleplay and in the novel, Ruth, Iris and Clara begin to form a family even without much nurturing from Margarethe, and their characters are more well-defined than their mother's. Iris's position as the "ugly" stepsister gives the teleplay an intriguing element, and director Gavin Millar uses the focus on Iris effectively. All her conditioning has led Iris to believe she is not attractive to men, and therefore must plan a way to support herself. (It's interesting that Margarethe pronounces nothing about Ruth. Perhaps the mother assumes this girl is so obviously impaired that no comment is required.) When the master chooses Iris as a subject for a painting, she believes her *ugliness* makes her interesting to him, when it's clearly her intelligence that draws him. Perhaps because she feels no pressure to be beautiful, Iris hones her powers of observation and wit.

Conversely, Clara sees her beauty as a handicap to be hidden from the world. She fears staring eyes and objectification. When the master chooses to paint her, she *assumes* it's her lyrical beauty he wants to capture. She dreads the sitting and the attention that will follow. The world, she believes, sees her as a beautiful thing, not a person. It's she who hates the stepsisters and stepmother, not the other way around.

Gradually, Clara welcomes the company of her stepsisters, who want to know her, not just stare at her. She also welcomes the chance to stay at home while Iris goes daily to study art. She likes making pets of the mice and "hiding away" in the kitchen. As a joke, Clara smears her lovely face with ashes because they make her less perfect. She obeys her step-mother and stepsisters so docilely because she *welcomes* this position and the change it brings. In a true reversal of before and after, Clara names herself Cinderella and embraces the hearth.

Clara's second makeover, then, does not make her newly beautiful; she already holds that status—great beauty—all over Haarlem, and it has made her miserable. In the teleplay, after Iris and Casper attempt and fail to transform Clara for the ball, the fortune-teller appears to show Clara her mother's dress, shoes, and jewels. A radiant Clara finally knows the truth about the fortune-teller, and she rides off to the ball in a golden coach, happy to reassume her before beauty now that she no longer fears it. While the gifts from Clara's mother make a nice allusion to Grimm in the film, the novel has a very different makeover scheme. Maguire has no fortune-teller to act as a fairy godmother. Instead, Iris, Ruth, and Casper create Clara's makeover. *They* plan for Clara to attend the ball; *they* manage the dress and jewels, and *Ruth* finds a beautiful pair of dancing shoes that shine like glass. The novel attempts to reinterpret the stepsisters, so this version of the makeover fits. There's sisterly love instead of a deus ex machina to save the day.

The teleplay, however, insists on a fairy godmother. That character has come, so consistently, to center the tale, that most current tellers feel pressure to provide her requisite magic. In the novel, those who know and love Clara propel her into the fashionable world, where she learns to accept herself. The television production of *The Confessions of an Ugly Stepsister* would be stronger if Iris had a similar self-affirming makeover. At the ball, it seems as if this might happen. The Prince, incredibly beautiful with porcelain skin and cotton candy hair, languishes on a throne, trapped into meeting a long line of hopefuls. When her turn comes, Iris points her plainness out to him and remarks on the discomforting nature of being made to meet this way. Out of all the others he has met, the Prince notices and likes Iris's spunkiness and wit and asks her to save him a dance. Could this revision actually alter the story so drastically? Could a *stepsister* catch the heart of the Prince?

Apparently not. As soon as he sees Clara enter the ballroom, before she has even opened her mouth, the Prince is smitten. His interest in Iris apparently dissolves as he develops the same fish face, gaping mouth, and goggle eyes that all the other Princes wear when they see Cinderella enter. The two obviously match; they even look alike. In the film, they dance and make conversation. In the novel, their attraction becomes physical, and Clara comes home a woman, perhaps even pregnant with the heir to the throne. At first Iris feels disappointment, even jealousy. What happened to the Prince's interest in her? Her envy dissolves as Iris realizes that Casper does love her, and he, after all, is her first choice. But even in this tale, which examines the mazes of character, physical beauty again wins wealth and high position.

In the novel, however, Iris *does* have a moment of pure insight that tempers everything that follows. On the way to the ball, she truly sees herself, as she is; she describes herself, the artist in her observing a subject:

> Though her nose was long and unregenerate, and her lips thin ... her color was good.... Her eyes were cast down ... and the lashes that sealed them were too thin to notice, and the brows that overarched them drove inward, a gesture of contemplation. So perhaps she was an intelligent thing, despite her lack of education.... She seemed, if not at peace with herself, then at least interested in developing herself, whoever she might be [106].

It's this, and many other introspective moments, that make Maguire's Iris a fascinating character. In the television version, though, someone always reminds viewers that Iris is not *physically* beautiful. Back in high school, there was a phrase we all understood as a signifier of plainness. "But Eunice," someone would comment, "sure has a great personality." No one had to add that Eunice would not be homecoming queen.

That kind of thinking ultimately undercuts Miller's adaptation of *Confessions of an Ugly Stepsister* and gives it a retrograde motion. While the novel's point seems to be to question the worth of beauty and to contemplate definitions of ugliness, the screenplay ultimately confirms the current notions of beauty, making the production very much a creation of our time. Jenna Harrison's (Clara) perfection reinforces the idea that beauty means specific attributes: an oval face, large blue eyes, sparkling teeth, clouds of blonde hair, and a slender, graceful form. The camera worships Clara; she's often backlit, a technique that gives her a halo and throws every ringlet around her face into sharp relief.

Azura Skye, cast as Iris, gets to define ugliness, as opposed to such perfection. But how can viewers believe that Iris would *ever* be seen as plain, when Skye, a conventionally pretty young woman, looks like Drew Barrymore? The first time we watched *Confessions*, we both thought the Master's portrait of Iris would show what *we* saw—a lovely girl. From that image, she would learn the truth about herself (in the novel, the Master claims he *was* painting Iris's beauty). Instead, the expressionistic work opts for emotion over likeness. Not so the realistic portrait of Clara. Apparently, we are to read plainness as the lack of the perfect: hair not quite so abundant, a sharper chin, and so on. Clara herself reinforces this by telling Iris that even if she is not beautiful she is "interesting to look at," a phrase which recalls high school anxiety. Then there's Ruth, who more clearly does not fit a conventional beauty formula and who gets to add comedy, but rarely has a line to speak.

In the novel's surprise ending, readers learn that *Ruth,* not Iris, has been telling the tale. While others have been stamping her as dumb, sometimes calling her a beast, Ruth has been watching and remembering every detail. It's she who puts the story down in a form that will last. It's she who has the last word. The film completely ignores this final twist, choosing a male voiceover to begin and end the film. The last page of the novel sends readers back to the beginning to realize that Ruth is the "ugly" stepsister of the title. Millar's adaptation gives the story a male frame and allows the "ugly" in the title to stand for Iris.

A more thoughtful production than the 1950 or 1997 Disney versions of Cinderella, *Confessions of an Ugly Stepsister* shows that beauty might be a crippling encumbrance, but it leaves no doubt about the way that beauty looks, and it sidesteps two of the most important events in its literary source. The television production refuses Maguire's revisionist makeover, which gives the power of transformation to the sisters. It also refuses the concept that the "ugliest" sister could have the most complete view of the tale and the most beautiful words with which to tell it.

Ever After *(1998)*

For both of us, the most satisfying Cinderella rewrite so far has to be Andy Tennant's *Ever After.* Tennant places and keeps the focus on Cinderella, transforming her from a flat, folktale character into a real person, promising, as did *The Confessions of an Ugly Stepsister,* the complete truth. Using a familiar novelistic technique for conferring reality on what is to follow, Tennant opens his Cinderella tale with a frame story: An elderly noblewoman (Jeanne Moreau) has called the Grimm brothers to her castle to set them right about "the little cinder girl," who, she claims, actually lived, "once upon a time." The Grimms argue that theirs is more correct than Perrault's unrealistic version. Displaying the glass slipper as proof, the noblewoman tells the "true" tale.

Before summarizing this "real" Cinderella, it makes sense to consider another level of reality that affects *Ever After*—casting. Jeanne Moreau, who became a star during the French New Wave cinema movement, invests the frame introduction to *Ever After* with glamour and with the reminder of a "new" approach that produced classics. With their famous family connections, Anjelica Huston and Drew Barrymore bring the glow of Hollywood's own fairytale of power and magic to the film. All three strong women give the production the clout it needs to succeed in rewriting a familiar story.

Individually, each woman has proven pull and range. Moreau, who stood for everything capricious and enchanting about women as Margaret in *Jules et Jim* (1961), weaves a spell that gives the film an international context—a fitting start for a folktale. Academy Award winner Anjelica Huston, star of *The Grifters* (1990) and *Prizzi's Honor* (1985), whom Louis Giannetti called "one of the joys of the contemporary cinema" (*Understanding Movies* 255), keeps the stepmother from being a flat character from the moment she steps regally, appraisingly, down from the coach to meet her new stepdaughter. Barrymore adds some film history of her own to the role of Danielle De Barbarac (Cinderella). Since she first appeared as Eliot's little sister Gertie in *ET* (1982), Barrymore has had the power to keep her audience rooting for that half-innocent, half-wise child. Ronald Reagan, "the Teflon president," reigned when *ET* was released, and for the last twenty years Barrymore, too, has had the ability to move forward, untouched by past damage. The ridiculously impetuous short marriages? The time spent in rehab? The bad film choices, like *Poison Ivy?* (1992). The recent *Playboy* centerfold? These events matter less than the collective memory of that engaging child. We *know* Gertie's still in there.

We yearn to see Barrymore reborn, and films like *Never Been Kissed* (1999), *Riding in Cars with Boys* (2001), and *The Wedding Singer* (1998), in which her character's self-actualization is played out, have brought her great success. The videocassettes for *Ever After* and *Never Been Kissed* make it easy for Drew junkies to cross-reference her films since each carries a trailer for the other. What could be a surer bet than casting her as Cinderella, a role that hinges on the power to be remade?

The idea of *becoming* remains central to this complex "historical" adaptation of Cinderella, which unfolds in sixteenth-century France. Briefly, we see Danielle De Barbarac as a child (Anna Maguire) on the day she is to meet her new stepmother, Baroness Rodmilla De Ghent (Anjelica Huston). She's a feisty tomboy who shocks her new stepsisters, Marguerite (Elizabeth Earl) and young Jacqueline (Alex Pooley), and stepmother. Danielle's father laughs at her behavior, and it's clear, when he soon dies of a heart attack, that his last loving thought is for his little girl, not his new wife.

Time jumps, and Danielle, a young woman, sleeps on the hearth, where she has been reading the last book her father brought her, Thomas

Moore's *Utopia*. Danielle and the other servants labor to keep the manor intact while the Baroness sells off valuables to maintain her lifestyle. Danielle's fortunes have changed, but she's still spunky. When a thief steals her father's horse, she peppers him with a windfall of apples. The thief turns out to be Prince Henry (Dougray Scott), who longs to escape from the palace, and who pays for the horse with gold pieces. Danielle dresses as a courtier and uses the gold to buy back a family retainer the unfeeling Baroness has sold.

Disguised as a member of the nobility, she again meets the Prince. He would not look at a servant, but he notices an enchanting courtier with modern ideas about equality. Danielle's intelligence attracts Henry, who has been resisting his arranged marriage to the Princess of Spain. Prince Henry begs for Danielle's name, and she blurts out "Nicole De Loncre," her mother's name.

The Prince secretly courts "Nicole." She comes to love him, and cannot bring herself to tell him she's really a commoner and a servant. As Nicole, Danielle inspires Henry to use his throne for good. He listens to her, and to Leonardo Da Vinci (Patrick Godfrey), who is artist in residence (go figure) and who advises the King and Danielle, as well as the Prince. In a compromise, the king gives Henry three weeks to find a wife or to marry the Spanish princess, and he plans a masked ball to announce the wedding.

Rodmilla, meanwhile, has been seeking Henry's attention for her cruel, beautiful daughter Marguerite (Megan Dodds), without much success. Increasingly, Rodmilla suspects that her stepdaughter, Danielle, has caught the prince's attention. Too many coincidences link her to Prince Henry and to Nicole the mysterious courtier no one seems to have seen— Nicole De Loncre. Rodmilla plants the rumor that "Nicole" is already married, and locks Danielle up on the night of the masked ball. (Of course she escapes.)

In this Cinderella tale, the ball functions as a showdown. Believing that his true love has deceived him, the Prince plans to announce his marriage to the Princess. Then Danielle appears, beautifully dressed, unmarried, and with eyes only for him. As the Prince leads her to meet the King and Queen, an angry Rodmilla tells Prince Henry he has chosen a commoner. Shocked, Henry casts Danielle away. Venting her rage, Rodmilla sells her stepdaughter to a lecherous neighbor. Danielle, still feisty, saves herself before Henry, who has relented, comes to save her. Finally, Danielle accepts Henry's hand, and Rodmilla and Marguerite find themselves serving as laundresses in the palace.

This plot summary shows how carefully Susannah Grant, Andy Tennant, and Rick Parks's screenplay of *Ever After* provides motivation for much of the action in folktale versions of "Cinderella."

Danielle obeys because she is trying to save her precious home and friends and fellow servants.

The Baroness hates Danielle because her father loved her best. Marguerite feeds on the hate, and calls Danielle "Cinderslut." Jacqueline, ignored by her own mother, sees the injustice done to Danielle and finally acts to counter it.

The Prince finds Cinderella unique and *does* recognize her without the slipper, but he recoils from the idea of marrying a commoner. This revisionist adaptation discusses issues of class that usually go without comment.

Grant, Tennant and Parks also have fun blending Cinderella sources. Although the Grimms have been called in for *correction*, their version *is* much closer to the tale the noble woman tells them than to Perrault's. Like Perrault's Cinderella, Danielle has a pair of glass slippers, and she is sweet, pretty and good-natured (not cloyingly so).

But parallels to the Grimms' "Aschenputtel" abound. Danielle loves nature, and Tennant is not afraid to mark her affection with mud and sweat. This story also focuses on Danielle's trials and her family loyalty. This version has no fairy godmother, and no magical tree or doves, but her mother's dress and slippers help transform Danielle. With a nod to the Grimms, the film ends in revenge of a less violent variety as stepmother and the most evil stepsister become servants.

Ever After isn't pure Grimm either because it offers a truly new slant on the main character. Unlike other film Cinderellas, Danielle has a name, and her essence matters more than her physical beauty. As Peters Travers says, "Barrymore's take on Cinderella is more Betty Friedan than Brothers Grimm. No Prince would mistake her for a docile dolly" (114). As Danielle saves the faithful servant, stays up late to read, and reflects on her stepmother's hatred, we come to know her. Her brilliance and wit become apparent when she saves the Prince from a marauding band of gypsies. She and Henry have gotten lost in the woods, and she sheds her dress to climb a tree and get their bearings. While she is "aloft," gypsies surround Prince Henry. The Prince warns her not to come down, but, when she sees the gypsies have stolen her gown (really Marguerite's), she shimmies down in a rage. Charmed by her fire, the gypsy chief tells her she can have anything she can carry off. Instead of the gown, Danielle gingerly lifts *Henry* over her shoulder and lugs him from the clearing.

The camera generally keeps us close to Danielle. We feel the texture of her life. Her tasks, wearing a yoke to plow, searching for windfalls, feeding the pigs, hunting for truffles in the forest, look real—no faux dirt here. Danielle's interactions with the other servants, who are her friends, make the manor a home, not just a stage on which Cinderella awaits her transformation. Unlike Disney's Cinderella, who gazes at the palace and primps in soap bubbles, or Rodgers and Hammerstein's Cinderella, who sits "in [her] own little corner," Danielle is a young woman *living* her life, not waiting for it to begin. The "more believable sorcery" of Danielle's reality replaces the magic in the traditional tales, and "the feminist spin" works (Hutchy 50).

Danielle's relationships with Rodmilla, Marguerite and Jacqueline (Melanie Lynskey) show complexity and shading. Both stepsisters watch their mother's reaction to Danielle. Marguerite feeds on her mother's anger and feels free to abuse Danielle, but Jacqueline measures the abuse her mother and sister perpetrate. Her attitude towards Danielle changes as she watches. In a climactic scene, Danielle slugs Marguerite for taking her mother's dress, and Marguerite responds by burning *Utopia*. Jacqueline knows a line has been crossed. We can understand her developing empathy for Danielle.

Rodmilla has character-revealing moments in which we see why she became a wicked stepmother. She loved her husband, and sees him "looking out" from Danielle's eyes. Her attempt to shut off her own pain leads to her resentment of Danielle. Rodmilla shows how she has cultivated coldness in a brief conversation after the masque. "Was there a time, even in its smallest measurement, that you loved me at all?" Danielle asks her. "How can anyone love a pebble in their shoe?" Rodmilla answers.

Danielle's makeovers (more than one—like Disney's Cinderella) make sense within the context of the story. In her before state, she's fresh and young and attractive, but Tennant is not afraid to mark her with the signs of poverty. As a servant, she wears one dull and tattered dress for most of the film, and her face and hands bear the traces of hard work. Unlike the other Cinderellas, Danielle first makes herself over for a noble purpose. To save her servant from deportation she must climb the ladder of class (a sub-genre of makeover films), and her friend Gustave helps her.

"I'm just a servant in a nice dress," she tells him, as she comes out from behind a screen wearing the signifiers of the palace set, a lovely gold and blue velvet gown and high-heeled shoes. She looks substantially as she looked before, just cleaner, and, as she notes, more naked. Gustave helps her to fix her hair, and he directs her not to look down if she is to convince others she is a courtier. Later, for love of the Prince, Danielle assumes this courtier's disguise she first wore out of necessity.

Her second makeover comes on the night of the masked ball, so it shares that similarity with other versions of Cinderella. Rodmilla has locked Danielle into a cellar room and takes her daughters off to the ball. No fairy godmother comes to release her, but her friend Gustave asks Leonardo to help. As Clara does in *Confessions*, Danielle wears her mother's dress and shoes, but she knows these are not enough to affect the change she imagines. A commoner, a virtual servant, cannot marry the Prince. Danielle tells Da Vinci, "A bird may love a fish, Signor, but where will they live?" We do not see the process of transformation, but the result tells us how the artist has answered Danielle's question. He has powdered her face lightly, added glittery beauty marks, and crafted her a pair of filmy wings. Most Cinderellas in their after state are "merely lovely," but Danielle's transformation works like a metaphor. She needs to ascend. Surely Henry will look at her wings and shining face and *see* she is an angel. Even though the object of a masked ball is disguise, Danielle's makeover reveals her true self.

While the other "arrival" scenes we have examined cue Cinderella, as if she was a pageant contestant, this one has a twist. The camera follows Danielle as she climbs the stairs, a white figure with gossamer wings silhouetted against the blue sky. It swings above her, and then faces her, and we hear what she says, "Breathe, just breathe." Then, for a moment, from her vantage point, the camera shows us the Prince, as if we were looking through Danielle's eyes. In the sequence that follows, both Henry and Danielle share the camera's gaze. The way seems clear for them. After this high comes the low of the Prince's rejection. It seems fitting that Danielle's makeover does not invest her with power born of physical beauty alone. She has power already, and it has little to do with her appearance.

Tennant, Parks, and Grant rework the slipper motif to fit their Cinderella. Danielle loses her slipper as she runs from the ball, crushed by Henry's response. But foot size never matters, nor does the slipper play a part in identifying Danielle later. Henry doesn't need the slipper to find Danielle; he needs it as a reminder that he loves her. The slipper and a lovely drawing of Danielle's face, by Leonardo, become the bits of her that last through time. These remnants introduce the Brothers Grimm, and us, to her.

In their battle for the gown and slippers, Marguerite throws Danielle's precious copy of Thomas Moore's *Utopia* into the fire. This conflagration—more violence against Cinderella—signals a turn in the film. Soon, forgetting all the Moorean ideas of equality she has taught him, the Prince rejects Danielle. It's true that he reconsiders, but why would *she* still want *him*? Like the Prince in *The Slipper and the Rose*, Henry desires freedom

Ever After (20th Century–Fox, 1998). (*Left*) BEFORE: As Danielle DeBarbarac, Drew Barrymore's expression radiates the bittersweet hopefulness she brings to many of her roles. In this revisionist Cinderella tale, set in Renaissance France, Barrymore plays a real young woman, not a fairytale heroine. Her before signifiers—simple clothing, dirt, and sweat—are more than cosmetic. This shot signals Danielle's earthy existence. (She's hugging a haystack.) She has strength, feistiness, and a tender heart. The only things she lacks are the power and the funds to keep her household of friends and servants together. Willing to work to achieve her goals, Danielle seeks survival first, not a ball gown or a pair of glass slippers.

(*Below*) AFTER: Although her after attire lifts her into the courtier class, it doesn't change Danielle DeBarbarac's sweet expression. Here, she directs her redemptive powers at Prince Henry (Dougray Scott), who clearly needs them. Danielle offers him her charming gaze and her hand, but Henry stares smugly off into the distance. He's a clear candidate for a psychological makeover, which we see beginning as the film ends.

to choose his life, but he must be *led* to intelligent choice. As brighter of the two, Danielle will have to do the leading. Still, Tennant's vision provides a Cinderella capable of that, and, *finally*, a Cinderella we might want to know.

Carolyn Heilbrun recognizes the importance of mythic tales like "Cinderella" to our lives:

> Let us agree on this: that we live our lives through texts. These may be read, or chanted, or experienced electronically, or come to us, like the murmurings of our mothers, telling us of what conventions demand. Whatever their form or medium, these stories are what have formed us all, they are what we must use to make our new fictions…. Out of old tales we must make new lives [109].

Our modern lives provide us with few grand balls, but events like proms and weddings prove that we still enjoy enacting the Cinderella moment. If anything, the frenzy of preparation surrounding those events has increased. Obviously, we believe magic and power can be bought with the perfect makeover. Obviously, we turn to texts, like Cinderella stories and films, to help us envision the way those moments should go.

If we view these films as part of the web of culture from which we craft our lives, we must acknowledge their negative implications. Something more than the plain woman equals invisibility convention is at work here. Even when the Prince has already met Cinderella, he usually does not recognize her at the ball. After that amazing event, he *still* needs the slipper test to be sure she is the right one. This repeating motif—the slipper test—tells us that a potent makeover can lift a woman out of her *self*. She becomes an anonymous, if ultimately desirable, goddess, identifiable only by a token. No one should pay that cost for external beauty, no matter how desirable it seems. Many Cinderella films reiterate another equally dangerous makeover effect. Disney's scene of violence done to Cinderella by her stepsisters becomes a repeating motif, absent only from *Confessions of an Ugly Stepsister*. Even in the comic lyrics of a song, the serious message is clear. Beauty breeds jealousy. Often, it divides women into two groups: those who have physical beauty and those who don't. Those who don't have it want to "pull out all [the] hair" of those who do.

But these film adaptations also suggest positive change. Starting in the seventies, writers and directors begin to walk around the original tales, looking for doorways to new tellings. They consider how and why such a story could have taken place; they imagine the personalities involved; they recontextualize. Most importantly, though, they begin to see Cinderella as someone who might be more than a dreamy head and a pretty face, someone whose life goes on before and beyond her magical transformation. We need to see that new vision enacted over and over again, until this truth becomes an indelible part of the tale: we can lose our accessories and perfect hair, but we must keep our valuable selves intact.

Now, Voyager establishes one formula for Hollywood makeover films to come, but "Cinderella," the world's first makeover story, also echoes in the chapters that follow.

• *Three* •

Teen Makeovers

Cher's main thrill in life is a makeover. It gives her a sense of control in a world full of chaos.

—Dionne Davenport, *Clueless*

It would be hard to find a young American girl who hasn't seen at least one version of Cinderella, or owned a Cinderella Barbie, or played dress-up Cinderella with her friends. By the time she gets to be a teenager, the conventions of that old tale have become the familiar fabric of her life. Magazines such as *Seventeen,* which has been doling out makeover tips to teens for years, reinforce the magic: one good haircut can turn a Plain Jane into a knockout. And the prom, the high school ball, brings the story to life for millions of teenage girls each year as they shop, shop, shop (and spend, spend, spend) for the perfect Cinderella gown.

Other than Disney's *Cinderella* and its various incarnations over the years, however, teen makeover movies are a relatively new phenomenon. If we scan early Hollywood history, few films in general have been aimed squarely at teenagers. There were the Andy Hardy flicks (16 in all) of the 1930s and 1940s, starring Mickey Rooney and occasional sidekick Judy Garland. Then came the teen dramas of the 1950s and 1960s: *Rebel Without a Cause* (1955), starring James Dean and Natalie Wood; *A Summer Place* (1959), with Troy Donahue and Sandra Dee; and *Splendor in the Grass* (1961), with Warren Beatty and Natalie Wood. Charged with sexual tension, identity crises, and teen-parent conflict, these films co-existed with the formulaic Elvis musicals in which female leads were little more than interchangeable parts whose main function was to fawn over the gyrating superstar.

Also in the 1960s, Frankie and Dee Dee hit the beach while Gidget went Hawaiian, providing frothy fare for teens. The 1970s teen standouts amounted to *Grease* (1978) and *Saturday Night Fever* (1977), both starring the black-haired, blue-eyed icon of coolness John Travolta. It wasn't until the 1980s that Hollywood began deliberately targeting the teen audience in a big way with the Brat Pack films—*Sixteen Candles* (1984), *The Breakfast Club* (1985), *St. Elmo's Fire* (1985), and *Pretty in Pink* (1986)—all of which examine high school angst. *Risky Business* (1983), *Top Gun* (1986), and *Dirty Dancing* (1987) also proved popular with the MTV crowd. All in all, however, the list makes a paltry showing for the teen target. What's more interesting is that nary a teen *makeover* movie appears on the list. It took a non-makeover movie, James Cameron's megahit *Titanic* (1997), starring teen heartthrob Leonardo DiCaprio and the winsome Kate Winslet, to turn the tide.

Titanic struck a vein of gold for Hollywood. As one writer put it, the film "tapped into a completely unanticipated audience, all of those teenage girls who went to see the movie ten times. George Lucas once said that Jim had succeeded in creating a *Star Wars* for girls" (Gove). The film topped box office charts for nine straight weeks, won 11 Oscars, and ultimately brought in billions of dollars worldwide. Matt Soergel, film critic for the Jacksonville *Times-Union*, pointed to movie studio research that revealed "three out of five *Titanic* ticket-buyers are female. And more than 60 percent of those who've seen it twice or more are younger than 25 years old" ("Drowning")—like 15-year-old Cristin Riffle, who saw the movie "so many times now that she doesn't have to wait for the iceberg before she gets emotionally worked up.…' Actually, I cry the whole way through,'" she told Soergel (qtd. in "Drowning"). BBC News Online Entertainment Correspondent Tom Brook observed that movies like *Titanic* and Wes Craven's horror flick *Scream* (1996), "demonstrated to Hollywood executives that the teen market was most definitely underserved" ("Teen power").

According to a recent online media study, teens make up about 8.6 percent of the U.S. population, or 23.4 million 12–17-year-olds, and, in 1998, they spent approximately $141 billion ("Teens as Targets"). Since "48% of these young people go to the movies once a month compared to just 26% of adults" ("Teens as Targets"), we can assume that they're spending a significant amount of their expanding allowances on movie tickets. Hollywood got this message fast, so fast that 1999 was dubbed the year of the teen movie. *Cruel Intentions, Varsity Blues, The Rage: Carrie 2, 10 Things I Hate about You,* and *She's All That* represent just a few of the teen flicks that poured into the market in 1999.

Hollywood's mad scramble to squeeze some serious bucks out of this "underserved" but oh-so-lucrative consumer group resulted in some pretty forgettable films. *Born a Cheerleader* comes to mind. (Most films aimed at teen wallets aren't bound for the Oscars.) The industry grabbed for any storyline it thought would appeal. A couple of directors even updated literary works to make them more palatable for the moving-going youth. We'd put Amy Heckerling's *Clueless* (1995) and Gil Junger's *10 Things I Hate About You* (1999) at the top of the heap. Fresh and clever, these two films stayed so faithful to the spirit of their original works (Jane Austen's *Emma* and Shakespeare's *Taming of the Shrew*, respectively,) that they were dubbed "new originals" and captured the teen public's imagination.

Hollywood also tapped into the old Cinderella story. Hadn't this fairy tale proved lucrative telling after telling, generation after generation? The transformation of ugly duckling to beautiful swan had a timeless, universal appeal. Didn't every Plain Jane who slumped invisible down high school hallways dream about being Prom Queen? Why not repackage the tale for the hip and savvy American teens? Thus, the makeover genre passed to a new generation, already mass consumers of beauty products and trendy fashions. The movies in this chapter—*Clueless* (1995), *She's All That* (1999), *Josie and the Pussycats* (2001), and *Legally Blonde* (2001)—represent only a few of the makeover minions that take aim at teenage girls and all deliver that magic moment when a few brush strokes and some sexy, stylish clothes reveal our heroine's dormant beauty and bring the man of her dreams to his knees.

Not totally mindless fare, a couple of these flicks manage to surprise us with twists and turns on makeover conventions and traditional plot lines. There are also a few unexpectedly enlightening messages here for young women and some refreshing celebrations of female friendship. Taken as a whole, however, these movies are specifically designed to speak to teens with one thing in mind: attracting the ever-popular, always hunky, brutally hot Prince Charming.

Clueless *(1995)*

"Sex. Clothes. Popularity. Is there a problem here?" So reads the tagline of *Clueless*, written and directed by Amy Heckerling (*Fast Times at Ridgemont High*). One of the most commercially successful of the teen makeover flicks, *Clueless* also won over the critics. Hal Hinson of the *Washington Post* called it "buoyantly funny" in his review. Roger Ebert wrote in his review, "Heckerling walks a fine line between satire and put-on, but she finds it, and her dialogue could be anthologized." And Peter Stack of the *San Francisco Chronicle* said the film "hits funny bones in its delicious satire of ditzy shopping-mall material girls, à la Beverly Hills" ("*Clueless* Knows").

Most of the other reviews fall in line, but Ebert hits the mark. The film belongs to Heckerling, who brilliantly updates Jane Austen's *Emma*, a novel about a wealthy, witty, well-intentioned—but clueless—young woman who loves to play matchmaker until her schemes backfire on her. Heckerling makes Austen's classic accessible for today's teen audiences while staying true to the spirit of the original work. She also nails her predecessor's facility for sharp social commentary and snappy banter. Heckerling won the National Society of Film Critics Award for Best Screenplay and won a nomination for Best Original Screenplay from the Writers Guild of America.

Clueless stars Alicia Silverstone as Cher Horowitz, the most popular girl at Bronson Alcott High School in Beverly Hills. Over the course of the film, she manages to make over one of her teachers, a new girl in school, and her own soul. As her best friend, Dionne Davenport (Stacey Dash), says, "Cher's main thrill in life is a makeover. It gives her a sense of control in a world full of chaos." And herein may lie the truth behind the makeover genre's appeal. No matter who initiates the makeover, Henry Higgins or Cher Horowitz, *control* becomes the issue. There's something intrinsically thrilling and satisfying about shaping another's, or one's own, life course through a physical transformation—especially in times of political, economic, or cultural confusion. The makeover, while it may be challenging, is so literally "hands on" and eminently doable that it empowers both doer and subject. In many of these films, the effects of the makeover are immediate and dramatic, furthering the appeal impact for us. Maybe one of the reasons we like the genre is that sense of vicarious pleasure we derive in seeing a screen sister find ways to control the elements swirling around her. Maybe we keep returning to the makeover well hoping for inspiration. Sometimes we're disappointed; sometimes we hit gold.

In *Clueless*, Cher feels empowered by her talent for making other people over. Cher *is* already the after, right down to her designer shoes. She hangs with Dionne because they were both named after great singers of the past who moved onto infomercials, and because they both know what it's like to have other people jealous of them. They talk on their cell phones in Bronson Alcott's corridors and, when they need to gather their thoughts and regain their strength, they head for the galleria to shop.

Cher's closet looks like a Rodeo Drive boutique, complete with a rotating clothes rack, and her computer helps her select just the right ensemble for the day. She never relies on dressing room mirrors, preferring Polaroid snapshots instead. And she wouldn't be caught dead in anything "so last season." No meek and mild Cinderella here. She's rich, confident, and beautiful. She could have her pick of the pack, but Cher won't date high school guys—they're too much like dogs: "You have to clean them and feed them." This is a young woman who knows who she is—until her well-ordered life begins to unravel and she becomes a woman of substance. Cher's makeover moves from the outside in.

Cher's physical beauty does come with a kind heart and good intentions. She hovers over her father, Mel (Dan Hedaya), a gruff, high-powered attorney who makes $500 an hour but clearly adores his daughter, like a mother hen. She fusses about his cholesterol and runs their "classic" mansion (with the help of servants), which boasts a gigantic portrait of Cher's mother, who died during a "routine liposuction" when Cher was a baby, and he is never too busy to ask about her day, listen to her problems, and scare her dates. In one scene, Cher finally deigns to go out with a high school guy—the "brutally hot" new guy in town, Christian Stovitz (Justin Walker), a Rat Pack wannabe who drives a '50s Nash Metropolitan and calls Cher "Dollface." Mel warns him in no uncertain terms: "If anything happens to her, I got a .45 and a shovel. I don't think you'll be missed." In short, Mel keeps one eye on his briefs and the other firmly on his daughter.

Also keeping an eye on Cher is her stepbrother, Josh (Paul Rudd), Mel's son from a previous marriage and college hunk ("a bit of a Baldwin," Cher admits) who wants to follow in Mel's litigating footsteps. Like the Mr. Knightly in Austen's *Emma*, Josh lectures and criticizes Cher for her shallowness. To Josh, Cher is a selfish, "superficial space cadet" who moves in one direction: toward the mall. And when Cher decides to make a new transfer student, Tai Fraiser (Brittany Murphy), her "project," Josh tells her: "You're acting out on that poor girl like she was your Barbie doll." Ignoring Josh's admonitions, Cher tells him: "I am going to take that lost soul in there and make her well-dressed and popular. Her life will be better because of me."

Cher has some success to back up her claim. When she can't negotiate above a C in two of her classes, she devises a plan that will make her single, lonely teachers Miss Geist (Twink Caplan) and Mr. Hall (Wallace Shawn) "sublimely" happy so they will give out higher grades: get them interested each other. But Miss Geist, the Miss Weston of this piece, needs some work before the balding, diminutive Mr. Hall will notice her. The poor thing wears glasses, spills coffee down her frumpy blouse, and sports lipstick on her teeth. Her pantyhose have runs while her slip hangs below her outdated skirts. "This woman is screaming for a makeover," Cher tells Dionne. "I'm her only hope."

In one scene, Cher and Dionne descend on Miss Geist as she's leaving the school office. The camera moves in close and tight as the makeover mavens, all arms and elbows, pluck and pull at their fashion victim. "You have such pretty eyes. Don't hide under them," they declare as they rip off her glasses (shades of Charlotte Vale) and marvel at her tiny waist. While Cher plays with Miss Geist's hair, Dionne removes her teacher's red sweater and rearranges her poorly tied scarf to better call attention to the nice figure beneath the cream-colored V-neck top. When Miss Geist finally manages to break free, Cher and Dionne survey their work. "Not a total Betty," Dionne proclaims, "but a vast improvement."

In the next scene, Cher and Dionne find the new lovebirds eating lunch together on a park bench. "Old people can be so sweet," they observe, smiling. In the montage that follows, Mr. Hall wears a nice suit with a yellow power tie and matching pocket hanky while Miss Geist dresses in more sophisticated, tailored suits or feminine, flowing dresses in neutral colors. Her garish makeup has been toned down, her stylish heels fit, and her wavy hair softly frames her face. Cher receives major kudos from grateful students for the improvement in their grades, and her makeover success gives her all the encouragement she needs to take on the new kid in town. But the makeover device in *Clueless* also acts as a barometer of Cher's growth as a person. Her "projects" are not entirely selfish. She's genuinely happy that she brings two deserving people together, and the result inspires her comment, "I wanted to do more good deeds."

The opportunity enters with transfer student Tai, a hopeless "farmer," as class bitch Amber (Elisa Donovan) calls her. All eyes turn to the newcomer in gym class as the camera makes the classic tilt up from Tai's yellow men's sneakers and brown, baggy cords to her plaid flannel shirt (untucked) over a black tee. With thick brows and dyed red hair pulled back in a sloppy ponytail, she stands, eyes downcast and shoulders slumped, hugging a notebook decorated with drawings of spaceships close to her chest. "Would you look at that girl," Cher says to Dionne. "She's so adorably clueless. We've got to adopt her." Dionne objects: "Our stock will plummet!" But Cher insists. "Don't you want to use your popularity for a good cause?"

The makeover scene plays out to the song "Supermodel." Red hair color swirls down the drain. Foundation is foregrounded as Dionne carefully instructs Tai in how to apply makeup. A full-length mirror reflects snappy fashion choices, front and back, as Tai preens gleefully in a miniskirt, short blue sweater, cool shoes, and fluffy hair. Cher finishes her off with exercise and vocabulary sessions.

The result stops high school hunks in their tracks the next day as Tai struts between Dionne and Cher, posture erect, wearing a black and white plaid mini, sweater, dark hose, makeup, a natural and becoming hairstyle, and a fashion book bag. "Do you see how boys are responding? My heart is totally bursting," Cher tells Dionne.

Unfortunately, Cher doesn't stop with Tai's physical makeover. She insists on matchmaking, where she has substantially less success with her friend than with her teachers. Cher discourages Tai's attraction to skateboarder Travis Birkenstock (Breckin Meyer) and instead attempts to hook up Tai and the narcissistic Elton (Jeremy Sisto). Her efforts blow up in her face as Elton puts the moves on her instead of Tai.

Cher's state of cluelessness takes a turn for the worse when she goes after the smooth-talking, impeccably dressed Christian. In one scene, she descends her winding staircase in a white mini-dress as "Gigi" plays under the action. Christian waits at the foot of the stairs, Sinatra fedora in hand, but it's Josh—sitting at a table with Cher's father and his team of lawyers— who stares with mouth agape and gulps. "I'll go to the dance and keep an eye on her for you," he tells Mel, who smiles and nods wisely. Her Prince Charming spends most of the night dancing and talking with other guys, yet Cher remarks to Tai, "See how he's falling in love with me?"

Still not sensing that Christian is gay, Cher arranges a romantic evening at home and calls in Dionne to help make her over into a seductive vamp, complete with a short little red dress and a Veronica Lake coif. Her makeover efforts are lost on Christian, who spends most of the evening talking about art or watching *Some Like It Hot* and "Sporaticus," both starring his idol, Tony Curtis. "What happened?" Cher wails. "Did my hair go flat? Did I stumble into some bad lighting? I don't get it." It's Murray, Dionne's "keepin' it real" significant other, who finally convinces Cher that her prince charming is a "cake boy."

Cher saves her relationship with Christian by making him her favorite shopping partner but misfires on her latest project—the new and not-so-improved Tai. The makeover has left Tai with a full social calendar but an unpleasant edge. She sends Travis to sit with the "slackers" on the grassy knoll and, with the loss of Elton, sets her sights on Josh. When a despondent Cher returns home on foot after failing her driving test, Tai is waiting: "You've got to help me get Josh." Cher resists. "Do you really think you'd be good with Josh...? I just don't think you would mesh well," she tells Tai, who, on her way "outie," delivers a one-two punch: "You're a virgin who can't drive."

Stunned by the recent swirl of chaos in her structured life, Cher comes to three realizations: 1) "I've created some sort of a monster"; 2) "I'm just totally clueless"; and 3) "I love Josh." Resolved to gain control over her life, Cher makes a decision that reflects her growing maturity and innate kindness. And she turns to the one thing that she understands to help her—the makeover. "I decided I needed a makeover, except this time I'd makeover my soul. What makes somebody a better person?" Cher muses. Vowing to be a better person herself, Cher volunteers to head up the Pismo Beach Disaster Relief Drive, agrees to attend one of Travis' skateboarding events, gracefully accepts Tai's apology, and sensitively guides Josh through his declaration of love. Not bad for someone whose big day was once breaking in a pair of purple clogs. She also tones down her look, opting for softer colors and less trendy wear, like Elle in *Legally Blonde*. Josh has pushed her toward an awareness of the outside world, and she has responded by fashioning a soul equal to her physical beauty.

As teen makeover movies go, *Clueless* packs a positive message for a generation of young women in desperate need of good role models. The makeover here goes beneath the skin, empowering Cher to reach out to others without giving herself snaps. In this respect, she seems much like Charlotte Vale in *Now, Voyager* who uses her wealth and beauty for a worthy purpose, and, like Charlotte, gives makeovers to those who need them most.

Clueless became a star-making vehicle for Alicia Silverstone who won the American Comedy Award for Funniest Actress in a Motion Picture, the Blockbuster Entertainment Award for Favorite Female Newcomer, and the MTV Movie Awards for Best Female Performance and Most Desirable Female. She also won the National Board of Review's Best Breakthrough Performer award.

She's All That (1999)

She's All That, an amalgam of makeover giants like *Cinderella*, *Now, Voyager* and *My Fair Lady*, surprisingly received a modicum of respect from critics for its *effort* at wit and originality. Unfortunately, the "been there, done that" meter kicked in for us the moment we discovered the main story line: Tall, dark, handsome, and wealthy senior class president (his license plate reads MR PREZ) gets unexpectedly dumped by his tall, buxom, and bitchy girlfriend. To save face, he accepts a wager that he can turn the school's ugly duckling into a prom queen in six weeks. (Even Henry Higgins gets six months.) Directed by Robert Iscove and written by R. Lee Fleming, Jr., the film is a predictable rehash of much greater screen moments.

Rachael Leigh Cook plays artist Laney Boggs, the dorkiest and "scariest" girl in the senior class—dorky because she wears dark-rimmed glasses and a painter's apron over baggy bib overalls; scary because she spends her precious little spare time in the basement painting works about death and destruction. Laney's art class chums (the wicked stepsisters) whisper things in her ear like "You're not afraid to be dark—so why don't you kill yourself?" (Not to worry. They get their comeuppance.) Laney's problem, according to her art teacher, Ms. Rousseau (Debbi Morgan), is that there's so little of Laney herself in her work.

Later we learn that our heroine has never really dealt with her mother's early death. Like Cinderella before her, she took over the household duties, leaving little time to worry about things like her own appearance. Laney looks after her little brother, Simon (Kieran Culkin), and her

She's All That (Miramax, 1999). Rachael Leigh Cook and Freddie Prinze, Jr., star as Laney Boggs and Zach Siler in this teenage melding of the Cinderella and Pygmalion tales. When Zach accepts a bet to turn the school's biggest dork into a prom queen, he doesn't bargain for love and a makeover of his own. He not only falls for Laney but also finds a depth in their relationship that none of his superficial friends can provide. Acting the part of fairy godmother, too, he comes knocking at her door, complete with the junior varsity soccer team for cleanup duty, his sister for makeover duty, and a flirty red dress (for himself?). In this shot, Zach and Laney are enjoying a private moment at the beach when his friends arrive. Note Laney's before look: hair pulled back in a knot, sloppy shirt over paint splattered overalls, and glasses. His interest really peaks when she takes off her baggy clothes to reveal a shapely figure in a sexy black bathing suit.

father, Wayne "Dr. Pool" Boggs (Kevin Pollak), who owns his own pool cleaning business and watches *Jeopardy* religiously, shouting out wrong questions to every answer. Elden Henson plays Laney's friend and voice of reason, Jesse Jackson (don't ask). Laney has been a self-imposed outsider for so long that when Zach Siler (Freddie Prinze, Jr.) targets her as his six-week project, she asks him, "Is this some kind of Dork Outreach program?"

The arrogant and self-absorbed Zach thinks only of his image as he saunters through the halls and checks out his smirking photo on a prominent pillar. But the rich boy soccer star has his own problems, we discover. His is the fourth highest GPA in the entire class, and he has been accepted to every major Ivy League school, but he won't admit that to his workaholic father (Tim Matheson) who wants his son to follow in his footsteps and attend Dartmouth. Zach, it seems, hates having his life all mapped out for him. Like most prince charmings, he resists parental authority and duty. His awakening begins when his girlfriend, Taylor Vaughan (played to the hilt by Jodi Lyn O'Keefe), the most popular girl in the school, returns from spring break in Daytona Beach sporting a new armpiece: former *Real World* "star" Brock Hudson (Matthew Lillard), now headed for Loserville, a guy so stuck on himself that he has his name and picture tattooed on his bicep.

At first, Zach only wants to show Taylor that she's "totally replaceable." His ego has been bruised, but he puts up a cavalier front. He tells his slimy friend, Dean Sampson (Paul Walker), "You strip away the attitude and makeup, and all you have is a C-GPA with a Wonderbra." Dean goads him with the bet, and Zach is ripe for goading. Enter Laney, who wins the ticket to Zachville by tripping up the steps, spilling books and painting supplies for yards around her. Not a lot of originality here. But Zach doesn't have a high acumen for nothing. He bides his time and finds his way in through art, Laney's one passion. He makes an appearance at The Jester, an art house, where Laney appears as a white apparition, except for her dark framed glasses, in a number called "Be Silent, Be Still." Afterward, she tests him by calling the new member in the audience to the stage for an impromptu set. Zach steals the show with his hackysack routine, "Never let it drop," a metaphor for his life. For Zach's family, appearance and status are everything, and he's scared to death of letting them down.

An impressed Laney lets Zach walk her home—and here comes the element of the makeover genre that has endured since *Now, Voyager*. Laney clomps along beside Zach on a darkened street with her bad posture, stringy hair, bib overalls, and thick glasses. They stop, look into each other's eyes, and Zach delivers those famous lines: "Do you always wear those glasses? Ever think about contacts? You're eyes are so beautiful." Of course they're beautiful. As Roger Ebert points out in his review of the film, "It is an unbreakable rule of this formula that the ugly duckling is a swan in disguise: Rachael Leigh Cook is in fact quite beautiful, as was Audrey Hepburn, you recall, in *My Fair Lady*. Just once I'd like to see the *Pygmalion* formula applied to a woman who was truly unattractive."

Like most makeover heroines, Laney's before signifiers barely conceal the loveliness underneath. Even when the heroine doesn't realize or acknowledge her beauty, as is the case with Laney, the hero suspects it, and the audience accepts it without question. Part of the viewing experience lies in anticipating the single, confirming moment when Venus stands before mere mortal man in all her glorious beauty. "We knew that. We were right," the audience sighs.

In *She's All That*, Zach gets clues to Laney's attractiveness when she removes her glasses in the following scene and later when she removes her overalls at the beach, revealing a beautifully stacked body in a black, low-cut bathing suit. He smiles knowingly from afar and then shows up at her door with a little red dress for her. He wants to take her to a party. She makes excuses. "I've got to clean." No problem. He ushers in the JV Soccer team for housework detail. "I'm a mess." No problem. He introduces his sister, Mackenzie (Anna Paquin). "I'm hair and makeup," Mackenzie proclaims and whisks her charge upstairs (clue) to be made over. Though the plot premise echoes *My Fair Lady*, Zach is no Henry Higgins. He conducts no tutoring sessions, nor does he supervise her physical makeover. Zach simply provides the dress, the mice (soccer players here), and the fairy godmother (his sister)—shades of Cinderella. His struggles are minimal compared with Henry Higgins'.

The scene cuts back and forth between Mackenzie's magic and Wayne, Simon, and Zach in the den ... waiting. The mice come and go. Afternoon turns to evening. "You really have to trust me," Mackenzie tells Laney as she begins her transformation. The bushy brows are the first to go. Too much like Bert on *Sesame Street*. Pluck, pluck. The hair goes next. It doesn't really complement the face shape. Snip, snip. "You really never wear makeup?" Mackenzie asks. Laney's affirmation shocks the young fairy godmother who has been applying the stuff like a pro to her own lovely face from the moment we meet her on film.

Finally, the unveiling arrives. Mackenzie appears in the doorway and announces: "Gentlemen, may I introduce the new, not improved, but different, Laney Boggs." (We love the insertion of "not improved, but different" to herald Laney's entrance.) Zach slowly gets up and moves toward the bottom of the stairs, a cautiously hopeful look on his face. Cut to the *Now, Voyager* shot: a medium close-up of the stair railings. In slow motion, a pair of red strappy heels appear descending the stairs. The camera pulls out to a medium shot of a shapely pair of legs and the hem of a flirty red dress. The tilt up shows Laney turning the corner of the staircase where she pauses in her perfectly fitted, dress with a square-necked bodice, spaghetti straps, and lots of cleavage. Her hair is shorter, framing her face softly. Her lips are full and red. Eyes downcast reveal beautifully applied makeup and brows plucked to perfection. Now she looks like everybody else: same hair, same dress, same shoes. She could walk right into *Clueless*, which suggests that to be seen as beautiful, you must comply with current trends. A *Friends* haircut and a Limited dress will do the trick. Zach's reaction—mouth slightly agape, eyes wide, glistening, and fixed on the goddess before him—stamps APPROVAL on Laney, who suddenly trips and falls into Zach's waiting arms. He's smitten.

Neither Laney's new look nor Zach's new attitude, however, can save our heroine from the disappointing events of the party. Other guys stare as Laney passes, but her venture into the ladies' room finds one of the ugly art class stepsisters lying on the floor, drunk. Laney's efforts to help are met with sarcasm and nasty comments. When the girl finally passes out, Laney paints her face like a clown and walks out—only to be met by a jealous Taylor, who pours a drink down her red dress and says, "You're vapor, spam, a waste of perfectly good yearbook space." Laney's had enough. She runs from the party, falling outside. Zach follows. "I swore I'd never let them see me cry," Laney tells him as he gently puts his jacket around her. He replies, "Sometimes when you open up to people, you let the bad in with the good."

If this Prince Charming is wise, he also has a conscience. He's troubled by the bet he made, and his guilt keeps Laney at arm's length even though he wants to get closer. Laney asks Jesse (her friend), "Am I kissable?" She senses that Zach wants to kiss her, she sees his reaction when the scheming Dean begins to woo her himself, and she watches as Zach rescues her little brother, Simon, from bullies in the cafeteria—yet he remains distant.

Zach's behavior confuses Laney, who has not reverted to her former dork state. Instead, her new look carries into the school corridors, where we see her in softer, more feminine outfits. Guys stare as she walks by. Someone nominates her for Prom Queen, which pits her against Taylor Vaughn, whose jealousy knows no bounds when she sees the "Vote for Laney" posters and hears the school rap group doing their "Laney—She's All That" number in the quad. Only Dean's malicious lies trump Taylor's reprehensible behavior. Dean wants to take Laney to the prom so he can "get some." He tells Laney the bet was Zach's idea and that Zach still has a "thing" for Taylor. A model of courtly virtue, Dean shows up at her house on prom night with flowers and the promise of a good time. As Kevin Thomas suggests in his review of the film, "the child-like cruelty that persists in what are, after all, young adults, reflects a persistent insecurity even within the most popular students."

Laney's dad plays fairy godfather here, encouraging Laney to turn in her painter's smock for a prom dress. She goes to the ball with Dean, but there's no grand entrance here. She's with the wrong man, after all. We never see her second transformation until Zach, arriving with his sister, spots Laney dancing with Dean across the room. She blends in so completely with the other couples that we don't recognize her until she steps into the light. She's wearing a fabulous long black dress and her hair is swept up into a sophisticated French twist. And, though she loses the bid for prom queen to Taylor, she wins a ticket to art school. Ms. Rousseau, who submitted the portrait Laney painted of her mother to a prestigious school, delivers news of the only award Laney really wants.

Ultimately, the night turns out to be a double victory for our unlikely Cinderella because she also wins Prince Charming's heart. Zach, frantic because Laney has left the dance with Dean and frantic because he understands Dean's ulterior motives for wanting to get Laney alone, races from hotel to hotel looking to rescue her from the evil Dean. He shows up, unsuccessful in his search for Laney, at her house to wait for her. When she arrives, it turns out that she has rescued herself from Dean's clutches. Like Danielle in *Ever After*, Laney is a feminist's Cinderella: intelligent, strong, and resourceful. As they stroll poolside, she accepts Zach's apology. He says, "I made that bet before I knew you, Laney, before I really knew me." He asks, "Can I have the last dance?" to which Laney responds, "No. You can have the first." Her father throws the light switch from within and thousands of small white twinkling lights create a sense of magic.

In this scene, Laney compares herself to another film Cinderella. "I feel just like Julia Roberts in *Pretty Woman*," she says, "except for that whole hooker thing." The camera swings up from the twinkling lights around them to the stars in the midnight sky. This unfortunate line negates the fact that Laney is a much stronger character than her *Pretty Woman* counterpart. Yes, her makeover has helped her cross class boundaries, but Laney's physical makeover is incidental to her intellectual and artistic pursuits, and she treats it as such. We know, too, that Laney would never be attracted to Zach if he also weren't smart and sensitive. The end, then, works against what some of the plot elements seem to set up—that physical beauty isn't the whole package. Her own comparison to pretty woman Vivian suggests a dependence on Prince Charming that runs counter to Laney's independent spirit, mixing the message of a potentially successful makeover film.

Josie and the Pussycats *(2001)*

Harry Elfont and Deborah Kaplan's *Josie and the Pussycats*, based on the cartoon series, takes a hypocritical stab at corporate America's greedy, unrelenting marketing tactics that encourage rampant teen consumerism. On the surface the film looks like a banner for freedom of choice, hanging high above its clichéd makeover moral: be happy with who you are. But *Josie* ends up being guilty of the same thing it claims to revile, sending yet another mixed message to teen audiences. The incredible number of product placements underscores the film's theme, and they provide a double service for the corporations whose logos appear in frame after frame and whose names come tripping off the tongue in scene after scene. As critic Kenneth Turan observes, "*Josie* manages to profit from the very thing it's supposedly skewering" ("Bubble-Gum").

The main plot of the film involves "The Pussycats," a girl group whose gigs at Riverdale's bowling alley keep them running in the fast lane to nowhere until they are literally almost run over by fiendish rock star manager Wyatt Frame (Alan Cumming). He and his maniacal MegaRecords boss Fiona (Parker Posey), in league with an unnamed government organization, have created a megaprocessor that adds a few extra tracks to rock CDs—subliminal messages that brainwash teens into buying specific products and worshiping particular icons of pop culture. "We turn the world into one TV commercial," Fiona proclaims. But when their current band-of-the-moment, DuJour, starts to get wise, Fiona orders Wyatt to get rid of them and find a new sensation—immediately. Enter Josie and her sister friends whose adventures in the music business get them much more than they ever bargained for.

The film opens with hundreds of teenie boppers screaming hysterically, hitting that ear-splitting decibel level that only teenage girls can. "I just want to touch them," one girl cries as a limo carrying DuJour comes into sight. The group emerges, performs a quick rendition of their hit "Backdoor Lover," and boards a plane. Big mistake. Their petty bickering makes us almost grateful when the plane goes down. Wyatt, who has parachuted out, is left to create a new band practically overnight.

Meanwhile, life in Riverdale is tough for passionate, red-headed wannabe star Josie McCoy (Rachael Leigh Cook) and her bandmates: ditsy blonde fluff kitten, Melody Valentine (Tara Reid), and tough but sensitive African-American girl, Valerie Brown (Rosario Dawson). They grind away, playing music no one wants to hear and take verbal abuse from three catty girls in a Tracer. The Pussycats do have one thing (well, two things) going for them, however: cat-eared headbands and each other. They hug and kiss and swear that friendship will always come before fame. Right. But Josie has more problems than making it to the top. She's in love with Alan M (don't ask), but he only sees her as a friend, someone who will fix his truck, give him advice about the "smelly guy" at work, and listen to the "original" songs he plays on his acoustic. Lest we forget these are cartoon characters here, we have the inane dialogue and stereotypical representations to remind us.

It takes Wyatt Frame to shake up their world. He signs The Pussycats to a mega-contract before even hearing them play, and, before we can say John Frieda, whisks them off for a makeover session, or makeover parody, as it turns out. The standard before signifiers—glasses, stringy hair, frumpy clothing, cloddy shoes, bushy eyebrows, and bad posture—are not in evidence here. The girls are simply a flattened out version of their after vision. They wear typical jeans and tees, hair slightly messy, some makeup. Their appearance says average, normal, nothing more—certainly none of the flash and dazzle of rock stars.

As they enter the salon, the three stand shoulder to shoulder. Wyatt Frame stands behind them. The ceiling is low and the framing is tight, giving them no avenue of escape. In the center of the room, standing grouped like bowling pins, the stylists ready for battle (reminiscent of the makeover scene in *The Princess Diaries*). One low angle shot privileges a hair dryer, large and looming like a weapon in center frame, held by some disembodied hand. In the background, looking tiny and afraid, we see The Pussycats, cowering, blocked in by Wyatt. The angle shifts upward as the stylists run toward their three targets. A rapid succession of close-ups—hair sheers, styling gel, mouse, lipstick—signals that the makeover is now in progress. A quick pan right reveals The Pussycats' reflections in a long mirror as the team works them over. They look fearful, dubious at best. The cool blue filters on the camera lens and ice blue smocks of the stylists suggest an overall detached, unfeeling attitude. These makeover magicians are simply turning out a product, like real-life Josie Britney Spears.

Britney began her career as a Mousketeer, but when she started a solo career, she was a sex kitten, wearing school uniforms and sweat pants in her first videos. Then wham! She went from being a young girl to a woman. (She once wore a totally transparent jumpsuit to the Grammy Awards.) Britney was so hot that Pepsi hired her for their commercials in which she danced with a Pepsi tab instead of a ring in her navel. Britney would feel right at home in *Josie and the Pussycats*. She's definitely a product as much as a performer.

Meanwhile, back at the salon, the Pussycats are being poked, tweezed, colored, manicured, masked, and blow dried, but eventually they start to have fun with the makeover. When the scene shifts to wardrobe, we hear an up-tempo tune. The brainwashing has begun. The Pussycats emerge from the salon much later, a glittered, glamorous versions of their former selves. The hair is puffier, the color more intense. The makeup is heavier, more pronounced. The clothes are rock n' ready stylish, all sparkles and spangles, revealing much more skin than their previous duds. The illusion is complete as they stand outside looking up at a gigantic marquis bearing their pictures and the name "Josie and The Pussycats," But Wyatt has a warning: "Don't worry. If you screw up, we'll just put somebody else up there." His comment, like so much of the movie, offers a stinging indictment of the unpredictable music business.

But a dark cloud hangs over this makeover. The montage that eventually follows this scene shows the whirlwind publicity process to the tune of "Pretend to be Nice." Wyatt has taken the group to the top of the charts in one short week. The photo sessions, the headlines, the billboards, the limos, the product endorsements, and the screaming fans carry a phony, manufactured, hollow ring. Something is amiss. Melody sees shadows out of the corners of her eyes. Strange messages, such as "Beware of the music," appear mysteriously on the steamy bathroom mirror. And Wyatt drives the first wedge between Josie and her friends by privileging Josie's name and making her the star. It seems all of the products have Josie's picture on them. Val gets jealous. Wyatt then makes a racial comment to Val and deliberately excludes her when handing out invitations to the party Fiona is throwing in their honor. Later Fiona will order Wyatt to "Keep Josie—and put those two pussycats to sleep." Can The Pussycats' pledge of friendship survive such scheming?

Much of the plot focuses on Josie—her man troubles, her brainwashing, and her eventual discovery of Wyatt and Fiona's plot to control the youth of America. She has brought Alan M along on this ride, and he has remained in the background, strumming his guitar and eating pizza, for the most part. But when Josie emerges from her dressing room, ready for Fiona's party, wearing a very low-cut leopard print gown slit to almost the hip, she gets her dreamboat's attention. He stands stunned, rooted to the floor and holding a pizza box as he drools at Josie's revealing outfit, her glistening skin, seductive makeup, and perfectly coiffed hair. When he finds his voice, he utters the famous male line from countless makeover movies: "I've never seen you ... Wow." When they do manage some time together, they are chased by screaming fans and take sanctuary in an aquarium where they play out a brief romance in silhouette (a technique obviously borrowed from Woody Allen's *Annie Hall*) with an Evian billboard clearly visible in the whale tank.

The lovers are soon parted when Wyatt laces one of Josie's CDs with subliminal messages to turn against her friends and see herself as a prima donna. She manages to efficiently and cruelly alienate everyone close to her until she takes a fall in her glass platforms, knocking her headphones to the ground. In true comic book fashion (all we're missing is the bubble with the light bulb above her head), Josie gets an idea. She's being brainwashed and maybe, just maybe, the megaprocessor has something to do with it.

Josie's showdown with Fiona on the night of her big concert, while thousands of prefab fans cheer in anticipation, confirms her suspicions. Mr. MovieFone's mellifluous messages have indeed been controlling the "playdough minds" of American youth. "I'm not going on. I'm nobody's pimp," the enlightened Josie tells Fiona as they duke it out in the film's climax. The Pussycats are reunited, and the megaprocessor is destroyed, exposing Fiona's and Wally's true identities. It seems they've been masquerading in makeovers. She's really Lisping Lisa, and he's Whiteass Wally—two high school losers, teased and taunted by their classmates, whose obsession to be popular drove them over the edge. Of course, they get together. The concert goes on, and The Pussycats take the stage—as themselves. "Decide for yourselves," Josie yells to the confused crowd, which goes wild as the band plays "We're Fine." And just to make this sugary ending sweeter, Alan M crashes the stage in the middle of the number and kisses Josie.

Critics roundly panned the film, and rightly so. *Josie and the Pussycats* virtually chokes on its intended satire of the rock industry, conformity, and mass consumerism. The makeover element, however, is what ultimately underscores the film's message: be true to yourself. Once The Pussycats catch on to the subterfuge, their glitter fades, and they play out the concert looking much as they did in their before state, suggesting— dare we say it—all that glitters is not gold.

Legally Blonde *(2001)*

Legally Blonde, starring the enormously talented Reese Witherspoon (*Election, Pleasantville, Sweet Home Alabama*) as West Coast sorority princess Elle Woods, sends all the right messages to its target audience: 12 to 18-year-old girls. Too bad the critics didn't dig a little deeper beneath the film's tagline "This summer go blonde!" On the surface, *Legally Blonde*, directed by Robert Luketic and written by Karen McCullah Lutz and Kirsten Smith (*10 Things I Hate about You*), looks like just another boobs and blondes flick. However, in the current *Extreme Makeover* cultural climate where ubiquitous icons of impossible beauty, the Barbie doll bodies, rule and where young women lack self-esteem to the point of mutilating their own bodies or starving themselves to death to achieve the ideal mainly because they think that's what men want, the film makes powerful arguments for having the "courage of conviction" and a "strong sense of self" and serves them up in a palatable way to the female demographic.

Even the music supports these messages, as Superchick sings "One Girl Revolution." The film opens with cross cutting between Elle's sorority sisters signing a card for Elle and Elle getting dressed. The juxtaposition of shots establishes the close connection among the sisters and their affection for their Delta Nu president. One young woman says, "Elle's gonna love it," and two others kiss the envelope before they slide it under her door. This opening scene is key since *Legally Blonde* offers a good example of bonding around gender instead of reinforcing the typical competition between women. In fact, what female competition does exist here between Elle and Vivian Kensington (Selma Blair) takes both women on a journey of self-discovery that ends in friendship.

The opening couple of scenes also establish Elle as a person who knows who she is: confident and beautiful, in a non-model way. At first we see her in fragments: blond hair, a shapely leg as she shaves, nice nails. A pan across her dresser and her room reveals a woman whose signature color is pink. Cut to Elle slipping her dainty foot into a hot pink platform sandal with a heart-shaped buckle. When the camera takes a full shot, we find a bubbly, buxom, blue-eyed blonde with a killer smile as she opens her card that reads "Good Luck. Elle and Warner forever." Like Cher Horowitz before her, Elle is the after, and she's clearly the most popular young woman on this fantasy California campus, CULA.

The following scene serves a double duty. It actually sets up the courtroom scene in the movie's climax as well as demonstrates what happens to women who disrespect their own gender. Elle is shopping for the "perfect outfit" with two sorority sisters. She thinks her steady, Warner Huntington, III (Matthew Davis) is going to pop the question at dinner, and she wants to look her best. A snotty shop clerk spies Elle with her friends and says to another employee, "There's nothing I love more than a dumb blonde with her daddy's plastic." She rips the sale tag off of a dress and says to Elle, "We just got this in yesterday." Elle plays along: "Is this low viscosity rayon? With a half loop top stitching on the hem?" Shop woman nods, hesitatingly, and replies, "Yes, of course." And then Elle delivers the lines that let the audience know that she's more than meets the eye: "It's impossible to use half-loop top stitching on low viscosity rayon. It would snag the fabric. And you didn't just get it in. I saw it in the June *Vogue* a year ago. So, if you're trying to sell it to me for full price, you picked the wrong girl." No dumb blonde here. As Roger Ebert writes in his review of the film, "Despite the title and the implications in the ads, this is a movie about smart blondes, not dumb ones, and she is (I think) using her encyclopedic knowledge of fashion and grooming to disguise her penetrating intelligence." Elle descends the stairs that evening to find her sisters all lined up to wish her well and see her off. One squirts breath freshener in her mouth; another spritzes her with perfume. Warner, wearing shades (always a bad sign) and chewing gum, wisks her off to dinner where he proceeds to tell her that he wants to break up with her. He's going to Harvard Law School, and he needs to be more serious. "If I'm going to be a senator," he says, "I need to marry a Jackie, not a Marilyn." Shocked and devastated, Elle responds: "You're breaking up with me because I'm too blonde? My boobs are too big?" She runs out of the restaurant. Cut to Elle crying as she walks along the street. Warner pulls up next to her in the car. "I have to think of my future," he says.

> ELLE: "But everybody likes me. I grew up in Belair, across from Aaron Spelling. That's a lot better than some stinky old Vanderbilt."
> WARNER: "I told you—I need someone serious."
> ELLE: "But I'm seriously in love with you."
> WARNER: "You're going to ruin your shoes."
> ELLE: "Okay."

She climbs into the car, but Warner dumps her at the Delta Nu house and drives off without a backward glance.

By this time, we're Elle fans, too. Her upbeat, generous nature is hard not to like. So what that she's a little flashy. She's got soul, and this Prince Charming is not worthy of her descent into chocolates and soap operas. Their breakup becomes the catalyst for the rest of the plot. With a little help from her friends, Elle gets a manicure and a new attitude. This 4.0 GPA fashion merchandising major is going to Harvard to get Warner back. All she needs is a 175 on her LSATs.

The scenes of Elle studying for her exams are intercut with clips from her video entrance essay and point to the contradiction between her looks and her intelligence. Although some viewers might argue that Elle

Legally Blonde (MGM, 2001). BEFORE: One of the pleasant surprises in the teen makeover genre, *Legally Blonde* promotes strong female bonding, not competition, and extols the virtues of self-confidence and courage of conviction to an impressionable teen audience in dire need of those messages. Delightfully enacted by Reese Witherspoon, Elle's strong sense of self and indomitable spirit make her attractive to both men *and* women. In this scene, her sorority sisters wish her well with Warner (Matthew Davis), a guy who dumps her—she's too blonde and buxom—for a "serious" girlfriend. (Since he's going to Harvard, he needs "a Jackie, not a Marilyn.") Here she clowns with two of her sisters in her signature color, pink, looking every inch the carefree, breezy California girl.

uses her physical endowments to get past the Harvard Board of Directors, the video is done with such creativity and humor that we end up rooting for her. For example, one scene in her video has Elle walking across campus wearing a flirty low-cut pink dress saying "I feel comfortable using legal jargon in everyday life" when she hears a wolf whistle behind her. She turns and shouts, "I object!" Her non-traditional essay has the stuffy Harvard board looking for excuses to admit her to law school. And, when Elle passes the LSATs with a 179, we cheer as loudly as the Delta Nus. In truth, all of our makeover heroines have one major thing in common—they are all basically decent human beings who expe-

Legally Blonde (MGM, 2001). AFTER: Warner's serious girlfriend, Vivian (Selma Blair), with her serious laptop can barely conceal her contempt for fellow Harvard law student, Elle Woods, in this classroom scene. Though Vivian tries to undercut Elle at every turn, she eventually comes to respect Elle's sense of honor and fair play, and the two become friends. In this shot, we see Elle in transition. Aware that she needs to blend in a bit with the Harvard crowd, she begins to tone down her playful, colorful California ensembles. She gives that legal eagle look a bit of her own style until, by the end of the film, we see her addressing her graduating class at Harvard in her cap and gown. Elle has gone to the head of her class, but she's done it without compromising who she is inside.

rience cruelty, pettiness, jealousy, and prejudice before their ultimate triumph. Audiences respond to their warmth, suffer their indignities, and cheer them on.

But life at Harvard challenges even Elle's positive personality, and her transformation from "Malibu Barbie" in her pink leather suit, sports car, and with her constant Chihuahua companion, Bruiser, to sophisticated—yet still irrepressible—legal eagle is a gradual, bumpy journey. Elle's bright California colors and trendy clothes stand out against the drab blues and grays of East Coast academia, and her cheerful, friendly attempts to fit in are met with palpable prejudice from snobby Ivy Leaguers. David (Oz Perkins), Enid (Meredith Scott Lynn), and Aaron (Kelly Nyks) look on in astonishment and disdain as Elle reveals that she and Bruiser are Gemini vegetarians and recounts a story about talking Cameron Diaz out of buying a "heinous" angora sweater. "Whoever said orange was the new pink was seriously disturbed," she proclaims.

Desperately wanting to blend in, Elle dons an electric blue suit and man's tie. Her hair is pulled back in a ponytail, and she's wearing thick-framed glasses. "I totally look the part," she says to her reflection in the mirror. Confident that she's struck just the right tone with her ensemble, she runs into Warner, leaving him speechless when she tells him she got into Harvard Law School and heads to her first class with Professor Stromwell (Holland Taylor). At first, Stromwell thinks Elle's a joke, too. As Elle sits in the front row with her heart-shaped note pad and pen with pink angora, Stromwell zeroes in to make an example of her. The low-angle camera on Stromwell makes her appear to tower over Elle, who hasn't read the assignment in advance. Stromwell dismisses her and tells her not to come back until she's prepared. In the end, however, Stromwell recognizes Elle's intelligence and grit and eventually becomes the younger woman's mentor.

A second blow comes when Elle learns that Warner is engaged to the smirking, pearl-wearing, diamond-flashing Vivian Kensington, who does everything in her power to humiliate Elle. Vivian excludes her from study groups, even when others, including Warner, would have her join. "Our group is full," Vivian says. "Is this like an RSVP thing?" Elle asks. "No, it's like a smart people thing," Vivian hisses. She cruelly sets up Elle to attend a "costume party" that isn't a costume party at all. When Elle shows up in a sexy bunny costume, Vivian snickers, "Nice costume." This time, Elle strikes back: "I like yours, too. When I dress up as a frigid bitch, I try not to look so constipated." On the other hand, Warner thinks she looks like a "walking felony." But when Elle tells Warner that she's applying for one of Professor Callahan's (Victor Garber) first-year internships, he says patronizingly, "You're not smart enough, sweetie."

In the meantime, the only two people who are nice to Elle are third-year law student Emmett Richmond (Luke Wilson, the real Prince Charming here), and manicurist Paulette (Jennifer Coolidge). Good-looking and kind, Emmett gives Elle advice on her professors, supports her decisions, and ends up falling for her himself. He never rescues her. He doesn't have to, but he does provide the opportunity she needs to prove her ability in a murder case. Paulette becomes a sister-friend. She offers support and encouragement to Elle, and, in exchange, Elle helps Paulette get her dog back from her brute of an ex-husband who "followed his pecker to greener pastures" and gives the shy manicurist some "bend and snap" tips on how to communicate with the hot UPS delivery guy who's already interested in Paulette. Their genuine affection for each other, despite their class and cultural differences, illustrates Elle's ability to embrace people of all backgrounds.

She has a good, forgiving heart. In one scene, she comes to dorky David's rescue. He's trying to ask out a co-ed who won't give him the time of day. Enter Elle, who stages a scene that suggests he is a stud and then walks away. The co-ed, now impressed that David could attract someone as beautiful as Elle, suddenly changes her mind about that date with David. Though Elle is treated badly by her classmates, she never holds it against them, and, in the end, wins not only their respect but also their friendship.

Elle's physical transformation follows the same trajectory as her academic progress. We see her sitting in Professor Callahan's class, now taking notes on a laptop computer, dressed in a chic black, sleeveless turtleneck sweater with her blonde hair pulled neatly away from her face. She blends in with the rest of the students. Her intelligent, out-of-the-box answers to her professor's provoking questions gain respect from him and the other students, as well as win her one of the coveted first-year intern slots, much to the astonishment of Vivian, Warner, and Enid who round out the rest of Callahan's team. Professor Callahan, who assembles a team each year to tackle a real-life case, is defending physical fitness queen Brooke Windham, who is accused of killing her wealthy, older husband.

Elle enters the courthouse for the first briefing wearing a beautiful black dress with a broad white collar and classy black pumps. She turns to Vivian, the person who has made Harvard life a misery, and says, "You look very nice today, Vivian." Vivian now returns the compliment.

Two other surprises await Elle in the briefing room. First, Emmett, Callahan's assistant, has joined the team. Second, it turns out that Elle knows the accused Brooke Windham, a fellow Delta Nu and her exercise instructor in California. Though Brooke refuses to provide an alibi for the time of the murder, Elle insists she couldn't have killed her husband. "Exercise makes endorphins. Endorphins make you happy. Happy people just don't kill their husbands. They just don't." Her syllogism turns out to hold truth when Brooke, who establishes a rapport with Elle, entrusts her Delta Nu sister with her alibi. She was having liposuction when the murder occurred but can't tell because it would ruin her career. "Your secret's safe with me," Elle assures her.

Another common thread among our makeover heroines is their integrity. To a woman, they stand for something. They have honor, and the best of them stand by their friends. Elle won't give away Brooke's secret to Callahan, though he gets angry with her. "I can't break the bonds of sisterhood," she says. It's Warner who urges her give it up. "Who cares about Brooke?" he asks. "I gave my word, Warner," Elle responds. Vivian overhears and later goes to Elle's room where the two do some bonding of their own. "It was classy of you not to tell Brooke's alibi," Vivian offers. Vivian seems shy, almost tentative. She realizes she made a mistake about Elle and is trying to reach out to her. She confesses that she's upset that Callahan always asks her to fetch his coffee. They laugh about some of Warner's flaws, but never in a cruel way. Then Vivian discloses that Warner was waitlisted when he first applied to Harvard. He was only admitted after his influential father made a call. Elle's expression says it all. Warner is a loser.

But Vivian still hasn't learned to trust another woman. She overhears Callahan putting the moves on Elle, but she doesn't hear Elle's rebuff (another positive message that no one should put up with or give in to sexual harassment). She thinks Elle got her position by sleeping with her professor until Emmett, who knows the truth, sets her straight. "I've made a horrible mistake," Vivian finally admits. She finally understands Elle's mantra: "Have a little faith in people. You might be surprised."

At the beauty parlor, Professor Stromwell overhears Elle telling Paulette what happened. "All people see when they look at me is blonde hair and big boobs. No one's ever going to take me seriously.... It turns out I am a joke," she cries. Suddenly she hears Stromwell behind her: "If you're going to let one stupid prick ruin your life, you're not the girl I thought you were."

On this advice, Elle wins the day in court. Brooke fires Callahan and hires Elle, who uses her vast knowledge of hair care to get the real murderer to confess and exonerate Brooke. "The rules of hair care are simple and finite," she tells a waiting press. Though highly improbable, the ending is totally satisfying since another common element in the makeover genre is a bit of revenge. Warner wants Elle back. "You are the girl for me," he coos. Elle responds, "If I'm going to be a partner in a law firm before I'm 30, I need a partner who is not such a complete bonehead." Justice is sometimes sweet.

It's the resolution of the film, however, that underscores that critical message to young women and makes *Legally Blonde* an important teen makeover movie. At graduation, Stromwell introduces the class-elected speaker, Elle, who has been invited to join one of the most prestigious law firms in Boston. Elle takes the podium in her cap and gown, looking sleek and sophisticated, and delivers a short speech about what she has learned:

On our very first day at Harvard, a very wise professor quoted Aristotle: "The law is reason free from passion." Well, no offense to Aristotle, but in my three years at Harvard, I have come to find that passion is the key ingredient to the study and practice of law and of life. It is with passion, courage of conviction, and strong sense of self that we take our next steps into the world—remembering that first impressions are not always correct. You must always have faith in people, and, most importantly, you must always have faith in yourself.

The crowd erupts in cheers as Hoku's song "A Perfect Day" plays under a series of visuals with subtitles indicating what happens to key characters. Of course, Elle ends up with her real Prince Charming, Emmett, the man who has had faith in her from the beginning. The subtitle reveals that he's proposing to Elle that night.

As we look at this new generation of makeover movies, we find some encouraging signs. Since more women are directing, we may see more films the caliber of *Clueless*, directed by Amy Heckerling. We may see more young heroines with substance, intelligence, talent, compassion, and wit, like the characters in these films. Their physical transformations may begin with the purpose of attracting that object of desire, but, along the way, the makeover teaches them something about themselves, gives them confidence, and makes them even better individuals. They understand the meaning of female friendship. And, they end up controlling their own destinies instead of depending on a man (read Prince Charming) to do it for them.

In some respects, these characters remind us of those feisty femmes of the 1930s, which Molly Haskell calls one of the "few truly 'liberated' periods of cinema," where women could be aggressors in love, initiate sex, pursue men, or embody "male characteristics" without penalty, without coming across as "'unfeminine' or 'predatory'" (*Reverence to Rape* 91). In short, these are young women who can show us how to get what we want without losing our souls.

It might be interesting for audiences to keep an eye on these teen makeover films, to talk to their daughters and their daughters' teen friends about them. Do teens know that these films come from a long tradition? Do they know any versions of Cinderella besides Disney's? Do they recognize the conventions of the genre? Carol Gilligan and Lynn Mikel Brown's *Standing at the Crossroads* emphasizes the need for communication between generations of women. Too often, they argue, girls feel isolated, with only one cohort to guide them. They say older women should cultivate friendships with younger women.

MTV's new hit, *Made*, where each week some new needy, nerdy teen participant gets a makeover, suggests the timing couldn't be better for stepped-up communication between generations. As Terry Morrow points out, this show has good intentions, but delivers some mixed messages. "The show doesn't delve into the deeper reasons a teenage girl wants to alter her image," the subhead reads (D3). For example, in the first show, a 17-year-old girl from New Jersey with a weight problem wants to become a cheerleader. Why? As Morrow reasons, "Had she merely wanted to lose weight because she needed to, or because the weight made her feel bad about herself, then 'Made' could be more inspirational. Instead, she sets her goal to be part of a popular crowd" (D3). Morrow suggests that "a better example would have shown us a participant who learned the real worth of a person is within and without" (D3).

Certainly, the female characters in this chapter come to realize their value as people, whether their learning grounds are high school corridors, college campuses, or rock 'n' roll highways. Their physical makeovers, however, essentially gain them popularity and the hunky Prince. For the characters in the next chapter, the stakes rise to the wider world—a world where Prince Charmings run multi-billion dollar corporations, a world where makeovers catapult Cinderellas across class boundaries.

Four

The Ladder of Class

It's easy to clean up when you got money.
—Vivian, *Pretty Woman*

The makeover often signifies not only a new look but also a repositioning for the heroine in Hollywood films, reflecting the particularly
American notion that class boundaries can be crossed or leveled. The
female characters in *Sabrina* (1954, 1995), *Funny Face* (1957), *Grease*
(1978), *Working Girl* (1988), *Pretty Woman* (1990), and *Maid in Manhattan* (2002) show us that an updated do, a little makeup, some contact
lenses, a designer outfit, and a stylish pair of shoes can open some pretty
big doors. Whether her move is up the class or corporate ladder, the physical makeover is the key, the entre to a better world—and better fit with
the man who lives there.

The dynamics of this scenario differ greatly from some films of old.
In *It Happened One Night* (1934), *Libeled Lady* (1936), and *Woman of the
Year* (1942), for example, our heroines move in circles high above the men
who woo and win them. They are often spoiled, rich, and feisty, with a
fierce wit and independent spirit. Initially, our heroine hooks up with
some milktoast of a guy with lots of money and little personality. Then
he comes along—a man she can't push over, a man her wealth and social
position can't influence. With his middle-class, all-American values, he
teaches her a thing or two about *real* life and *real* men. Their misadven-
tures spell "made for each other," and their happily-ever-after suggests a
blissful state of verbal sparring.

The heroine's makeover in these early films is not so much physical
as psychological. She's already a stunner, decked out in all the finery that
money and breeding can buy. Instead, her transformation lies in what she's
willing to sacrifice for the hero. To keep this man, this worthy opponent
and potential life partner, she must shed only the signifiers of her class:
her haughtiness, her frivolousness, her empty pursuits, her empty-headed

friends, her dull fiancé. Keeping her intelligence and wit always in play since that's partly what attracted the hero in the first place, she must come down off her proverbial "high horse" and embrace the virtues of the common man. He gives her grounding; she gives him a leg up in social status. It's a fair exchange, perhaps, and one reason their relationship seems made of studier stuff than that of latter-day heroes and heroines.

From Billy Wilder's 1954 version of *Sabrina* to the present, the makeover generally functions as the catalyst for the *heroine's* change in social status. The physical transformation gets her noticed by a man who would never otherwise look at her, let alone consider her as potential mate. Sometimes in these films (which we discuss in Chapter V), the hero himself initiates the makeover, though his reasons for undertaking this monumental task are usually motivated by his monumental ego. Photographer Dick Avery (Fred Astaire) in *Funny Face* needs a fresh "face" for the cover of *Quality* magazine. Professor Higgins (Rex Harrison) in *My Fair Lady* wants to win a bet from Colonel Pickering. Corporate raider Edward Lewis (Richard Gere) in *Pretty Woman* needs a beautiful armpiece for the New York social scene. In *Up Close and Personal*, Warren Justice (Robert Redford) wants to create a crack reporter in his own image. All serious men with serious money, at the top of their professions, they *are* the rich and famous. They take what they want and consider feelings later, if at all. A beautiful woman is leverage, part of the master business plan designed to help get them what they need. In each case, the hero reaches down from his lofty perch and lifts a diamond in the rough to his level using his power and influence to make her over into an image that befits him. In exchange for her repositioning, the heroine softens the hard edges of this control freak and shows him that there's more to life than work and money.

In some scenarios, the hero may already know and like the before, but, often because they are from two different worlds, never thinks of her in a romantic way until her metamorphosis. The transformed creature descends the stairs or walks into the room. Our hero looks up, catches his breath, and stands rooted to the floor—slack-jawed and paralyzed with awe and mystification. Who is this apparition before him? When he finally recognizes the girl of his dreams, like turns to love. Her makeover acts as the bridge between worlds and her beauty the only dowry necessary to enter his.

Sabrina *(1954)*

One of Hollywood's most famous repositioning makeovers occurs in *Sabrina*, Billy Wilder's 1954 screen version of Samuel Taylor's 1953 play,

Sabrina Fair. Audrey Hepburn stars as Sabrina Fairchild, the chauffeur's daughter infatuated with the dashing David Larrabee (William Holden). After spending two years in Paris (the makeover capital of the world), Sabrina returns transformed into a charming, glamorous woman who finally gets David's attention. Older brother and workaholic Linus Larrabee (Humphrey Bogart) has other plans for David—a marriage to an heiress that will increase the already hefty Larrabee fortune. Sabrina is in the way, so he sets out to distract her, to woo her himself. In the process, he falls for her and finally realizes what he's been missing.

Sabrina's voiceover, which begins with "Once upon a time," sets up the fairytale motif throughout Wilder's film, and the opening scene visualizes her narration on life in the "castle." After the extreme high-angle long shot of the Larrabee Long Island estate—the ever-present, silent character and reminder of the enormous gulf between the classes in a "classless" society—we see Sabrina helping her father, Thomas Fairchild (John Williams), wash one of the Larrabees' many expensive vehicles. Sabrina is dressed in classic Cinderella style befitting her station in life: her long hair in a ponytail, her jumper fitted at the waist, her feet bare. The before signifiers are minimized as Sabrina wears no glasses, no cloddy shoes, no frumpy clothes. There is no hint of an ugly duckling here, as there is with Bette Davis' Charlotte Vale.

Like Cinderella, Sabrina's beauty is hard to disguise. She is framed and photographed to enhance her features. The camera gazes as longingly at her as she gazes at David. Wilder's frequent, lingering close-ups of her exquisite face and lithe body suggest immaturity, not plainness. The close-ups also make sure that the audience connects immediately and emotionally with her character who must make the journey from gangly girlhood to woman "in the world" sophistication in order to break the class barrier. Along the way, she picks up the signifiers of the cosmopolitan female—the contemporary hairstyle, the chic ensembles, the confident smile. The makeover works as a plot device, guaranteeing Sabrina's place in the Larrabee lifestyle (read rich and famous). The new Sabrina "fits," like one of her Givenchy gowns.

Several technical devices help signal the before and after as well as the class chasm. The exposition shots of Sabrina as a moonstruck young girl show her on the outside looking in. She watches the lavish Larrabee parties, zeroing in particularly on playboy David Larrabee, from her perch in a tree by the garage, above which she and her father live. (Sabrina's mother is dead, another plot identification with the Cinderella story.) When David leaves the party with one of his conquests for the evening, he literally runs into Sabrina and casually remarks, "I thought I heard

Sabrina (Paramount, 1954). BEFORE: With her ponytail, bare feet, and fitted "Cinderella" jumper, Sabrina (Audrey Hepburn) looks every inch the chauffeur's daughter, yet her attention is not focused on washing the Larrabee Rolls—the status symbol which takes up most of the frame and divides her and her father. She looks longingly off frame, toward the castle, dreaming of the prince who lives there. The spiral staircase, a typical motif in makeover movies, looms slightly out of focus at this point but promises ascension to another level. The open space around Sabrina suggests freedom of movement, too, while Mr. Fairchild (John Williams), pinned between the garage and the car, has little room to move and so concentrates on the task at hand.

somebody." Crushed, she responds, "No, it's nobody." And she is nobody to David without the signifiers of class and breeding. She follows David to his favorite trysting place, the indoor tennis court, and watches him romance a silly socialite through the window. All we see are her huge, expressive eyes watching from the outside.

Dejected and despondent, she returns to the garage and climbs the staircase to her room. The staircase, a frequent motif in these makeover films, suggests the heroine's journey. The climb up usually symbolizes challenges and struggles ahead, and here it serves as a subtle reminder of her place in this society. In fact, Sabrina is constantly reminded of her

11506-35

Sabrina (Paramount, 1954). AFTER: Audrey Hepburn's "love affair" with Hubert de Givenchy lasted a lifetime. He designed most of the couture costumes for *Sabrina*, including this perfectly fitted, exquisitely embroidered, strapless ball gown the title character wears to the Larrabee's party. A chic coif replaces the childish ponytail, while sleek pumps show off a shapely ankle. The picture of wealth and sophistication, she now holds David's (William Holden) gaze as steadily as he clasps her hand, lifting her into his upperclass world of champagne and parties.

station in life, even by her father, who tells her, "Don't reach for the moon, child." He decides to send her to cooking school in Paris, solidifying her future in the servant's quarters. But Sabrina has other plans. Crushed by David's indifference and a future below the stairs, she decides to end it all. After writing a childishly dramatic note to her father that reads, "Don't

even have David at the funeral—he probably won't even cry," she fool-
ishly attempts suicide by closing the garage doors and starting all of the
cars in the Larrabee fleet. Linus actually saves her in an ironically funny
scene as she explains, "I was just checking the spark plugs for my father."

The catalyst in the film is Sabrina's trip to Paris and her fateful meeting with 74-year-old Baron St. Fontanel in her cooking class. The
makeover must happen before anything else in the film can take place.
Though a member of the European uppercrust, the Baron recognizes Sabrina's unhappiness and potential. "You might as well be looking for the
moon," he tells her, echoing her father's warning. Referring to her adolescent ponytail, he advises, "You must stop looking like a horse." The
Baron realizes that in David's circle, appearance is everything. In order
to go to the ball, she must *look* like she belongs there.

We never see how this fairy godfather works his magic, but, two
years later, we see the results of his efforts. The sophisticated Cinderella,
on one of her last nights in Paris, is writing a letter of a very different
kind to her father. Wearing a chic white robe, her hair cut short in the
current Paris fashion, listening to strains of "La Vie en Rose" from the
street below, Sabrina writes that she has learned to be "in the world and
of the world" and predicts "I shall be the most sophisticated woman at
the Glen Coe Station."

Even with this glimpse of the new Sabrina, the transformation is
startling as Wilder cuts to the quintessential signifier of sophistication,
the poodle in his rhinestone collar, and tilts up to the after: Sabrina in
her beautifully fitted suit, white hat, earrings, and makeup that enhances
her chiseled features. David, in his flashy sportscar, screeches to a halt
before her. She's got his attention. Like most heroes at this point, however, he has no idea who she is because he's never *really* looked at her
before. "I could have sworn I knew every pretty girl on the North Shore,"
he confesses to a delighted Sabrina, who confidently toys with him about
her identity until he pulls into the Larrabee estate and Linus says, "Hello,
Sabrina."

Sabrina's journey into the old European world has taught her that
beauty and confidence pay big dividends in David's world. Her coy, flirtatious behavior suggests that she's comfortable in her new skin. "Everything's changed," she tells her father, but he again warns her: "Remember,
you are still a chauffeur's daughter, and you're still reaching for the moon."
This time Sabrina responds, "No, Father, the moon's reaching for me."
Sabrina's makeover opens the door to the world she's always wanted. Her
arrival at the Larrabee ball that evening in a stunning strapless gown is
a classic Cinderella entrance. Men gasp and women stare while Sabrina

smiles and sways to the music. She moves in this world now with grace and ease. Even the servants, watching from their places, whisper that she has "such poise, as if she belonged up there." The smitten Prince Charming, David, ditches his fiancé—fast—jumps a stone wall and whisks the chauffeur's daughter onto the dance floor. "Sabrina, Sabrina. Where have you been all my life?" he whispers in her ear. What a coup! As Jamie Bernard once said, "*Sabrina* is an example of one of women's favorite revenge fantasies—that the guy who wouldn't give you a second look would someday come begging when you have blossomed into the belle of the ball" (*Chick Flicks* 119).

One of the disturbing things about Wilder's film version lies in the ultimate brittleness of this heroine, which is a far different depiction than Taylor's original stage version of the Sabrina character. This Sabrina is oblivious to the fact that David is engaged to another woman. She has carved out her territory, and his name is David Larrabee. Though she may have confidence and sophistication, she seems almost amoral in her total disregard and compassion for Elizabeth Tyson, David's intended. In fact, Hepburn's Sabrina has no female friends or confidants. She has loved David all her life, and now she has the ammunition (provided by her makeover) to get him. It's matriarch Maude Larrabee, however, who reminds Sabrina of her level when she greets her with "You must come over and cook for us sometime." The not-so-subtle comment makes no impact on Sabrina, who is too busy reveling in the life she wants and fixating on reeling David in. "Would you like to kiss me, David? A nice steady kiss?" she asks him. The makeover has empowered and emboldened her, but the results are not necessarily flattering.

Intelligent and shrewd, Sabrina does understand that the Larrabees might object to her designs on David. The fact that she has come between the Larrabee/Tyson plastics merger sends eldest son and CEO Linus to the indoor tennis court where Sabrina is waiting for David, an incapacitated David, as it turns out. To keep him from meeting her, Linus tricks David into sitting on two champagne flutes that he has tucked into his back pockets. While he's having the shards extracted from his bottom, Linus goes to meet Sabrina. "You look lovely, Sabrina. Very grown up," he says. She knows he's been sent to "deal" with her, but she won't be bought off. "She doesn't want money. She wants love. The last of the romantics," Linus explains to Mr. Larrabee, who is in an agitated state about the "girl over the garage." Interestingly, during this conversation with his father, Linus attempts a makeover of his own. Desperate to distract Sabrina from his strategically engaged brother, Linus must get her attention, so he searches for the signifiers of his youth like his college sweater and cap. He only ends up looking silly, and his makeover fails because it is rooted in the past instead of the present.

Ultimately, through lies and deception, Linus succeeds in wooing Sabrina away from David, and in the process falls for her himself. Our heroine wins the chairman of the board, but men decide her fate at the boardroom table. Sabrina really has little say in the outcome of her future. Her makeover gains her entre into an elite class but no control. Even her one skill, cooking, is rendered unnecessary by her rise in social status.

Hepburn's Sabrina does not embody the spirit of women sitting in the audience as much as she offers them a model of what they might aspire to if only they could make themselves over: a good marriage to a man of means who would take care of her for the rest of her life, shades of Cinderella. But few women looked like Audrey, though they gave it their best shot. (Fifties fashion magazines featured slim models sporting Hepburn's cropped tresses, and "real" women copied the look.) Hepburn had the body of a fashion model, the bearing of a queen, and the face of an exotic, elegant angel. Her metamorphosis from gamine to sophisticated beauty in *Sabrina*, as well as other of her films, made her the quintessential armpiece for mature men with money and breeding, like Bogie's Linus or Fred Astaire's Dick Avery in *Funny Face*.

In 1957, Hepburn was paired with a man old enough to be her grandfather, Gary Cooper, in *Love in the Afternoon*. Coop plays Frank Flannagan, a man of refined tastes who dallies with married women to avoid commitment. Attracted by Ariane's (Hepburn) freshness, innocence, and romantic sensibilities, Frank literally sweeps her off her feet in the film's final scene as she runs alongside his departing train. Unable to say goodbye, she babbles and trots after him, her neediness almost too painful to watch.

It's precisely because of her ability to express this neediness and to bring out the protective instincts in her leading men that Hepburn became the female screen role model for a war-weary society. She posed little threat to the status quo. In the end, *Sabrina* is little more than a star vehicle for Audrey Hepburn and her French designer, Hubert de Givenchy. There's little spark between Hepburn and the aging Bogart. Their on-screen pairing pales in comparison to Hepburn's scenes with William Holden, with whom she actually fell in love during filming.

Sabrina Fair *(stageplay, 1953)*

Wilder's adaptation bears little resemblance to Samuel Taylor's 1953 dramatic version, *Sabrina Fair* even though Taylor helped Wilder and

Ernest Lehman write their screenplay. Much of the warmth and wit of the play are lost in translation, and the three main characters—Sabrina, Linus, and David—differ considerably from their dramatic counterparts. Wilder kept the fairytale motif, as the play also begins in narration—a young girl on stage opens with "once upon a time"—but Taylor's play moves immediately to a lovely scene between Maude Larrabee and her longtime friend, Julia Ward McKinlock, a magazine editor who is convalescing at the Larrabee estate. Their affection for each other is obvious as they reminisce about their past and Julia's time in Paris, which leads to a discussion of Sabrina, who happens to be returning from Paris where she's been living for five years. Thus, the audience meets two powerful, strong women; experiences a sense of female bonding and companionship instead of competition, from the beginning; and learns something about Sabrina before they see her. Here's how Maude describes her chauffeur's daughter to Julia:

> Sabrina was an earnest, scholarly little mouse, who graduated from a small women's college with all the high honors, and went to Paris for all the wrong reasons. There's so little romance in young people these days, have you noticed, Julia? And so little gayety [*sic*].... You went to Paris with the romantic hope that everything you'd ever wanted to happen would happen. And it did. Sabrina went to Paris to be a file clerk in one of those world-saving American projects called "NATO," or "SHAPE" [10].

We learn later that Sabrina advanced from file clerk to secretary to private secretary with a secretary of her own, but Maude remembers her as a "dun-colored, sallow little wisp ... very timid, very shy, quite intelligent, and ... terribly athletic" (13).

The Sabrina who returns, however, looks and acts quite differently from Maude's vision. At her entrance, Taylor describes Sabrina this way:

> Sabrina Fairchild is about David's age, and will look very much as she does now when she is very much older, for she is one of the lucky ones in whom youth and age will never be measured by days and years. She is beautifully and tastefully and expensively dressed in traveling clothes that show off a very good figure. No one could look more chic. She is not pretty, but her face is appealing and bright with animation and reflects the inner glow of a girl in love, for Sabrina Fairchild has fallen in love with the world and is carrying on a passionate affair with it [21].

Taylor puts the emphasis on Sabrina's inner strength and beauty, not the physical makeover. As with Charlotte Vale, Sabrina's makeover has given her self-confidence but hasn't made her brittle. Her warmth toward Maude brings out Maude's maternal instincts, and, later in the play, Maude "takes the girl in her arms and holds her in a long embrace," saying, "I wish you had been my daughter" (77). Mr. Larrabee, the eccentric patriarch who spends his retirement going to funerals, likes Sabrina instantly. So does Julia, who, after meeting Sabrina in Act I, turns to Maude and asks, "Tell me, Mrs. Larrabee, have you any more dun-colored, sallow little mice growing up in odd corners of the property?" (27). Both women are taken by the younger woman's intelligence (Sabrina speaks fluent French), charm, and genuineness. Margaret, Maude's maid, greets her little "Brina" with tears, embraces, and the exclamation "You've come home such a beautiful lady!" (27). In short, Taylor's female characters are quite fond of one another, and supportive, which gives an entirely different feel to the play.

Sabrina's father, however, feels his daughter has crossed the class line and tries to check her enthusiasm, to which Sabrina responds, "I'm sorry, father. I shall keep my place as soon as I know it" (23). In the beginning of Act II, he says to his daughter, "You were such a nice, quiet girl. How could anyone change so much in five years? You were so likeable!" (34). An injured Sabrina says, "You needn't fear, father.... Paris will wear off. Cinderella's been to her ball, but now she's back in the chimney corner, with no Prince Charming to seek her.... Anyway, I've got such *big* feet" (34).

Neither of the Larrabee sons shares Mr. Fairchild's sentiments. Both are instantly attracted to Sabrina. In fact, one of the most interesting differences between the play and Wilder's film version is the interplay among these three characters. Linus, the eldest son who "took a settled old American family business and built it into an international empire before he was thirty-five" (18), is the playboy, not David. He has a twisted sense of humor that extends to dating his brother's ex-wife. Though obviously loving toward his family, he is ruthless in business. Life is a game to Linus, and the game's about control. And he believes in marriage, which is precisely why he's never married. In his first scene with Sabrina, he wheedles several key pieces of information from her that illustrate his keen insight, persistence, and charisma. She's named after Milton's water nymph who saves a virgin from a fate worse than death in *The Masque of Comus*. She's run away from Paris to escape a wealthy Frenchman, Paul D'Argenson, who wants to marry her and who eventually shows up on the Larrabee doorstep to take her back. And she loves being domestic but fears being domesticated. She says, "The trouble with marriage is that men want to give you the world, but it has to be the world they want to give you. And what of the other worlds outside the window?" (45). Men don't have "the exclusive right to run from domestication," she tells him (45). This speech would be akin to Cinderella saying, "Yeah, the castle's great, but what's outside the moat?"

Sabrina's ideas about life and love, her open and direct manner of conversing, her youthful passion, and her sense of humor intrigue Linus and captivate David, who has a relatively minor role in the play. After spending one night talking with Sabrina, David wants to marry her. He tells Maude and Linus:

> This girl is different from any girl I've ever known.... When you're with Sabrina, you find yourself suddenly talking about things you've always wanted to do and that you've forgotten. You become aware of all the things you've missed and all the things you're missing. She's so much in love with life, there's so much feeling of life in her, that you want to take hold, you want to have her, because maybe if you do, you'll have what she has [54].

It seems, however, that everyone else knows about David's intentions before Sabrina, including Mr. Fairchild. He opposes the match because his daughter would be marrying above her station, though we eventually discover the chauffeur is a millionaire because of his investments in Larrabee stock. Sabrina has her own reasons for not marrying David:

> You took me for granted. Oh, yes. Look deep, David. You took it for granted that I would curtsey and say, "Yes, sir," didn't you...? And that's what's always been wrong with the story. Everyone takes it for granted that Cinderella will marry Prince Charming when he comes knocking on her door with that diamond-studded slipper. Nobody considers Cinderella. What if she thinks Prince Charming is a great big oaf? [67].

Besides, she doesn't love him. She loves Linus, and, in a delightful twist, asks him to marry her. He responds, "Will you save me, Sabrina? You are the only one who can" (82–83). As Gerald Wood points out in "Gender, Caretaking, and the Three Sabrinas," "Empowered by her own will and choices, Sabrina needs only companionship from Linus as she saves him from his isolating need to own people 'without being owned' himself" (73).

This is a far cry from Wilder's version, and we have to wonder why this strong, independent, intelligent character never made it to the screen. Taylor's stage Sabrina upset the "natural" order of the American society in the 1950s, and, in an era still reeling from Joseph McCarthy's House Un-American Activities Committee hearings, such an "unconventional" character might have been interpreted as too much of a deviation from the wholesome, traditional roles embraced by the peacetime propaganda machine. Hollywood, especially, had been hard hit by those looking for a communist under every rock, and, perhaps, just wasn't prepared to put a woman with a mind of her own, a woman who ran from being domesticated, a woman who actually proposed to a man, on the screen. Whereas the theater might have escaped scrutiny because of its smaller scope and influence, the powerful, pervasive movie-making industry was a prime target for McCarthy's bizarre witchhunts. Thus, Taylor's original stage vision, entitled "Sabrina Fair: or, A Woman of the World," becomes simply *Sabrina* for the screen—an adaptation as watered down as the title implies.

Sabrina *(1995)*

In 1995, Sydney Pollack (*The Way We Were, Tootsie, The Firm*) decided to remake Wilder's 1954 hit with two newcomers to film—Julia Ormond as Sabrina and Greg Kinnear as David. It was a gutsy decision to update a popular classic, let alone cast relative unknowns, but Pollack reduced the risk factor by casting superstar Harrison Ford as Linus Larrabee. The timing would have been perfect for an adaptation of Taylor's stageplay, but Pollack basically follows Wilder's plotline and misses the opportunity to shift the focus of the story back to Sabrina and Linus.

Pollack does return to the female-centered story that we have with Taylor's play and Prouty's *Now, Voyager*. Julia Ormond's Sabrina studies fashion photography in Paris and has a stunning fairy godmother and mentor in *Vogue* editor Irene (Fanny Ardant), who aids in her transformation. While there, she meets a hunky French photographer who falls for her. Their relationship never takes off because Sabrina still pines for David, whose fiancée, Elizabeth Tyson (Lauren Holly), is a medical doctor instead of an empty-headed heiress. There is no Mr. Larrabee. Maude (Nancy Marchand), who has made the cover of *Fortune* magazine, now runs the Larrabee empire with her son, Linus.

The gulf between the classes has closed a bit over the years, although, as Gerald Woods writes, "Fairchild becomes wealthy by overhearing the investment strategies of the Larrabees, implying that the wealthy have information not usually available to the lower classes" (75). On the other hand, when the contemporary Sabrina mentions that she's the chauffeur's daughter, it's Linus who says, "This is the '90s, Sabrina." Later, when a business partner calls her the "chauffeur's daughter," Linus yells, "Don't call her that!" And some point is also made of Mrs. Tyson (Angie Dickinson)—now a millionaire's wife—being a former flight attendant. Political correctness not withstanding, Pollack's *Sabrina* never achieves the true spark of Taylor's original story. Keeping his moonstruck heroine's fixation on David in the second film version diminishes the character's strength, wit, and spirited interchanges with Linus, her intellectual equal in the stageplay.

Because class isn't a huge issue in Pollack's *Sabrina*, the "ladder" isn't a hard climb. But the makeover must still be in play before any movement upward for our heroine. David would never notice Sabrina in the before state and, remember, that he is her target. "You're absolutely transformed," he tells her in one scene. "I haven't seen you in years. I'm not sure I've ever seen you." Both the 1954 and 1995 film versions focus the story on Sabrina's gradual realization that the man she has obsessed over her whole life is not the man for her instead of keeping the spotlight on Linus and Sabrina's relationship as Taylor did in his play. Therefore, Sabrina's makeover must be dramatic enough to get *David's* attention. (Interestingly, in all three versions, Linus instantly recognizes the after and takes it casually, much to Sabrina's disappointment.)

Wilder, seemingly unable or unwilling to de-emphasize Hepburn's natural beauty, simply transformed his heroine from beautiful gamine to beautiful woman—which seemed to be change enough for William Holden's David. Pollack dramatizes the transformation by making the before signifiers for Sabrina more pronounced and more Charlotte Vale-like. He camouflages Ormond's considerable good looks with thick glasses, long and heavy hair, shapeless jumpers, and cloddy shoes. There's more of an emphasis, too, on her shyness and awkwardness. Her well-read, enlightened father (John Wood) encourages his daughter to stop mooning about over David and use her talents: "There's much more to you than this obsession." But the night before he packs her off to spend two years with *Vogue* in Paris, Sabrina feels the need to confess her feelings to David. She tentatively knocks on his door, enters, and unburdens herself while she thinks he's in the bathroom. Linus appears instead, sending a stammering, mortified Sabrina running from the room.

To intensify the effect of Sabrina's transformation on David, Pollack never allows us to see the makeover moment on screen even though he spends a considerable amount of screen time showing us the klutzy Sabrina in her Paris environment. Initially, she can't understand or speak French so she has no idea what her co-workers are telling her to do and screws up a major fashion shoot. She clods along the streets of Paris looking much like she did before she hit the big city. Several critics cried foul. Sabrina spends all that time in Paris, and we never get to see her evolu-

Sabrina (Paramount, 1995). AFTER: Standing on the intrinsically heavy right half of the frame, the "new" Sabrina (Julia Ormond), the picture of Paris sophistication, gets not only our attention but David's, as she flashes him a wide smile. Gone are the awkward signifiers of her adolescence and her "before" look: long hair, bushy eyebrows, shapeless jumpers, sneakers, and glasses. After spending two years in Paris, she returns home only to find that her cosmopolitan makeover is as out of place above the garage as it is here, amid the quaint shops and antique stores.

tion from frump to fashion diva? Not fair, they complained. But the delay gives the metamorphosis impact, just as it did in *Now, Voyager*. Decked out in a sleek black pant suit and wide-brimmed hat, looking every inch the model, Sabrina stands waiting for a ride home. David spots her. She greets him as if she's known him all her life. Mystified and smitten, he gives her a lift, and the rest of the plot follows Wilder's 1954 version except for a few key elements.

Though she comes home a stunner, this Sabrina is warm, a bit less sure of herself, again, like Charlotte. When David invites her to the Larrabee ball, an event she's watched for years from her tree perch, Sabrina, visibly nervous, *descends* the staircase (visible only from the waist down) wearing an emerald-colored gown with a glittering bolero jacket, walks the path connecting her world and David's, and stands hesitating, watching the festivities from the garden gate. She spots David and waits.

Sabrina (Paramount, 1995). Through their own innate goodness, makeover heroines tend to soften their Prince Charmings. Julia Ormond's Sabrina is no exception. A bit more hesitant, shy, less egocentric than her 1954 counterpart, this contemporary Sabrina values female friendships and realizes that David Larrabee (Greg Kinnear), the man she has loved all her life, is engaged to Elizabeth Tyson (Lauren Holly). Throughout the film, we see her struggle with that conflict and her growing attraction to older, single brother Linus (Harrison Ford). Ultimately, he chooses her over his corporate empire, and here we see them in Paris. He has discarded his executive tie and briefcase for a more relaxed, natural look that matches her own. Now who's wearing the glasses?

There's a moment when their eyes meet, David walks toward her, they exchange hellos, he extends his hand, and pulls her into his world.

This gesture, then, becomes the enabling force behind Sabrina's climb to much higher stakes—Linus. But there's no bold, brittle man hunter here. Dancing with David, Sabrina responds to his question, "Do you know how beautiful you are?" with a soft, slightly embarrassed, "No." Like Charlotte, this Sabrina knows that the external transformation is superficial. When David gushes, "You're dazzling," Sabrina stares in disbelief. She doesn't feel different on the inside. When she realizes that it's Linus she loves, she tells him, "I went to Paris to escape. I wrote in my stupid journal. I cut my stupid hair. I came back stupider than ever."

What's even more interesting in the 1995 version is Linus' transformation, a makeover both internal and external. The corporate shark finds a conscience. He's ready to blow a billion-dollar deal so Sabrina won't have to return to Paris alone. Running through the airport to catch the Concorde, Harrison Ford looks the part of a man in love—excited, sweating, unsure—and when a flight attendant asks if it's his first time on the Concorde, he responds, "It's my first everything." He greets Sabrina upon her arrival in Paris, standing beneath the streetlight, his hair tousled, his shirt opened at the collar. He has jettisoned the glasses, the tie, the hat, the umbrella, and the briefcase, all signs of his corporate world, and come to Paris to be saved. In a shaky voice, he says, "I've been following in footsteps all my life. Save me, Sabrina Fair. You're the only one who can."

Sabrina's makeover may get her noticed and gain her acceptance into his class, but her warmth and resolve attract Linus. At one point in the film, he says: "I like Sabrina. I always have. I don't care what she's done to her hair." It's a hopeful remark suggesting that he sees beyond the superficial, too. In the contemporary version, we're left with the sense that this Cinderella has some wisdom and something useful to teach and that Prince Charming actually cares about what she has to offer. In this respect, Harrison Ford makes a much more believable Linus Larrabee than Humphrey Bogart, who comes off as stiff and bored, or just bored stiff, as though he'd rather be anywhere than on the movie set. Hepburn's Sabrina simply turns down his hat brim while he hooks his umbrella on the belt of a man passing by. He never says "Save me," and we're left to wonder why Sabrina would embrace him so quickly. Nothing about their relationship rings true, and not even Hepburn's youthful passion can eke out any screen chemistry.

Funny Face *(1957)*

In "Audrey Hepburn: Fashion, Film and the 50s," Elizabeth Wilson argues that, in the end, no matter what role Hepburn playing, she is "incapable of being damaged or shop-soiled, yet there is a poignancy in her films that comes from the metamorphosis that invariably lies in wait: her passionate innocence is encased in *haute couture*, her beauty gets embalmed in happy endings that solve nothing" (38). Nothing gets resolved in Wilder's *Sabrina*. She sails off with multi-millionaire Linus, but will these two ever find *terra firma*? Stanley Donen's *Funny Face* offers yet another example of Hepburn paired with an older man deciding her fate, a man who literally encases her in *haute couture* and all but quashes her independent spirit. In fact, *Funny Face* suggests '50s females' forced retreat from self-actualization into surface appearance.

Jo Stockton (Hepburn), a Greenwich Village bookstore clerk, dreams of going to Paris to meet Emile Flostre, professor and "father" of empathicalism, the study of empathy, or, as Jo explains, "the most sensible approach to true understanding and peace of mind." The opportunity presents itself when editor of *Quality* magazine, Maggie Prescott (Kay Thompson), her fashion photographer Dick Avery (Fred Astaire), and their chorus of Greek tittering models (all without a lick of empathy) crash the "movingly dismal" bookstore for a fashion shoot. Jo is on a ladder (always visible in the frame) shelving books when they barge in, bang into the ladder, and send her reeling across the room. In the ensuing chaos, Jo is pushed to the bottom of a spiral staircase, forced down another spiral staircase below floor level, and ultimately shoved and locked outside on the street to wait for hours while books are flung everywhere to create the right mood.

A tad more sympathetic than the rest, Dick stays to help her clean up the mess, and here we get a sense of Jo's strongly held convictions. She chides Dick for photographing "silly dresses on silly women." And when he says that "most people think they're beautiful dresses on beautiful women," she quickly responds, "A synthetic beauty." Jo (perhaps an allusion to Jo in *Little Women*) hasn't time for such artificiality. With her pale and beautiful but unadorned face; unfashionable, mousy hair; black mock turtleneck sweater over a black skirt covered with a long tweed vest; thick, black stockings; and sensible shoes, she looks the part of a beatnik bookworm.

As she and Dick talk, Jo is on the ladder; he's next to her, higher in the frame. Suddenly, as she's telling him about Flostre and empathicalism, he pulls the ladder towards him, leans down, and kisses her—a perfectly fatherly kind of kiss. She scuttles him out the door while the kiss provokes her long and sappy rendition of "How Long Has This Been Going On." The peck he gives her hardly warrants lyrics that set up the conflict between individual principles and love, but it sends her dancing across the bookstore whirling an abandoned wide-brimmed hat and vivid pink scarf, a brightly-colored symbol of her eventual compromise for love and stark contrast to the dimly-lit bookstore.

Though the film pokes fun at the world of high fashion, it manages to convey the idea that what women really need to cure them of their intellectual pursuits is the right man. When Dick develops the photos from the shoot, he notices Jo's photogenic possibilities. "If we do her over and fix her up, she'd be great for us," he tells Maggie Prescott, who is looking for "The Quality Woman" for the next issue. "That *thing* from the bookshop? Her face is perfectly funny," she wails. But Dick thinks it has "character, spirit, and intelligence"—fine words that eventually prove empty, at least on his part. Maggie acquiesces. Before we know it, Jo is standing

Funny Face (Paramount, 1957). BEFORE: All of the before signifiers in the world—cloddy shoes, thick hose, frumpy costume, scarf, bushy brows—can't hide the fabulous face of Audrey Hepburn as Jo Stockton. We need no poster to tell us that she's quality underneath that disguise, and that all she needs to wipe that scowl off her face and move up that ladder is l-o-v-e. Jo makes her physical transformation into gorgeous swan with the help of fashion photographer Dick Avery (Fred Astaire), but does it kicking and screaming most of the way. In this shot, she stands before the threshold of a new self, hesitating before the towering doors of the modeling agency that will propel her into the world of *haute couture* and "synthetic beauty," as she calls it.

Funny Face (Paramount, 1957) AFTER: Winged victory springs to life in this incredible shot of Hepburn's Jo Stockton, as she flies down those stairs, all her beauty unveiled. "Take the picture!" she orders Dick Avery, who, until this moment, has been the one in charge. "Wait a moment," he cries as he fumbles with his camera. "You've outgrown me." And so she has.

in her office with an armload of books (the only way they could get her there was to pretend they wanted to buy some books) looking every inch the before, especially with the black triangle scarf added to her bookstore ensemble.

This first attempt at making her over proves a total failure, but the scene, though meant to be funny, illustrates the typical cruelty of the makeover magicians toward their makeover targets. Maggie pulls back on Jo's shoulders, trying to correct her posture. She yanks off the scarf and roughly grabs her face saying, "The bones are good." Then the makeover maven addresses the ditzy model troops now closing in on Jo: "Girls, eyebrows up, a light powder, a little rouge. She needs a marvelous mouth. The hair, the hair—it's awful. It must come off!" Maggie runs for a gigantic pair of scissors as she cries, "We may as well get started. Get that dreadful thing off of her." To her credit, Jo fights back. "You lunatics," she says. "I don't want my hair cut. I don't want my eyebrows up or down. I want them right where they are. There's no functional advantage in a marvelous mouth. I'm leaving now." And she runs out the door, finding sanctuary in Dick's darkroom where he sings the film's theme song and convinces her to think of modeling as an opportunity. In exchange for being "The Quality Woman," she'll get a trip to Paris and a chance to meet Flostre the philosopher.

Jo tries to rationalize her new profession as a means to an end instead of a loss of integrity, and, at least for awhile, Jo manages to hold on to her integrity. She leaves designers and makeup artists waiting for hours while she hangs out with the café crowd in Paris' Left Bank wearing her "Modern Bohemian Black" ensemble—black turtleneck, black slacks, black loafers—as fashion historian Anne Hollander called it. Alison Lurie explains in *The Language of Clothes* that this look "originated in Paris after World War II and soon became the standard costume of beatnik intellectuals, artists and students" (192). The outfit represents a fragile freedom for Jo as she dances unrestrained, perhaps for the last time, to "release" and "express" herself in the dark, smoky café. Her wings will soon be clipped as Dick retrieves her and ushers her back to her responsibilities.

Again, we never see the makeover—just the anticipation of it as Prescott *et al.* anxiously await her unveiling. Finally, *couture* designer Paul Duval (Robert Flemyng) appears and makes this announcement: "My friends, you saw here a waif, a gamine, a lowly caterpillar. We opened the cocoon, but it is not a butterfly that emerges. It is a bird of paradise. Lights! Curtain!" On cue, the curtain rises and a vision emerges against the dark backdrop. The camera slowly dollys in to Jo, now a goddess in a Givenchy gown of peach satin. But the bird of paradise is a caged one as she walks down the runway erect, her movement restricted by the form-fitting long gown. The total effect of the makeup, earrings, sophisticated hairdo, and Cinderella crown evokes stunned silence and then cheers from the ecstatic onlookers. They surround her. "How does it feel?" they ask. "It feels wonderful, but it's not me," Jo responds. "Her passionate innocence has been encased in *haute couture*" (Wilson 38).

The transformation allows Jo to soar high above her "movingly dismal" bookshop in Greenwich Village, and the ensuing photo shoot montage, depicting her in one luscious designer outfit after another, shows her growing comfort with her new look and status. Initially, Dick guides her. "Just do whatever I tell you, and don't worry about it," he commands, giving her motivation for every mood. When she takes control, telling him not to worry about what she's going to do and just take the picture, Dick confesses, "You've outgrown me." She confesses that she loves him.

Maybe if the film had ended here, it might have been more satisfying. Instead, Dick's thin veneer of male enlightment begins to peel when Jo finally meets Professor Flostre, who turns out to be a sleazy hypocrite interested in a lot more than discussing empathicalism with her. Dick is jealous. "You're never going to see him again," he shouts, and then he delivers the ultimate blow: "He's about as interested in your intellect as I am." Wow ... whatever happened to "character, spirit, and intelligence"? What happened to the man who asked, "Aren't there any models around who can think as well as they look?" He sings the Gershwins' "S'wonderful" and dances off into the sunset with Jo, in a wedding dress, who has completely capitulated to him after discovering Flostre's real intentions. As Wilson suggests, this "happy ending" solves nothing. Once again, Hepburn ends up with a man who could be her father, maybe her grandfather, in a tentative union that implies women need protecting and saving from their own ideals and intellect.

Grease *(1978)*

The musical *Grease* sent women spiraling *down* the ladder of class faster than greased lightning. In Randal Kleiser's 1978 musical, based on Jim Jacobs and Warren Casey's Broadway hit about a year in the life of 1950s Rydell High seniors, our heroine moves from pure and wholesome "Sandra Dee" to slinky, leather-clad "Pink Lady" in order to please her T-Bird, greaser boyfriend. When Kleiser cast two 1970s pop icons, singer Olivia Newton-John and actor John Travolta, in the lead roles, audiences went wild and boxoffice registers went "cha-ching." "In general, the combination of teen angst set to charmingly raunchy uptempo tunes and the nostalgic fixation this country keeps with the "ideal" fifties has kept money pouring in from stage, screen, and soundtrack for over two decades. But it's the Hollywood version most people remember and still watch today, largely because of the sheer magnetism of the two young stars, their onscreen chemistry, and the makeover, delayed until the very end of the story.

The film opens on a beautiful beach. Waves roll to shore to the tune of "Love is a Many Splendored Thing." Two teens, Sandy Olsen (Newton-John) and Danny Zuko (Travolta), play out their summer romance, frolicking in the froth. She's all white, blonde, and wholesome. He's tall, dark, and handsome—hormones racing. When he makes his move, Sandy rebuffs him with "Danny, don't spoil it!" He tries again: "It's not spoiling it, Sandy. It's only making it better." The lovebirds part, passion unfulfilled, thinking they may never see each other again until, presto, Sandy shows up at Rydell High for the first day of school blithely unaware that Danny goes there, too. (Did Danny forget to mention the name of his high school?) "Do I look okay?" she asks Frenchy (Didi Conn), the kind-hearted beauty school wannabe and member of Rydell's female gang, The Pink Ladies. "Sorta cool," Frenchy replies diplomatically.

Sandy looks like the girl-next-door from Down Under with her blonde, straight, shoulder-length hair neatly trimmed, her crisp white blouse, matching bright yellow sweater and full skirt, and white flats. She's pure. "Too pure to be 'Pink,'" Rizzo (Stockard Channing), the class slut, tells Frenchy. As Alison Lurie points out in *The Language of Clothes*, "brilliant yellow, the color of the sun, is associated with youth, life, and hope," and Sandy is nothing if not optimistic. In the face of moving to a new country, changing schools, losing a summer love, and finding out her Prince Charming—as Riz calls him—lives and reigns as Rydell's jive-talkin', cool-walkin' leader of the T-Birds, she remains remarkably hopeful and sweet.

Devastated that Danny camouflages his real affections for her because of his too-cool-to-care image, she agrees to a sleepover at Frenchy's with the Pink Ladies. It's a study in contrasts as Frenchy, Riz, and Marty (Dinah Manoff) parade about in their scant nighties and jumbo curlers, drinking wine and smoking ciggies. Sandy sits in a long, white nightgown laced to the collar. Her blonde hair is held back with a simple, pale blue ribbon. She doesn't drink or smoke, and Frenchy's attempt to pierce her ears ends with Sandy sick in the bathroom while Riz sings "I'm Sandra Dee," a tune whose lyrics mock Sandy. Thus, the first attempt at a makeover fails because even though Sandy is "hopelessly devoted" to Danny, she's not ready to chuck her clean-cut image and descend to his level.

Instead, Sandy challenges Danny to make himself over from greaser to jock, and, in a funny scene sequence, we see His Coolness trying out for several varsity sports to impress the girl he still wants; however, we never see the results of his makeover until the end of the film. Delaying Sandy's and Danny's physical transformations until the main climax of the film. heightens the conflict. Which one will make the ultimate sacrifice to cross over? This one's a no-brainer, especially after Danny wins the National Dance Contest with Cha Cha DiGregorio (Annette Charles). He also wins a race against rival gang The Scorpions while driving the T-Bird's lean, mean, racin' machine, which they've transformed, with the help of shop teacher Mrs. Murdock (Alice Ghostley), from a dilapidated clunker into "greased lightening." Sandy watches Danny take his kudos from afar. She sings a song about wishing she was more than what meets

Grease (Paramount, 1978). (*Left*) BEFORE: Wholesome. Pure. Virginal. This shot of Olivia Newton-John's fresh-faced Sandy Olsen speaks volumes about our before heroine. That wide-eyed, innocent stare, childish bangs, and toothy smile suggest a young woman in love with life, a "good girl" who's not going to give anything away until "Mr. Right" comes along. But when she falls for Rydell High's top greaser, Danny Zuko (John Travolta), Sandy finds her clean-cut image an obstacle to their eventual happiness. (*Below*) AFTER: With the help of Frenchy (Didi Conn), Sandy slides down that ladder of class to fit into Danny's world of fast cars and black leather. Her risk pays off, big time, as Danny's "chills" leave him drooling at her hot red Candies.

the eye. Frenchy joins in, and helps her see that she must change herself and still be proud of who she is. It would be hard to find a clearer cue for a makeover in all of film.

We see Danny's makeover first, during graduation festivities. His physical transformation consists of substituting his black leather jacket for a school sweater. It seems Danny has lettered in track. When fellow T-Birds tease him about it, he finally has the courage to tell them that Sandy is just as important to him as they are, and he's going to do whatever it takes to get her back. However, he doesn't have to work very hard. The camera moves from a reaction shot of the gang members' startled faces to Danny's wide-eyed stare to, yes, Sandy's shoes: bright red, high-heeled Candies. Next comes the tilt up shot that mimics Danny's gaze—past her skin-tight, black stretch slacks to her black leather jacket. Sandy now wears lots of makeup, earrings peek from beneath her blonde hair, which has been curled and poofed, and a cigarette dangles from her bright red lips. She's hot! Her sultry comment to Danny, "Tell me about it, stud," brings him to his knees, literally. After gyrating to the tune "You'd Better Shape Up," they fly off into greaser heaven in their made-over car "Greased Lightening"—an ending possible only because of Sandy's deliberate choice to remake herself into his image.

While Sandy makes the transformation from virgin to slut in *Grease*, Tess McGill moves from sex object to business professional in *Working Girl*, decidedly more adult fare.

Working Girl *(1988)*

After almost two decades of white male action adventure fare, Hollywood rediscovered women and women's issues. In truth, the industry could no longer ignore reality: sisters were doing it for themselves. More and more women were becoming executives and juggling their jobs, their families, and their social lives. They were clawing their way up the ladder of success, often under enormous pressure, and, since they made up a large portion of the movie-going public, they were demanding films that reflected their own lives and their own concerns and struggles. In the late eighties, a handful of movies appeared that finally reflected contemporary problems of contemporary women trying to break the glass ceiling. *Baby Boom* (1987), *Broadcast News* (1987), and *Working Girl* (1988) all dealt with women trying to balance a career and a personal life. They also depicted the pitfalls of working in a patriarchal culture.

One of the most important makeover films to come along in decades was *Working Girl*, written by Kevin Wade and directed by Mike Nichols. Although billed as a corporate Cinderella story (one of the trailers starts with "Once upon a time there was a secretary from Staten Island"), the film spoke to millions of women, namely secretaries, who were stuck on the low rung of a very big ladder. But the film also addressed another huge issue for women at the time: how women who make it to the top treat the women below them. In *When Women Call the Shots*, Linda Seger explains how this issue manifested itself in the movie-making business:

> In the 1970s and 1980s, as they moved into the corporate structure, women were aware that they were playing by men's rules. Some were good players but got criticized for being too much "like a man." The stories circulating around Hollywood in the 1980s about tough and abusive female bosses were many. Some felt the abusive woman boss acted that way partly because of insecurity, partly because she was not comfortable with the accoutrements that go with the job—the toughness, the aggressiveness, the competitiveness. They didn't seem to wear as well on women as men. (Although some would say they don't wear well on either gender.) Women were taking jobs in a system they didn't design, imitating a gender they didn't belong to, trying to accomplish objectives they never defined [54].

Later, she writes, "As more women entered the industry, they began to find ways to balance their own personal style with the demands of the business" (55).

Seger's explanation aptly describes the main narrative arc of *Working Girl*, starring Harrison Ford (Jack Trainer), Sigourney Weaver (Katherine Parker), and newcomer Melanie Griffith (Tess McGill). Tess is just one of hundreds of frizzy-haired secretaries who ride the Staten Island Ferry into Manhattan each morning and disappear into skyscrapers wearing their miniskirts, textured hose, cheap jewelry, and layers of makeup.

What sets Tess apart from her working stiff sisters is sheer guts and determination to better herself. She skips lunch so she can attend speech classes and graduates from college with honors by attending night classes. She's light years ahead of her fisherman boyfriend, Mick (Alec Baldwin), who buys her tacky red and black lingerie (à la Fredrick's of Hollywood) for her birthday. "Just once I'd like a present that I could actually wear outside of this apartment," she tells him. And she's smarter than most of the Wall Street lotharios she works for who ask her to fetch toilet paper, steal her ideas, and then turn her down for the Entre Program so she can move out of the secretarial pool. Director Nichols says in "How Plot of 'Working Girl' Can Apply to Real-Life Role" that Tess has "great ability for the job she wants to do. But she doesn't talk right, she doesn't look right, and in the upper reaches of Wall Street and industry, that's a huge drawback. Eighty percent of the battle is style" (qtd. in Turk 1).

When her boss tries to fix her up with a slimy, coke-sniffing executive (played by Kevin Spacey) who slops champagne all over her and forces her to watch porno films in his limo, Tess fights back. She sprays him with champagne, leaps out of his limo, and, back at her computer, types "David Lutz is a sleazoid pimp with a little dick" into the stock exchange ticker board. Her antics get her a transfer to the Mergers and Acquisitions Department—and a female boss.

Katharine Parker has everything that money and breeding can buy. She's been educated at the finest schools, knows all the right people (Andy Warhol's done her portrait), and dresses according to the edict of Coco Chanel: "Dress shabbily and they notice the dress. Dress impeccably and they notice the woman." She strides into the office in her gray, fitted suit with white, shell pearls (one strand), gray gloves, and raincoat confidently draped over her shoulders. Sitting behind her enormous desk, she gives Tess the ground rules. They're a "team" and as such they have a uniform. "Simple, elegant, and impeccable," she tells Tess. "You don't get anywhere in this world by waiting for what you want to come to you. You make it happen. Watch me, Tess. Learn from me."

Katharine has all the appearances of being a mentor to her secretary, but Katharine's too involved with Katharine to really care what happens to Tess. She swims through Wall Street waters like a hungry shark thinking only about where its next meal is coming from. She throws a party to introduce herself to all the right people in town and treats Tess like a servant. In her bright, red dress, Katharine charms her guests while forcing Tess to push around a steaming dim sum cart, which leaves her dripping with sweat, her long hair frizzier than ever.

Yet Tess does learn a thing or two from Katharine and tries to make herself over, at least physically, in her boss's image. She gradually sheds the signifiers of her lower class background. "Rethink the jewelry," Katharine tells her. In the next scene, we see Tess in the restroom jettisoning the chunky jewelry and softening her makeup. She comes to work in cheaper versions of Katharine's classy white blouses and simple but elegant black skirts. Her makeover has nothing to do with getting a man and everything to do with getting ahead. As J. Emmett Winn writes in "Moralizing Upward Mobility: Investigating the Myth of Class Mobility in *Working Girl*," "Tess sees the 'rules' of the game as putting her out of bounds; hence, style and image must become the way she gains access to the upperclass strata" (44).

The turning point in the film happens after Katharine's skiing accident puts her out of commission and out of the country for awhile. Lackey Tess is left to "take care of things" both at the office and Katharine's apartment where she stumbles across Katharine's recorded memo to speak with investment broker Jack Trainer about an idea to resolve Trask Industries' financial problems. Tess listens in horror, realizing that her mentor, the woman who has encouraged her to "bring me your ideas," has stolen Tess's plan. Not the end of Tess's troubles, she returns to Staten Island only to find her lover, Mick, having sex with another woman.

Mick's almost comical response—"What, no class?"—as he looks up to find Tess standing in the doorway signals a different meaning to Tess than the one he intended. She's going to "make it happen" for herself. (We already know she's good with payback.) She devises a plan to get some class, with the help of Katharine's clothes and a "serious" haircut from her friend Cyn (Joan Cusack). "If you want to be taken seriously, you need serious hair," she tells Cyn as she schemes to crash a party to meet Jack Trainer and follow through on her original idea for Trask Industries with his help. Her description of the little black dress she intends to wear provides a perfect metaphor for her modus operandi. "This is it," she says to Cyn. "It's simple, elegant. It makes a statement. It says to people, risk taker. Not afraid to be noticed. Then you hit 'em with your smarts."

In the next scene, we see Cinderella at the ball. There's no entrance and no tilt up shot, not even a staircase in the frame. We simply see a full shot of Tess sitting at the bar in Katharine's $6,000 dress. (In *Pretty Woman*, we'll see Julia Roberts seated at a bar in another expensive little black dress.) She's gorgeous to be sure. Her hair, a quieter strawberry blonde, is cut in a sophisticated, wavy, chin-length bob. She wears a simple pair of earrings and lets the dress do its work. The off-shoulder, elegant number gets Prince Charming's attention. Jack locks in on Tess and makes a direct dash to the barstool next to her. He realizes that he has a ten o'clock appointment with her for the next morning, but he keeps *his* identity a secret. He doesn't want to talk business. He wants to drink shots of tequila and look at her. When she tells him, "I have a head for business and a bod for sin," he's hooked. But Tess has had two shots of tequila on top of a Valium that Cyn gave her. This Cinderella passes out in her yellow coach so Jack takes her back to his apartment and tucks her into bed.

Jack's attraction to her, though inspired by the way she looks, quickly turns to respect as he hears Tess's plans for Trask Industries. Would he listen to her ideas without the makeover? Doubtful. Would he work with her to finalize the deal if he knew she was a secretary from Staten Island?

Working Girl (20th Century-Fox, 1988). BEFORE/AFTER: With her big, frizzy hair, heavy makeup, and flashy jewelry, Tess McGill (Melanie Griffith) could pass for any of the nameless secretaries in the Manhattan beehive. But the jut of that chin suggests a determination to fly above the drones, and she becomes a queen—without the stinger. By the final scene, she has pulled herself up by her own intelligence and hard work, toned down her outward appearance to look the part of the executive, and become a real role model for working *women* everywhere.

Probably not. But as long as the illusion is in place, he backs her brilliant ideas and opens doors for her that otherwise would have remained shut tight. Once inside the boardroom, Tess holds her own with a cadre of senior male executives, and she impresses Mr. Trask, whose daughter's wedding she crashes in order to get a meeting with him. When Cyn expresses her concern over Tess's cloak-and-dagger act, Tess snaps, "I'm not going to spend the rest of my life working my ass off and getting nowhere just because I followed rules that I had nothing to do with setting up."

Tess's makeover has evolved to the point where she no longer fits in Cyn's world, her old world. When Tess attends Cyn's engagement party at one of their old haunts, her transformation is evident and the differences between the two women more pronounced than ever. Cyn, still almost clown-like with her big, big hair and multi-colored eye shadow, accepts her station in life. In fact, assistant costume designer Gary Jones says research showed that New York secretaries who saw the movie loved Cusack's character and the way she looked (Turk 1). Tess's black designer suit and white blouse look out of place, and her successful efforts to shed her thick New York accent set her apart. Mick says to her, "You look different.... The hair, the duds, and the briefcase.... You look good, classy. Did you have to go to traffic court or something?"

Just as Sabrina's father muses that his daughter is caught between the world of the garage and the mansion, so Tess seems out of place in both Staten Island and on Wall Street. She has reached the point of no return. She realizes she cannot go back down that ladder. Instead, she must keep looking up.

Her attraction for Jack turns to romance and then to love as they set to finalize the deal with Trask. All goes well until Katharine hits town and then hits the ceiling when she finds out what Tess has been up to. To complicate matters, it turns out that Jack is the man Katharine wants to marry. She bursts into the board meeting brandishing her crutches, proclaiming that Tess is her secretary and accusing Tess of stealing *her* idea. The interesting thing is that the men, including Trask, believe her because of her forceful, aggressive, confident manner. They understand that persona. Tess, embarrassed and now unsure, apologizes and then flees the room, leaving Jack stunned and Katharine to take the credit for all of her work. Up one rung, down seven.

As fate would have it, Tess runs into Trask, Katharine, Jack and their entourage one more time. And this time, Tess has the courage to stand up to Katharine and convince Jack that the idea was really hers. "If I'd have told you I was just some secretary, you never would have taken the meeting," she flashes. He takes her side and shoves her into an elevator with Mr. Trask, thus giving Tess the opportunity to explain to Trask alone how she came up with her plan to use radio to save Trask Industries from a Japanese takeover. Once off the elevator, he confronts Katharine, asking how she came up with the idea, and when Katharine can't respond, Trask fires her "boney ass" and gives Tess a job with his company.

Working Girl could have ended here, in the Mergers and Acquisitions Department bullpen with the villainess roundly defeated while Tess and Jack kiss amidst cheers from Tess's fellow secretaries. But it doesn't. Jack may have lifted Tess up a couple of rungs on the corporate ladder, but their romance isn't the main focus of the story. Trask may have had the good sense to believe in her enough to give her a chance, but Tess pulled herself up by her own boot straps and authored her own makeover; therefore, the honest ending, the ending that makes *Working Girl* more than just another romantic comedy, must be the one that privileges Tess in her new working environment.

For the film to have real impact for real women, we must see her success, we must see what she does with it, and, most importantly, we must see how she now treats those who work for *her*. After a brief scene with Jack, who gives her a lunchbox and sends her off to work, we see Tess, now poised and elegant, enter Trask Industries on her first day. Still modest and humble, she takes a seat at the secretary's desk, until her secretary points out that she has her own office with windows. Stunned, Tess gets up and slowly walks into her office, leans against the window sill, her back to the skyscrapers visible behind her, and stares at her secretary, who, anticipating the worst, nervously asks about Tess's expectations of her. Will Tess repeat Katharine's mistakes, we wonder? Never. In a soft voice, she says, "I expect you to call me Tess. I don't expect you to fetch me coffee unless you're getting some for yourself. The rest we'll make up as we go along." Her relieved secretary smiles broadly, gratefully, and closes the door, leaving Tess to revel in her new surroundings and call Cyn.

Working Girl, like the Statue of Liberty and the American flag—icons of opportunity frequently visible in shots throughout the film—offered hope to women sitting in the audience in the late 1980s who were trying to reposition themselves. In not privileging the easy, happily-ever-after romantic ending, the film sent women the message that they, too, could make themselves over and move up, and not necessarily for a man.

Maid in Manhattan *(2002)*

Maid in Manhattan takes place under that same New York skyline. It shares more than a location with *Working Girl;* Kevin Wade wrote the screenplay for both films, which have a similar urban Cinderella feel. The plot of *Maid in Manhattan* follows the well-trodden path.

Hotel maid and single mother Marisa Ventura (Jennifer Lopez) works well and diligently at her cleaning job and at parenting her brilliant ten-year-old, Ty (Tyler Garcia Posey). (Marisa's book for the subway is Alice Miler's *The Drama of the Gifted Child.*) Stephanie (Marissa Matrone), Marisa's best friend at work, knows about her career aspirations and encourages Marisa to apply for a management position at their upscale hotel, although Marisa's mother (Priscilla Lopez) thinks that Marisa should know her place and be happy she can pay the bills.

While cleaning a lavish suite where glamorous guest Caroline Land (Natasha Richardson) is staying, Stephanie coaxes Marisa into trying on a gorgeous Dolce coat that Caroline plans to return. Marisa gives in and puts it on. Meanwhile, Ty rides up in the elevator to find his mom and meets hot politician Chris Marshall (Ralph Fiennes) and his dog on the way. Ty asks if he can go along to walk the dog, and Chris, fascinated by a small child who knows his voting record, agrees.

When Ty runs into the suite, Chris follows and hears Stephanie call Marisa "Caroline." He sees Marisa in the expensive outfit, thinks she's a guest, and invites her to go along on the walk. Marisa, Chris, Ty, and the dog have a great time, although the paparazzi have a field day photographing the "new woman" in the flirtatious Chris's life. Chris's political guru Jerry (Stanley Tucci) cautions against involvement with any woman so close to his announcement for the Senate, but Chris invites Marisa to a posh charity affair. Worried that her hotel will discover what she's done, Marisa refuses.

A comedy of errors follows, all acted out in the context of Marisa's impending promotion to management. Stephanie has turned in the application for her, and Marisa has been accepted. Anxious to see her again, Chris invites "Caroline" to lunch, and the *real* Caroline (Richardson) shows up. Chris hates her, but she's smitten and avidly seeks his attentions. Chris can't find Marisa; he tells Jerry he will only go to the charity affair with her. Jerry relents, but he doesn't know her real identity, either. After a Cinderella makeover orchestrated by her friends, Marisa *does* goes to the "ball" to tell Chris she can't see him. He seduces her, and, before Marisa can tell him the truth, a jealous Caroline reveals the whole affair to the hotel managers. Marisa loses her job and the chance of promotion. A disappointed Chris, hurt by Marisa's lies, leaves.

Months later, Marisa has found a job at another hotel, and, still optimistic, she plans to enter the management track there. Chris comes back to town to announce his Senate Candidacy and Ty cuts school to attend the press conference, held at the hotel where his mother works. Ty points out to Chris that many politicians lie, and that most of them get a second chance. The story ends happily as Chris and Marisa embrace. A series of stills over the closing credits suggests that their lives continue together, and that both are successful.

The image of Jennifer Lopez looms over this story, coloring the film in every way. There's Lopez's background, her own class-inflected Cinderella story, in which she rises, by persistence, focus, and amazing luck, from her beginning in the Bronx to fame in the pages of sleazoid gossip rags, on the covers of fashion magazines, on the music channels, and on our movie screens. She's had some dark moments (like the affair with rap-ster Sean "Puffy" Combs), which she doesn't talk much about. She prefers that people remember her as "just a simple girl from the Bronx who worked really hard" ("I Always Knew" 5). Currently, she's reeling from a much publicized breakup with Ben Affleck. Her single, "Jenny from the Block," aptly describes her reversal of fortune; the video reveals quite a bit of Lopez and even more of her glamorous lifestyle. Lopez's life provided her with the perfect material for this before and after role, and perhaps her experience helped her step out from behind her high-profile persona to *be* Marisa the maid, which she does very well. As Joe Leyden notes, "Lopez gives a generous and self-effacing star performance, leaving the impression of a team-player bent on serving the material, not a diva intent on upstaging her co-stars" ("Nice 'n' easy").

Michael O'Sullivan isn't so willing to suspend disbelief. He hints that Lopez's celebrated beauty might be a hindrance: "Give me a second before I start reviewing *Maid in Manhattan* ... to recall the last time I rented a room in New York City (heck, anywhere for that matter) where a member of the housekeeping staff looked that bootylicious. Ah, now I remember. *Never*" (WE36). A biased and downright mean assumption supports O'Sullivan's "cute" opening. Why *couldn't* a maid be beautiful? When was the last time O'Sullivan looked, *really looked*, at any of the housekeeping staff anywhere? We'd bet *never*. Actually, although Marisa Ventura's before hardly qualifies as a Charlotte Vale revival, Lopez does manage to look like one of those extraordinarily pretty girls you see working everywhere, not like a movie star.

At home, and on her way to work, Marisa wears just the kind of trendy, inexpensive clothes you would expect a beautiful young woman without much money to pick: tight, flared pants and tight sweaters. She bundles her dark hair back carelessly and doesn't wear much makeup. But plain? No way. The set and the camera work suggest her situation. Marisa enters the hotel by descending from the street (going down that ladder) into a nondescript basement door (not much like the grand entrance that welcomes guests). We follow her down the hallway, and the camera keeps these shots tight, making the dull walls press in on Marisa. At work, Marisa's frumpy maid uniform (gathers around the waist—oh, no!) confers a special kind of invisibility; she's still quite beautiful, but no one seems to notice, reading her uniformed figure as "service person" instead of *person* person. (The real truth behind O'Sullivan's assumption lies in this unfortunately common brand of blindness.) Marisa cleans Chris Marshall's bathroom when he checks into the hotel, and he barely glances at her. (*Ever After* makes Danielle's life real; she works, and she sweats. As *Pretty Woman* barely discloses the seamy world real hookers have to endure, *Maid in Manhattan* nods to, but downplays, the realities of being a hotel maid.) After their first, romantic meeting, she serves luncheon in his suite (the lunch with the real Caroline), and she enacts an elaborate pantomime of disguise. Marisa holds flowers and food in front of her face and passes most of the high contact tasks to the butler, her good friend, Lionel Bloch (Bob Hoskins). If Chris Marshall really looked, though, he'd see her.

This whole rigamarole makes an interesting statement about the anonymity of certain, gender-coded positions: maid, secretary, prostitute. Say any of those three words and a hazy female presence probably pops into your mind. In this chapter, several of the heroines use makeovers to help them flee the ghetto of poorly-paid and under-appreciated slavery that characterizes these jobs. In *Maid in Manhattan*, all Marisa has to do to temporarily escape invisibility is put on a Dolce and Gabbana coat. Her after says that designer clothing stamps its wearer *special, desirable, rich.* Any trace of the class inferences a maid's uniform carries disappear as Marisa slips on the incredibly creamy white, three-quarter length coat and matching pants. (Read white as a color only the wealthy can wear for a stroll in the park without worrying about dry cleaning bills.) Just that outfit, no change in her hair, or the addition of any makeup, make Chris recognize Marisa as one of his kind. Clothing works the same way in *Pretty Woman,* and in the real world, it's a pretty unappetizing capitalistic fact that a trip to Barney's might be worth more in terms of class than a year of good deeds at the soup kitchen.

But it isn't just Marisa's midtown look that impresses Chris. During their short walk in the park, and another brief conversation, her straight speaking makes him begin to understand that a visit to the projects could be more than a photo op. Like Prince Henry in *Ever After,* Chris needs a little prodding to see what good things his power might make possible. Marisa's brains and beauty, not just her coat, make him invite her to the charity affair, which becomes their "ball."

Marisa's Cinderella makeover for the ball, held in the Temple of Dendur wing of the Metropolitan Museum, repeats the Dolce and Gabbana idea: if you have the right stuff, you have the *right stuff.* No fairy godmother, but a bevy of quasi-underlings, people who handle but can't buy luxury goods, help Marisa, and this is no hostile take over, like the makeover scenes in so many films. Instead, Marisa enjoys the gifts lovingly bestowed on her by her friends. She chooses her beautiful blush-colored dress in a spree of trying-on that rivals Julia Roberts's similar extravaganza in *Pretty Woman.* Ty picks his mother's delicate ivory slippers (this *is* a Cinderella story, after all), and a good friend from an upscale jewelry shop loans her a special edition Harry Winston necklace that Caroline recognizes. This time, fancy hair and perfect makeup go with the gorgeous clothes, and the after tells viewers that Marisa's glamour is hardly dependent on borrowings from Caroline's closet. She may not have the money, but she *does* have the taste. Walking down the ramp into the temple wing, she could be a young, fragile Nefertiti. Do you think this Prince recognizes her? Of course he does, and the Cinderella moment initiates their one night of love—a big departure from traditional Cinderella stories. This maid's a mom, so she can drop the virginal pose.

It's the "Prince's" reaction to Marisa that fuels Caroline's wrath. *Maid in Manhattan* could easily avoid the convention of female-to-female meanness by concentrating on the difficulty Marisa faces as she juggles the roles of *maid* and *guest.* Instead, Kevin Wade uses cattiness to get some laughs. While some of the film rings true, Wade's bitchy character, Caroline, plays a one-dimensional evil stepsister. Caroline's not terrible to Marisa, although she expects to be waited on. She even recognizes Marisa's eye for fashion—once she asks Marisa for her opinion on an outfit, and she takes the suggestion (a very Perrault incident). She's not as snobby as her friend Rachel (Amy Sedaris), who takes everything Marisa says as insubordination and sass.

When Caroline sees that Chris loves the lovely maid, though, she only wants revenge. How dumb is this? Caroline is beautiful, apparently wealthy, and gainfully employed. Chris attracts her because she's on the rebound; her crush is hardly serious. Why does she need to demolish Marisa? We think Kevin Wade cloned Caroline from Katharine in *Working Girl* to create an easy catalyst for tension. The whole situation feels too similar and too contrived. Occasional and unnecessary schtick with the maids also crosses the line into stereotype-land. The women dissolve into cartoons; their butt-swinging happy dance makes the trailer, but their love and support for Marisa doesn't. Why must they be the three fairies from *Sleeping Beauty* jazzed up, instead of simply loyal friends?

We expected more, too, from the scenes between Marisa and her mother because director Wayne Wang so delicately revealed the fault lines between mothers and daughters in *The Joy Luck Club* (1993). Here, however, he depends on too little to suggest the nature of their relationship. Much more interesting than any catty Caroline incident, Marisa's drive to climb the ladder and her mother's inclination toward stasis could use a little explication.

Yet, the good things in *Maid in Manhattan* outweigh its lurches into convention. It would be stupid to argue, on the basis of this film, that class is no longer an issue in the U.S. Of course it is, as the whole invisibility factor shows. It takes more than a Dolce and Gabbana coat to finesse your way into one of the reigning political dynasties. But *Maid in Manhattan* has a beating heart, not only a collection of clichés. Marisa isn't ashamed to be a maid, but she isn't an idiot. She fully understands that knowing her true identity would affect Chris's feelings for her, and she tells him so. Still, she's no Cinderella sitting in her corner, or Sabrina aiming for a rich husband (either brother will do). Also the child of a servant, Marisa, like Sabrina, doesn't act servile. She speaks her mind; she works hard; she reads; she's a good mother; she knows she can be more. She's a reminder that in America, a servant's child can attempt and believe in upward mobility. But there's a big difference in the two heroines' methods of ascending the ladder. Sabrina, playing cutthroat all the way, angles for a step up via marriage, but Marisa, like Tess in *Working Girl*, depends on herself, not romance, for advancement. Independence, intelligence, and tenderness can belong to members of every class. It's the well-heeled, very white, upper class, British Caroline, not Marisa, who's shallow and stupid.

   Maid in America also reminds us of the dilution of ethnic tensions. Even thirty years ago the casting of Lopez and Fiennes as lovers would surely have given the film a *West Side Story* spin. Today, the cast, like the audience we saw the film with, looks like the America we brag about. Milan Paurich, in his review, calls the story "hopelessly dated," (D8), but our audience didn't agree. They cheered Marisa on, and they clapped when the film was over. The Manhattan skyline may have taken a hit, but ideals truly made in America are still thriving. *Maid in Manhattan,* like *Working Girl,* refuses cynicism (like Paurich's) to remind us how passionately we believe in the value of *every* life. *Pretty Woman,* one of the most talked about makeover films of the twentieth century, paints a different American landscape.

Pretty Woman *(1990)*

   In *Working Girl*, Tess McGill does not wait for her knight to rescue her, and no man has a hand in her makeover. She puts herself through school and makes things happen for herself, never compromising her integrity. Yes, she gets a lift up the class and corporate ladder, but Jack simply opens the boardroom door a crack. Her ideas and fortitude actually save the day. *Maid in Manhattan's* Marisa follows suit. Unfortunately, we can't say the same for Garry Marshall's *Pretty Woman,* starring Julia Roberts as hooker Vivian Ward and Richard Gere as corporate raider

Edward Lewis. The fact that the film was referred to in the press as a modern-day Cinderella or Pygmalion story only serves to gloss over its inherent anti-feminist ideology, which most critics and scholars got but movie-going masses chose to ignore. As one critic said, "It's a movie at odds with its feel-good purposes" (Howe N37). Because of this and the movie's major emphasis on class and social positioning, ultimately through marriage, we've put *Pretty Woman* not in the Cinderella or Pygmalion chapters but in "The Ladder of Class."

The plot of *Pretty Woman* is deceptively simple. Edward Lewis buys huge corporations in financial trouble and then dismantles them, piece by piece, without a shred of remorse for the jobless masses he leaves behind. (He never gets emotionally involved. It's just business.) He has an ex-wife and a girlfriend who's just broken up with him because she talks to his secretary more than she talks to him. He's got a chip on his shoulder the size of the Empire State Building. He can't drive because he's been chauffered around most of his life, he's afraid of heights, and he has issues with his now-deceased father. It seems his wealthy sire ran off, taking his money and another woman, leaving his mother to die of a broken heart (we assume). To get even, Edward goes "all the way" through school, becomes a billionaire, and raids daddy's company. He revels in his revenge and his money, which affords him "the best" of everything.

One night he borrows his smarmy lawyer's (played smarmily by Jason Alexander) Lotus and gets lost on Hollywood Boulevard on the way back to his hotel, the Regent Beverly Wilshire. Enter hooker Vivian Ward with directions and a way with an H shifter. She's had a rough life, we learn. It seems her mother used to lock her in the attic when she was bad. Did she scream and cry and develop issues? No. She pretended that she was a princess in a tower waiting to be rescued by a handsome knight on a white horse. After quitting school in the eleventh grade, the small-town girl escapes to the big city with her "bum" of a boyfriend and has to support herself by selling her body to make ends meet. Evidently, waitressing and parking cars didn't pay enough. But this beautiful, feisty working girl calls her own shots (no pimp, no drugs). She says who and when and where.

Through it all, Vivian's heart beats gold, and, after one night with her, Edward presents her with a "business" deal. He's willing to pay for an armpiece for the week he's in L.A. She can be bought, for $3,000. He waves his no-limit credit card and, almost instantly, transforms her into a dream babe. But wait. Clothes alone don't make a lady. She must have grace—and table manners. Hotel manager Bernard Thompson (Hector Elizondo), the fairy godfather of this tale, performs this Herculean feat

practically overnight. Vivian has now become "the best" and worthy to
be seen with such a man as Edward Lewis.

For the rest of the film, we see the changes each character affects on
the other. Edward transforms Vivian into the beautiful princess, and
Vivian softens the hard edges of the knight raider and fills his emotional
black hole. If it sounds too good to be true, it is. The movie, Jack Curry
says, with its "retro-romance right out of a storybook," confounds "preconceived ideas about what women want" (19). Filmmaker Lizzie Borden
puts it this way:

> *Pretty Woman* shows the knight-in-shining-armor notion.... If the right
> man comes along, the woman can be bought and taken out of her life
> and transformed. It's a false myth. It's the same fairy tale that women
> have been conned into believing for so long, which has prevented women
> so often from being realistic about what's there, what we want, how to
> make it happen. It's the old romantic tale that allows you to think your
> life will be saved by a man [qtd. in Seger 211].

Vivian even tells Edward at one point that she wants it all; she wants the
fairy tale. And though, when in the end Edward asks what happens after
the Prince rescues the fair damsel in the tower Vivian replies that "she
rescues him right back," it's always been clear that he holds all the power.
He's responsible for her makeover, and he can set her right back on the
streets again.

When the film came out in 1990, Jay Carr wrote, "There isn't an
American film this year that so nakedly (under its benevolent surface) and
so systematically humiliates a woman" (B30). He goes on to explain that
"what makes it demeaning to women is its view that the rich guy necessarily calls all the shots. It goes through the motions of having Roberts'
character take a stand. But its not-so-hidden motor is her submission to
Gere" (B30).

So why then is *Pretty Woman* one of the highest-grossing films of all
time, especially when its ideology reinforces the notion that women *want*
the fairy tale and *accept* that they are dependent on men? Several reasons
come to mind. First, "it's all about money." This line opens the film, and
for the next two hours we're seduced into believing another false myth:
that class boundaries don't exist in America, especially when money paves
the way up the ladder. As Vivian says to her hooker friend Kit (Laura San
Giacomo), "It's easy to clean up when you got money." We're willing to
bet that every woman who plunked down her hard-earned money to see
this film (some more than once) got this message.

In "A Modern Cinderella," Karol Kelley points out that Vivian's "status can be raised only through marriage, when she will take the position of her husband" (89). She holds out for the fairy tale and wins when Edward charges up to her apartment in a white limo, takes a deep breath (remember, he's afraid of heights), and climbs up to meet her halfway on the fire escape. We're meant to believe that because we leave them in the middle of the ladder at the end of the film that their relationship will be an equal partnership. Hardly. The gap between our hero and heroine is about as wide as it can get, but Vivian leaps from the bottom rung of the ladder to the top in one swoop when Edward decides to marry her.

Hand in hand with that big leap is the suggestion that Vivian gives to Edward as much as she gets. When she turns down his offer of a fancy apartment, a car, and a limitless credit card and walks out, Vivian says to Edward, "I think you have a lot of special qualities." In the role of hooker and therapist, she manages to allay his chronic need to get back at his father and put him in touch with his sensitive side. He calls off work, goes on a picnic in the park, and walks barefoot through grass. He's even able to walk out onto his penthouse balcony by the end of the film. Instead of raiding James Morse's (Ralph Bellamy) financially troubled corporation, Edward ends up becoming the old gentleman's partner in the shipbuilding business after Vivian tells him he doesn't make anything and he doesn't build anything. Through her, Edward reveals his redeeming qualities: his refined taste in music and a generous nature. Through her, Edward sees how insincere his "friends" really are. In exchange, Vivian gets her fairy tale. The temptation to believe that if it can happen to someone as far down the social scale as Vivian it can happen to anyone hovers irresistibly above us.

Love conquers all, and, according to psychiatrist Joanna Magda Polenz, "It is not surprising that this film was so popular because everyone wants to believe that there is nothing as great as love" (*PR Newswire*). And if that love is happening between two people as charismatic and beautiful as Julia Roberts and Richard Gere, all the more reason to sidestep the deeper issues here. The sheer magnetism of these two stars pulled people into theaters in droves. It was difficult to resist Roberts's fresh, open, unrestrained quality. Tall and slender with a huge toothy smile, big laugh, and cascading mane of wavy red hair, she lit up the screen as Vivian Ward. What man could turn away, even in her before state? (She won the Golden Globe for Best Actress in a Comedy/Musical as well as Oscar and British Academy of Film and Television Arts nominations for Best Actress.) Like so many other heroines of makeover films, Vivian's makeover stems from her lack of sophistication, not her lack of beauty.

Richard Gere had built a reputation as a hunk in films like *Ameri-*

can Gigolo (1980) and *An Officer and a Gentleman* (1982), but *Pretty Woman* set him up a notch. His graying locks, designer suits, soft voice, and powerful persona became the subject of female fantasy. He also won a nod from the Golden Globes for Best Actor. Audiences rooted for both of them in *Pretty Woman*.

Another reason for *Pretty Woman*'s enormous popularity lies in what's *not* dealt with in the film. With the exception of a brief scene in which a prostitute ends up dead in an ally (we never see the body—only tourists snapping pictures of it), the film whitewashes the whole prostitution business. Vivian witnesses the scene, shudders, and walks into a bar to meet Kit who has spent their rent money on drugs, though their devastating effects are never in evidence. As they sit at the bar, the tight framing and intense red filters suggest a feeling of claustrophobia. Vivian says, "Kit, don't you want to get out of here?" Kit replies, "Where the fuck you want to go?" Kit's fatalistic response dramatizes the sheer implausibility of Vivian's total makeover and journey to the top.

Most prostitutes are trapped in the life, but not according to Hollywood. It's interesting to note here that J. F. Lawton's original screenplay was "an anti–Cinderella story" with the "idea that men would rather buy women than respect them" (qtd. in Broeske 39). Lawton has Edward dump Vivian right back where he found her at the end of his script, but Hollywood went for the unrealistic, hooker-lives-happily-ever-after-with-billionaire-businessman ending and filtered out most of the sleazy elements of her underworld existence.

But the signifiers of this underworld, the red filters, persist for awhile and bathe Edward's suite on their first night together, connecting their worlds temporarily. As their relationship grows, hooker red gives way to the clarity of day. The before Vivian looks totally out of place in bright daylight. Edward gives her money to buy a dress for dinner. Vivian ends up on Rodeo Drive still wearing her call girl duds from the night before: blue mini skirt, white midriff top, over-the-knee black vinyl boots held up by a safety pin. Men and women stare. Bitchy shop girls won't wait on her, even with Edward's wad of money. "Nobody will help me," she cries to hotel manager Bernard ("Barney," she calls him). Her fairy godfather waves his wand, and soon she's dressed in a black lace cocktail dress dining with the rich and powerful. "Stunning," Edward says. "Female beauty is thus first shaped by or acquired with money and then validated through the male gaze," Dima Dabbous-Sensenig writes in her article "Who is the Prettiest One of All?"

Vivian's world gives way to Edward's with little evidence of her former life. Elizabeth Scala observes that even Vivian's hair is a cue for audi-

ences to suspend their disbelief and forget how she makes her money.
When Edward first meets Vivian, she is wearing a blonde wig. "Vivian's
real hair color remains hidden," Scala writes. "It is not until the next
scene, in which she sleeps alone, that her natural red hair color is uncovered. And for the rest of the film, as one forgets her initial role as Holly-

Pretty Woman (Touchstone, 1990).
(*Left*) BEFORE: Once hooker Vivian
Ward (Julia Roberts) takes off that blonde, bobbed wig and heavy makeup,
she looks just like thousands of other young women with long, tousled hair who
like to wear their boyfriend's oversized shirts. Isn't that the point of this movie?
Isn't every streetwalker just a regular girl whose dreams of marrying her prince
went terribly awry? These two shots reveal the natural beauty and charming
persona of Julia Roberts, one reason for this film's enormous popularity. With
her big smile, bigger laugh, and fun-loving spirit, she makes us forget that she
was ever a lady of the evening and wins the heart of billionaire tycoon Edward
Lewis (Richard Gere).
(*Right*) AFTER: By the time Vivian makes an appearance at the opera with
Edward in this stunning, strapless gown, she can even wear red without
reminding us that she's a hooker. In this profile shot, she gazes at the ruby
necklace that Edward holds out for her. "Only the best" is this Prince Charming's mantra. With his money and a little help from the hotel manager, he
has transformed a diamond in the rough into a priceless *objet d'art*, like the
vase on the table next to her. Vivian has become "the best," and he can't part
with her.

wood Boulevard prostitute, Roberts's own hair suffices—her own colors flying, as it were for the rest of the film" (36).

In truth, Vivian sheds the signifiers of her profession so quickly (one week!) that when Edward reminds us late in the film that she's a hooker by telling Stuckey, who uses the information to attack her in order to get even with Edward for blowing the Morse Company takeover, we're as shocked and hurt as she is. Edward saves her by punching Stuckey but isn't capable of making a permanent commitment to her until Barney, now captivated by Miss Vivian, spins him in the right direction. Barney has completely accepted Vivian's transformation—and who are we to argue with the fairy godfather? When Vivian leaves the hotel, he calls for the limo, kisses her hand, and says, "It's been a pleasure knowing you. Come visit us again sometime." This from Barney, who would never abide hookers at the classy Beverly Wilshire, carries a lot of weight.

Barney's got a few parting words for Edward, too. When Edward asks him to return the ruby necklace Vivian wore to the opera to the jeweler's, Barney looks at the necklace and says, "It must be difficult to let go of something so beautiful." Edward gets his meaning. And herein lies the real appeal of this film for female audiences—the transformation, or makeover itself. The idea that a woman can change her appearance, acquire some etiquette, fly up the social scale virtually overnight, and end up with a guy oozing with money, power, and good looks is mighty seductive. The film was "tremendously strong with women over 25," film analyst Martin Grove tells us (qtd. in Curry 18). And the second scene on Rodeo Drive, the one in which Edward takes Vivian shopping himself, is sheer wish fulfillment for women who have ever felt intimidated by snobbish shop clerks who look down their noses at the rest of the unwashed.

The scene begins back at the hotel. Edward, on his way to work, shakes Vivian and says, "Wake up. Time to shop." (Most of us just hit replay on that line alone. It seems she didn't buy enough the day before.) Vivian moans. The shop girls were mean to me, she tells him. "Stores are never nice to people. They're nice to credit cards," he counsels. Edward then escorts Vivian to Rodeo Drive, walks into an exclusive shop and tells Mr. Hollister (Larry Miller) that he's going to be spending an obscene amount of money and Vivian is going to need a lot of sucking up. "Profane or really offensive?" Hollister asks. "Reeeeeeeeeeally offensive," Edward tells him.

Thus begins one of film's most famous montages. We hear Roy Orbison's "Pretty Woman" as we are treated to a series of shots of Vivian (surrounded by shop clerks sucking up) trying on one stunning outfit after another while Edward, on the phone conducting business, nods his approval. When he has to go back to work, he leaves his credit card and no doubt as to how Vivian is to be treated. By the time the song ends and Vivian leaves, she's transformed from a hooker who spits her gum out on the street to a well-behaved goddess.

Walking down Rodeo Drive, men and women stare, this time because she's gorgeous and looks like she's been shopping there all her life. A full shot of her shows the complete makeover. Vivian wears a white dress, with buttons down the front, sleeves to the elbow, white gloves, a black and white heels, and black, wide-brimmed hat. Her long, wavy hair is now neatly pulled back in a chic do. Carrying several shopping bags, she walks past the window of the store where she was mistreated just the day before. She pauses, coolly saunters in, and asks the same women (now smiling at her), "Do you remember me, the person you refused to wait on yesterday? Big mistake. Huge. I have to go shopping now." Revenge is sweet in the makeover genre.

When next we see Vivian, she and Edward are headed for the San Francisco Opera, the substitute ball in this film as it is in *Moonstruck* (1987). He's in his tuxedo; she's in her red gown, ruby necklace, white gloves, and upswept hair. Vivian's transformation is so effective that she can even wear a red dress without the color reminding us that she's a hooker. "If I forget to tell you later, I had a really good time tonight," she tells Edward as the young elevator operator smiles. They step out into the hotel lobby. People gasp. Vivian and Edward look stunning together. They fit.

The bonding experience they have at the opera (she gets it) is really only icing, the minimal attempt to show that there's more to their relationship than looks. In truth, with his money and power and influence, and with very little effort on his part, Edward has bought and molded the perfect mate, a woman who now befits his station in life. Or, as Harvey Roy Greenberg rather colorfully puts it, "*Pretty Woman* preaches that once tutored, then backed in classy spending by the man of your dreams, you, too, can be transformed into the submissive Cinderfuckingrella of every rich lout's predatory dream" (11).

As we suggest in our discussions of *Sabrina* (both 1954 and 1995 versions), *Funny Face, Grease, Working Girl, Maid in Manhattan*, and *Pretty Woman*, makeovers let our heroines transgress the boundaries of a class. Usually they provide her with upward mobility (except in *Grease* where the movement is purposefully downward) since the hero dwells among the uppercrust. The makeover becomes the linchpin of these plots. She must transform to enter his world, to fit in his world where oftentimes appearance not only gets her across the moat but also unlocks the castle doors.

Each film here follows the formula that makeovers are performed on women who are already beautiful, as if to confirm what we already know. It isn't as if we're amazed by the metamorphosis from Plain Jane to Princess. We know it's coming. And how plain can Audrey Hepburn or Julia Roberts really be? We've come to instinctively understand the conventions of this genre. Yet we sit transfixed—watching things being put back the way they *should* be. The ultimate union of two beautiful people solidifies the message that class boundaries in America can be leveled, even if the leveling tools are a few makeup brushes and a blow dryer. The question becomes, "What freedoms have our heroines left behind on their way up the ladder?"

Five

Pygmalion Problems

Tonight, old man, you did it, you did it, you did it!
—Alan Jay Lerner and
Frederick Loewe, *My Fair Lady*

Cinderella's fairy godmother comes at her call, does her bidding, and disappears until the tale's end. Most Cinderella films, even the modern adaptations, repeat that pattern. Literal fairy godmothers do not appear in the films we place in "The Ladder of Class," but, each of those boundary-breaking "Cinderella" figures has a fairy godmother-like character, sometimes male, sometimes female, as an agent of change. What happens when that character makes a less abrupt appearance? This version of a makeover story—heavy on the creator's talent and anguish—has a mythic source.

Ovid tells of the woman-hater Pygmalion, a sculptor from Cyprus, who created a statue of the perfect woman, Galatea, and fell in love with his own creation (Hamilton 145–146). Taking pity on him, Venus turned cold marble into warm flesh, and the statue came to life. "Venus herself graced their marriage," Ovid concludes the tale, "and after that we do not know" Hamilton (50).

This is a happy ending? The myth tells us of Pygmalion's talent, his misogynistic tendencies, his obsession, and of Venus's magic and *her* pleasure at the resulting wedding. We smirk at the irony of a woman-hater possessed by the image of a woman, and we wonder at Venus's marvelous gift. But about Galatea, we know nothing, except that Pygmalion created her. Perhaps she came to life seeing before her a man who repelled her. Perhaps she cried at her own wedding. Maybe her first words to Pygmalion were "Take out the garbage," making him wish for marble again. Can a *man* craft a perfect woman? Can either creator or creation be happy in such a relationship? These Pygmalion films—*Pygmalion* (1938), *My Fair Lady* (1964), *Shampoo* (1975), *Up Close and Personal* (1996), and *Miss*

Congeniality (2000)—(lavish attention on their Pygmalions and provide more information about their Galateas, "goddesses" who come down from their pedestals. No sculptor gets exactly what he expected, and no "creation" finds herself in a perfect situation. Exaggerate the premise, as *The Stepford Wives* (1975) does, and the myth dissolves into terror.

Pygmalion *(stageplay, 1914)*

Most Pygmalion films draw from the famous dramatic incarnation of the myth, George Bernard Shaw's play *Pygmalion: A Romance in Five Acts,* which opened on the London stage in April 1914. Although Shaw obviously enjoyed creating his Galatea, in this case, Eliza Doolittle, a whining slavey of a Cockney flower girl, he loved his Pygmalion. Misogynist Henry Higgins, or as pre-transformation Eliza calls him, "'Enry Iggins," has the best lines, the star turn, and the last word. The action follows Higgins's bet that he, a linguist, can pass Eliza off as a duchess after six months of working to change the way she speaks from Cockney to upper crust. Eliza's new self emerges in glimpses, first at Higgins's mother's house where she stuns all other guests into silence with her correctly pronounced but horrific "small-talk," and finally after the ball, where she has had a great success, which Colonel Pickering and Higgins attribute to Higgins alone (no praise for Eliza).

But the joke's on Higgins. After Eliza leaves in anger, Higgins finally understands that he has become fond of her. What attracts him? Paradoxically, Higgins—who doesn't care about social graces—has helped Eliza learn them, but it's her spunkiness he says he likes, and Eliza had that to begin with. Eliza realizes that she no longer fits anywhere, and she's not the only member of her family who feels that way. Higgins has changed Eliza's father, Alfred P. Doolittle, from a loquacious dustman into a "moralist" by recommending him to an American millionaire as an original thinker. Both lives are altered, but for the better? The play ends ambiguously, no Venus and no wedding, with Higgins's absolute assurance that Eliza will return to him, and with Eliza's absolute assurance that she will not (306).

In the short preface to the play, Shaw says that he believes such a linguistic transformation can actually happen, and that linguists who practice class leveling should be considered heroes. This talk of heroics might encourage readers to take the subtitle of the play, *A Romance,* literally. By the simplest definition of the term, the story should be driven by the coming together of two lovers, who surmount obstacles to do so. But which two? *Pygmalion* is far from simple, and in his *Afterword*, Shaw makes this clear. He carefully considers Eliza's options as if she were a real person. Shaw says that Eliza and Higgins will remain friends, but that for them to marry would be a very bad idea, especially since "Eliza has no use for the foolish romantic tradition that all women love to be mastered, if not actually bullied and beaten" (601). Shaw goes on to explain, in his *Afterword*, that Eliza gets a posh flower shop and Freddy Eynsford Hill as a husband. Her transformation has given her independence from her creator.

Such independence rarely happens in Pygmalionesque makeover films, and herein lies the crux of most Pygmalion problems. Shaw complained that "our imaginations [are] so enfeebled by their lazy dependence on the ready-mades and reach-me-downs of the ragshop in which Romance keeps its stock of 'happy endings' to misfit all stories" (*Afterword* 598). The films we examine here bear out the truth of his remark, depending all too often on the "ragshop" happy ending, and not often enough on how a creator might be altered in the process of remaking or what a woman so entirely changed might become.

Pygmalion *(1938)*

In his Preface to Shaw's plays, Rex Harrison wonders how Shaw would have felt about the ending to the musical *My Fair Lady:*

> When I was playing the last scene ... with the near-implicit suggestion that Eliza is going to stay with Higgins, I often thought of Shaw.... The idea was anathema to him.... He was so against the banal the ordinary, the mundane. He thought of Higgins as an independent man....
> [Shaw's] heroes should not marry [xi].

But Shaw *had* been involved in an earlier production that implied a similar ending. Shaw is credited for screenwriting in the 1938 British film adaptation of his play *Pygmalion,* starring Wendy Hiller and Leslie Howard. (Examining the British film puts *My Fair Lady* into perspective.) Amazingly enough, the screenplay opts for exactly the ending Shaw thought so wrong. Henry Higgins sits alone in his study at the end of the film, and, at the last minute, Eliza appears, repeating a line she spoke when she first entered his home: "I washed my hands and face before I come, I did." Her appearance resolves the ambiguity of Shaw's original ending. Except for that radical change, the balance of the film, directed by Leslie Howard (who also stars as Higgins) and Anthony Asquith, remains faithful to the play. The Pygmalion myth, the play, and the film focus on hubris, class prejudice, and the unpredictability of love.

Wendy Hiller's before Eliza looks young and fairly healthy, but her broken hat, ripped hem and frowsy hair signify her poverty; she can't afford to be neat and clean (shades of Cinderella). Her costume reads as real, not as a designer's idea of what a poor person might wear. When it rains, Hiller gets wet and speaks her lines with her hair dripping down her face.

The film opens in the cacophony of an early morning Covent Garden market, and Hiller as Eliza blends into the crowd of chattering folk. The sounds remind us that what Higgins terms as "noise," the speech of the poor, has a lilt of its own. The scene shifts: it's the same location, but that evening. A rainstorm has chased all, rich and poor, under the shelter of the pillared church. When Eliza speaks alone, begging folks to buy "f'lars off a poor gel," her words show why Higgins can claim that her "oooow and garn" will keep her in her place. And how is *her place* perceived by others? In the play, and in the 1938 adaptation, Freddy Eyensford-Hill bumps into Eliza as he tries to get a cab. "Watch out there, Freddy," she cautions.

Because she uses his name, Freddy's mother questions Eliza. How does she know him? Eliza explains that she doesn't know him, that she was simply using a colloquialism, like, "look out there, Buddy," and that she's a "good girl," but the implication's clear (Shaw 519). If you look and speak as Eliza does, others might take you for a prostitute. Maybe, someday, you might have to resort to that. The prostitute incident gives a more powerful reason why this "squashed cabbage leaf," desires change.

Scenes implied by the play give the film an emphasis of its own. A revealing scene in Eliza's hovel of a room after the evening at Covent Garden where she meets Higgins adds some darkness. Shaw describes Eliza's room in the stage directions (527), and, in the film, her lodgings come to life to show what relief even a verbal makeover might bring. It might bring a flat with more that one room, more than one gas light, more than a pallet for a bed. Eliza gazes into a spotted mirror with longing that demonstrates her depth. She's more than a Cockney cartoon; Shaw knew that her room would show "the irreducible minimum of poverty's needs" *(Pygmalion* 527). Although the challenge of improving her "deliciously low" status attracts Higgins, he also notes her shrewdness. This Eliza has a sense of herself *before* she learns a new way to speak. Unlike many of the heroines in makeover films, and unlike Galatea in the myth, Eliza seeks her own makeover and is quite willing to pay for it.

Other scenes implied by the play demonstrate the sacrifice and drudgery that go into the makeover—no waving of wands here. Eliza's change begins with Phase I—a bath, the first all-over one she has ever had. Her amazement that she is to get *all wet* underscores the contrast between wealth and poverty, as does Eliza's modesty. She shrieks at seeing herself in a mirror. Shaw enjoys pointing out the differences between upper and lower class morality. Complete cleanliness alters her profoundly. Her own father does not recognize her. The major change has begun.

A montage reveals Phase II. Higgins has said he views her as a "thing," but he treats her as a teachable student. These scenes detail Higgins's talents and his methods of changing Eliza's speech. Neatly dressed in what looks like a school girl's uniform, Eliza strains to follow Higgins's chart-assisted lecture about the proper position for the mouth, lips, teeth, and tongue; she mimics his pronunciation; she huffs out her *Hs*, blowing out candles as she changes them from "aitches." "By Jupiter," Higgins says about her pronunciation of *cup*. "She's done it at the first shot." Pickering agrees that it's "splendid." Add Eliza's quickness to the portrait of her character. Punctuating these scenes of work with Higgins, glimpses of Eliza tossing in troubled sleep show that what she has learned runs through her dreams. *Whew.* Eliza's irrepressible personality breaks free in Phase III of her makeover, when Higgins and Pickering try her out on Higgins's mother. Hiller's body language shows Eliza's insecurity. She holds herself stiffly. She looks to Higgins before every move. She speaks only the syllables she has practiced, even when they make little sense. "The rain in Spain falls mainly in the plain" hardly fits seamlessly into conversation.

But, gradually, Eliza begins to loosen up. Freddy Eyensford-Hill's mirth at her utterances irritates her. In that frame of mind, Eliza deserts her script. Her face changes, and the other guests lean in to hear a dreadful tale of her aunt's death. Eliza says she is sure her aunt was "done in" by those who wanted her goods, not by influenza. She explains that the aunt "come through" influenza the year before, cured by gin. Now Eliza looks happy. Each rounded and perfect vowel divulges some horror. No makeover can squelch the suspicious, entertaining girl who tells this tale.

Or can it? Eliza breaks down during more strenuous coaching by Higgins and Pickering, this time on matters of etiquette, but she rebounds to enter Phase IV. Her physical makeover, like Charlotte Vale's, and so many others, is overseen by designers and hairdressers. We see her getting a mudpack and a pedicure while stylists argue about her coiffure. She emerges looking regal; externally, she has been ironed into a conventionally charming young woman. Of course, this is one of Shaw's points. In every scene of contrast between Eliza and the upper crust she wants to emulate, she shines, while they moulder. What a stodgy, boring lot.

In her fancy gown, sleek hairdo and tiara, Eliza suffers from the Cinderella effect. Although she is universally admired for her "charm," she has become a beautiful object, appreciated by those who value only others like themselves. Her final form seems the antithesis of anything Henry Higgins would want in the perfect woman, and Eliza makes it clear that an effete self isn't what she had in mind. It's nice to see Hiller burn when Eliza turns her wrath on her teacher.

Higgins has his own before and after. Leslie Howard emphasizes Higgins's before state of self-satisfaction. His every move speaks of assurance and comfort. He likes himself as he is—eccentric, abrasive, killingly funny, and alone. We like him that way, too. He knows his great power and has used it to the best of his ability on Eliza's father, and on Eliza herself.

Higgins's after state details his shock. How could he, the "confirmed old bachelor," have fallen for his protégé? In this film adaptation, it's easy to see how. Shot after shot shows Higgins teaching Eliza, drilling Eliza, prodding Eliza, rewarding or punishing Eliza. He has entangled his life with hers while they worked, and she has untangled his life by becoming a kind of under secretary, in charge of all the irritating minutiae of existence.

Shaw's play ends abruptly, leaving us to wonder about the outcome, but directors Howard and Asquith ask their audience to empathize with Higgins, and to feel satisfaction when Eliza returns to him. This resolution changes the trajectory of the story, making it more closely parallel the conclusion of the Pygmalion myth. It's *his* future that's been at stake, not hers. Did Higgins get what he expected? His expectations, always unclear, never went further than proving his power. He certainly never wanted a *woman*. Did Eliza get what she wanted? Not really. She will never achieve her goal of an independent life. The extraordinary interactions between Higgins and Eliza will conclude in convention. Higgins will give Eliza the position to which he has raised her, but Eliza will not use her painfully-gained independence. The conclusion hints at a frightening equation: poverty equals freedom. Even in the sub-plot, Eliza's father gains success through Higgins's recommendation, but he, too, loses his independence. His new middle class status makes him feel that he should marry Eliza's "stepmother."

The casting makes Eliza and Higgins more suited to be father and daughter than lovers. Howard was nineteen years older than Hiller, but the scenes of the two working together, an alliance against snobbery, make the ending palatable, if not perfect. Faithful to the play, the film allows Eliza to be quick and bright, and Hiller holds her own, even considering Howard's brilliant performance. Her Eliza has enough depth to make us hope Higgins will not completely overpower his creation.

My Fair Lady *(1964)*

Is the same true for the glamorous musical adaptation *My Fair Lady*? The British film throws the American version, directed by George Cukor, into stark relief. Oscar winner for Best Picture, this cinematic interpretation of Lerner and Loewe's Broadway blockbuster puts its own slant on *Pygmalion,* increasing its glamour, altering Eliza's character, and escalating the focus on Henry Higgins.

George Cukor spared nothing in this production. From the opening credits, superimposed over tubs of gorgeous Covent Garden market flowers, and from the opening scene of the hoi polloi parading down a theater staircase in their finery, Cukor opts for lavish color, mesmerizing motion, and gorgeous production numbers. Big isn't necessarily bad, but it is *different.* For grandeur and sweep, Cukor forfeits the intimate feel of the play and the 1938 film.

The choice to cast Audrey Hepburn as Eliza Doolittle profoundly altered Eliza's character. Julie Andrews had triumphed in the part on Broadway, proving she had acting skills, a voice, and, certainly, the stamina to reprise the role. Hepburn could not sing well enough to carry such a demanding role. Still, she could draw audiences, and Warner Bros. felt safer with her than with Andrews, who did not want to do a screen test. In *My Fair Lady,* Eliza's looks are Hepburn's, but her voice belongs to Marni Nixon.

The title *My Fair Lady,* not *Pygmalion,* offers the same reassurance as the first song in Disney's *Cinderella*: the heroine will be "fair." In Andrews, Warner Bros. would have had a lovely and talented newcomer, but in Hepburn they had an icon. Louis Giannetti reminds us how well Hepburn fit the makeover convention that mandates starting with a glamorous lead: "We couldn't imagine a star like Hepburn playing a woman of weak character or a coarse or stupid woman, so firmly entrenched was her image of an elegant and rather aristocratic female" (264). Posters for *My Fair Lady* featured the Hepburn everyone knew would emerge from Eliza Doolittle, as she had from *Sabrina* and *Funny Face.*

The trailer for *My Fair Lady,* includes a single shot of Eliza's before transformation, which might seem a daring choice, but a look at her shows how "safe" it was. Cecil Beaton (who won an Oscar for costuming) gave close attention to Shaw's very specific description, and Hepburn's first costume, more accurately than Hiller's, duplicates Shaw's ideas about Eliza's garb:

> She wears a little sailor hat of black straw…. Her hair needs washing rather badly…. She wears a shabby black coat that reaches nearly to her knees and is shaped to her waist. She has a brown skirt with a coarse apron. Her boots are much the worse for the wear [*Pygmalion* 518].

Although Shaw's components signify poverty, on Hepburn, the effect reads *adorable*; the fitted coat flatters her slender figure, and the mop of hair sets off her luminous complexion and lovely features. Shaw subtitled his play *A Romance,* but he says that Eliza "is not at all a romantic figure," and that her "features are no worse than [the ladies around her]" (518). No matter how she mugs it up, Hepburn, a romantic gamin, resists any attempt to make her look ordinary. Her features are *way better* than those of the ladies around her. The music and dance in this scene underscore Eliza's preciousness and her taste for romance. Shaw hated the idea of setting his plays to music (*Collected Works* ix), so he probably would have hated Eliza's first song, "Wouldn't it Be Loverly."

In one of the few changes from stage script to screenplay, the film action contributes to the idea that Eliza is already special. The stage directions call for a pantomime of a grand dinner during the number, with Eliza as one of the mimers (*My Fair Lady* 26). The film surrounds her instead with a male entourage of costermongers who twirl her, lift her, hand her into a produce cart, and offer her a cabbage bouquet. Obviously, they adore her.

"Wouldn't it Be Loverly" takes the place of the scene in the 1938 film that shows Eliza's room. Watching her capering about gives poverty a happier face than the glimpse of her cold, dark flat, and the lyrics add another twist that's missing from the 1938 adaptation. Eliza wishes someone she can take care of and who will take care of her. Her first song introduces her readiness for "someone," a sentiment missing from Shaw's play.

As the musical raises the romantic stakes, it sanitizes Eliza. The screenplay deletes the incident in which Eliza speaks Freddy's name and triggers his mother's suspicions. This Eliza may be cutely smudged, like Lesley Ann Warren was as Cinderella, but she's carefully kept above any "filthy" implications. Later in the film, in the only scene that places Eliza in an intimate situation with Freddy, they never touch. (In Shaw's play and in the British film adaptation, Freddy and Eliza kiss and embrace.) Hepburn's Eliza remains virginal, a "good girl."

In *My Fair Lady*, costuming and music emphasize Hepburn's beauty and vulnerability, and a comic mood prevails as Eliza goes through the makeover phases. In Phase I, Eliza's bath becomes an epic struggle involving Mrs. Pearce and several maids who cluster around a screaming Eliza. Shaw imagined Eliza wearing a Chinese kimono while she waited for some new clothes, and this is how Hiller appears. Cecil Beaton ignores this description. After her bath, Hepburn wears one of many girlish day dresses.

Hiller had one schoolgirl costume. Hepburn has lots, and she sports them during Phase II, which has a strong comic thrust. In the play, and in the 1938 film, Higgins and Pickering declare Eliza quick and bright from the start. This is not the case in the musical. Although Higgins later says Eliza "can do anything," the teaching sequence suggests otherwise.

My Fair Lady (Warner Bros., 1964). BEFORE: As unbending as the pillar behind him, Henry Higgins (Rex Harrison) takes the measure of Eliza Doolittle (Audrey Hepburn), the "squashed cabbage leaf" he has just met. She looks him over, too. She's a little intimidated, but not too afraid to assert her position as a "good girl." In the Pymalion-Galatea relationship that follows, both will be remade, but Eliza's initial feistiness, so apparent in this before shot, suffers in the process.

My Fair Lady (Warner Bros., 1964). AFTER: By this moment in the film, Eliza has a new, if limited, vocabulary of "proper" English. Her jaunty pose, however, signals that she understands she has a new kind of power resulting from her makeover. Eliza enjoys turning male heads in her debut as a beautifully-gowned lady. Henry Higgins's relaxed posture does not indicate that he has relinquished his hold over her. Higgins obviously enjoys what he sees, but he is still standing behind her, literally, like a puppeteer, trying to direct Eliza's performance. She is, after all, *his* creation.

Cukor uses a montage (as Asquith and Howard did), but these scenes show Higgins practicing a different instructional method. Let's call it linguistic tough love.

Higgins leaves Eliza for hours? days? to say her vowels alone, apparently to little avail. Over and over, she screeches, "Ahyee, E, Iyee, Ow, You," a prisoner shut in solitary. (Flash forward to *Working Girl* to find Tess riding nowhere on an exercise bike, listening to her boss's voice, trying to duplicate the sounds of success.) When he helps, Higgins's assistance has a cruel edge. He gives her a sheet of phrases to read and places Eliza near a tall flame emerging from a burner. When she says "H" correctly, the flame will flicker. Eliza makes good progress until she sets her paper on fire! Higgins is oblivious.

Because she can't say "cup of tea" correctly, Higgins holds a cup tantalizingly out of her reach. Later he fills her mouth with marbles to force her to enunciate. Poor Eliza swallows one. (This incident occurs in the 1938 version as well.) Higgins tells her not to worry, he's "got lots more," and pops another heinous marble into her mouth. As she wearily repeats and repeats, Higgins gives a delicious strawberry tart to his parrot, not to Eliza, who salivates for it. From the teaching montage, the audience must draw the conclusions that Higgins is a detached slave driver, and that Eliza is a bit slow—a very different impression than the montage in the 1938 film leaves.

But things change in the "Rain in Spain" scene. After endlessly repeating "The rhine in spine sties minely in the pline," her horrid version of the phrase, Eliza finally gets it right. (She says it correctly the first time in the 1938 film.) Higgins, Pickering and Eliza sing the catchy tune, "The Rain in Spain," falling under its spell. Looking particularly adorable, Eliza wears a dark green jumper with a crisp white high-collared blouse. For color, a violet and blue scarf accents her tiny waist. Her upswept hair with its fluffy bangs screams femininity. During this scene Eliza falls for Higgins (a moment that doesn't occur in the play or in the earlier film). In her suddenly perfect upper-class dialect, Eliza sings "I Could Have Danced All Night" to Mrs. Pearce. Eliza's linguistic breakthrough parallels her romantic one, and her tuneful declaration of love for Higgins overshadows her triumph over "OOOWWW" and "GAAARRNN."

In *My Fair Lady,* makeover Phase III has a stunning setting—the opening day of the Ascot races. Cukor treats his audience to a lavish production number, featuring members of the aristocracy dressed to the hilt in whites, blacks and grays. At Ascot, not in Mrs. Higgins's drawing room, Eliza encounters the Eynsford-Hills and tests her conversation. Shaw says Eliza should be, "exquisitely dressed," and should create an "impression of … remarkable distinction and beauty" (*Pygmalion* 559). Wendy Hiller, costumed in a ruffled, chiffon afternoon dress, added a stiff insecurity to this description.

It's difficult to imagine how Beaton could top Hepburn's Ascot costume. The gown and Hepburn herself, both drop-dead gorgeous, now deck videotapes and DVDs of the remastered film. Hepburn wears a high-necked, floor-length, white lace sheath that showcases her trim figure. A wide black and white ribbon, slung low around those slender hips, ties in a bow in the back. An enormous hat sits rakishly aside her head, and, to warm the black and white with a blush of color, a pastel, floral print mob-cap almost covers her hair.

The authors both remembered this costume from previous viewings of *My Fair Lady,* but we still oohed and ahhed. Hiller's Eliza reveals her insecurity. Hepburn, however, plays this scene like someone to the manor born. Hiller's Eliza warms up to the situation; Hepburn's owns it. She exudes poise, thrilled that she and that stunning costume are the magnet for all eyes. Hiller provides life, energy, and obscenity to contrast with the decorous entropy of the upper class. Although "bloody" gets edited out, Hepburn also steals the show with a hilarious punch line. Positioned against a stiff row of jaded race watchers, she leans forward passionately, finally screaming at her horse, "Move your blooming arse!" From this point in the film, however, costuming overpowers Eliza's character, each subsequent outfit reeking of expensive haute couture.

Hepburn's look dominates the ballroom scene, Phase IV of her makeover. Since we've already seen just how lovely and poised Eliza can be, she's got to look amazing to prevent anticlimax. *My Fair Lady* deletes the process of Eliza's final makeover—no hairdressers or stylists. This gives Hepburn's grand entrance more punch.

More than any other scene in *My Fair Lady,* Eliza's Cinderella glide *down* the staircase (significant, no?) recalls Hepburn's prior makeover credits. Her high-piled hair glistens with jewels, her filmy white empire gown emphasizes her long neck and regal bearing. Frozen into a similar image of distinction, Jo in *Funny Face* comments, "It feels wonderful, but it's not me." Eliza says nothing, but she exudes a palpable aura of sadness that fits the production year—1963. No baby boomer watching the film could resist a comparison to Jaqueline Kennedy's stately inaugural ball appearance, similarly coiffed, caped and gowned. *My Fair Lady* cast members noted the schizophrenia of living through Kennedy's assassination while they were shooting the production numbers.

Eliza's sadness fits the inner world of the story as well. She understands that she has become a statue—a nice reversal of the Pygmalion myth. As "fair lady," she fits nowhere: too grand for Covent Garden, too negligible for Westminster. Later, in the post-ball scene, Hepburn's scarlet-cloaked and silent presence *smolders* through Higgins's and Pickering's cackles of triumph.

Where *can* Eliza go? Higgins doesn't seem to care. Subsequent costuming suggests Eliza's only possible direction. When she leaves Higgins's house, she wears a particularly suggestive outfit. We have just watched her triumphant appearance at the ball, where she has been "hailed as a Princess by one and by all." No one could have looked sleeker, more stunning or more sophisticated. What a surprise, then, to see her dressed like a little girl. Her peach, two-piece ensemble has a short, swingy jacket that accentuates Hepburn's slight frame and minimizes her bust. The jacket closes with enormous buttons, like a toddler's coat. The frivolous scoop of her bonnet slants at an angle over her forehead and ties in a big bow. This get-up suggests another makeover stage: from flower-monger, to socialite, to helpless child.

Her next outfit underscores her helplessness. Eliza takes refuge in the home of Higgins's mother, her only female friend. When Henry tracks her down, she tells him, in a song, that she can manage without him. But the way she looks suggests she cannot. Dressed in the height of femininity, in a ruffled, filmy pink frock decorated with a giant rose, she resembles a hothouse flower. For all her words about independence, and for all Higgins's claims that he likes her feistiness, Eliza's fragile beauty and expensive clothing, bought for her by Pickering and Higgins, steals the scene and demonstrates her dependence.

An examination of Higgins's dialogue suggests the future tone of their relationship. Shaw's play gives Higgins and Eliza almost equal utterances (a little heavier for Higgins). But Lerner and Loewe's lyrics tip the balance. Higgins's songs, like "I'm an Ordinary Man," elaborate on his misogyny. His "Hymn to Him" claims that fixing their hair is all women do, and he counsels them to fix up their inner selves. (116). These lines are funny, but the sheer number of Higgins's words about women creates an onslaught. If you count the lines in his musical numbers, Higgins has 304 to Eliza's 172.

Rex Harrison's unique delivery adds more weight. Much was made about his speaking, not singing, his numbers because it proved that a great actor with a not-so-great voice could star in a musical. But his spoken "songs," like the misogynistic "Hymn to Him," have an additional impact. In a story about the power of language, it seems important that every crystal-clear word Harrison utters acts as part of the screenplay, while every syllable Hepburn (really Nixon) sings becomes a tone in a musical interlude, apart from the action. Higgins's "words, words, words" establish his dominance over Eliza. Add casting to the balance of power, and the scale tips again on Higgins's side. Harrison and Hepburn look like, and could be, father and daughter. (There's a greater age gap than the one between Hiller and Howard. In 1964, Harrison was 66 and Hepburn was 35.)

Eliza lapses into Cockney towards the end, hinting that Higgins will continue to tutor her while he is supporting her. In his loveliest song, Higgins sings that he has "become accustomed" to Eliza's face; the song fits Cukor's adaptation perfectly. *My Fair Lady* has Pygmalioned Eliza into an exquisitely beautiful face and has given her the soul of a romantic. Consequently, the ending feels more like a foregone conclusion than a surprise. In the translation from Shaw's play, to the 1938 film, to the Broadway musical and its film adaptation, Higgins's Galatea becomes progressively more glamorous and more dependent. The metamorphosis could be traced through *My Fair Lady* to *Pretty Woman,* where money is the most important aid to transformation, and where the heroine's options dwindle.

Higgins gets a Galatea whom he can control. Dressed in clothing he has bought her, speaking a dialect he has taught her, Eliza's chances of maintaining her feisty individualism seem slim to none. After all, the title of the musical is not *A Fair Lady,* or *The Fair Lady,* or just *Fair Lady.* It's *My Fair Lady,* and Higgins (who else?) speaks that possessive pronoun.

Shampoo *(1975)*

What if Henry Higgins had yanked three chattering flower girls from the gutter? What if they demanded that he fix up their *hair,* not their pronunciation? A Pygmalion's nightmare, *Shampoo* continues the theme of problematic makeovers. You might subtitle *Shampoo, My Hair Ladies.*

A sexual and political romp, *Shampoo* capitalized on Warren Beatty's status as stud extraordinaire. Recognizing this, *Time* reviewer Jay Cacks sees the film as an homage to Beatty, suggesting the subtitle *Advertisements for Myself* (4). In *Shampoo,* viewers get a biographical byte from three days in the life of swinging Beverly Hills hairdresser George Roundy (Beatty) beginning on election eve 1968, and ending the day after the election. The film follows Roundy's relationship as stylist and lover to three women, Jackie (Julie Christie), Jill (Goldie Hawn), and Felicia (Lee Grant). Roundy burns with ambition and seeks funding for a shop of his own, first from the bank, then from Lester (Jack Warden), who is Felicia's husband and Jackie's lover. George's life reaches a crisis when all "his" women abandon him. Even so, he seems certain to get the loan from Lester, who commiserates with him about the vagaries of females.

Critics applauded performances by all the female leads, including a devastating star turn by Carrie Fisher as Lorna, Felicia's daughter, and Lee Grant won an Academy Award for Best Supporting Actress. Audiences responded well to *Shampoo*, making it "Columbia's biggest hit in the studio's 50 year history, with rentals over $22 million, and ranking as the sixth most popular film for 1975" (Leibman 82). Almost unanimously, critics, like Pauline Kael, who called *Shampoo* "the sum of an era" (437), found the late sixties ethos dead on, but director Hal Ashby's political agenda heavy handed. (Visual reminders of the Nixon/McGovern race proliferate.) Many criticized *Shampoo* for trying to be more than it is—a farce. Few critics, however, focused on the politics of transformation, perhaps the film's most upsetting statement.

Although none of the characters vote or pay much attention to the televised footage from the McGovern/Nixon election that punctuates the film, the real television clips should evoke makeover memories from the audience. We remembered watching Nixon come back from his unsuccessful 1961 campaign against JFK. His 1968 race against George McGovern, too liberal and too Eastern for many voters, gave Nixon a chance to make himself over, to erase the man who had appeared to great disadvantage in the first televised presidential debates. While Kennedy's good looks, casual elegance, and intellect wowed viewers, Nixon projected a grubby, shifty-eyed, stubbly, and generally unappealing image. The Nixon whose face appears in *Shampoo* is the after version, white-shirted, focused, clean-shaven, a smiling good guy, real-world proof that the cult of personal appearance already dominated politics.

Women in *Shampoo* have internalized the lesson that Nixon had to learn so painfully: to survive, they must *always* look great. *Shampoo* refuses the makeover film convention of the typical before state, dispensing with any pretense of transforming an "unattractive" heroine. There's no Charlotte Vale with beetling brows and bulky body or tattered Cinderella on the hearth. All the women in *Shampoo* are beautiful, but all are constantly seeking to maintain their perfection, equating perfect hair with perfect happiness. Each one has a before and after makeover.

Their hair obsession ups the ante for Beatty's character. As *My Fair Lady* directs attention to Higgins's exertions, *Shampoo* follows Roundy. Armed with an unflagging libido and a blow dryer, he ceaselessly services his clients, assuring them they all look "great." But how long can this go on? *Shampoo*'s makeovers require constant tending, and none of the beautiful female characters ever fully believe Roundy's assurances. They could be read as three anxiety-ridden stages of woman.

Jill (Hawn), the ingénue, with her baby voice and baby-doll pajamas, adopts the sexy-child avatar familiar to all female survivors of the sixties. Alison Lurie gives this fad a jaded, backward look: "The baby-doll night-gown and the brief, lacy baby-doll dress attempted, with results that now seem ridiculous rather than seductive, to make grown women look like toddlers with a glandular affliction, or like severely retarded nubile teenagers" (80). Jill's image—she's a mini-skirted Nordstromesque hip-pie—screams "I am young!" Jill is George's current steady girlfriend, although *steady* fits neither character, and George keeps her acting and looking like a child. She whines for his attention, calling him away from the embraces of the others with false hyperventilation and complaints that her hair always comes "last."

For everyday wear (her before), Jill has toddler hair, all floppy bangs, loose curls and floating tendrils. For the election night bash that all the main characters attend, George makes Jill into a glamour baby. He pulls her front hair back, catching it at the crown, to cascade down with the rest, an approximation of a little girl's dress-up do. This nicely comple-ments her pale blue micro-mini party dress and poufy rabbit jacket.

Jill isn't the only 1960s film character with little girl clothes and hair. Julie Christie wore schoolgirl costumes and a similar pulled-back hairdo in *Dr. Zhivago* (1965) to underscore Lara's schoolgirl innocence, a state that drove her mother's lover mad. She evolved into a more mature woman as Zhivago's mistress, trading the cascading hair for a French twist. In the real world, Jackie Kennedy reversed that motion by adopting an unchar-acteristic innocence for a key event in her life. The unquestionably sophis-ticated Jackie chose a lacy, low-waisted, party dress for her marriage to Ari Onassis in 1968. She pulled her hair back in a version of Jill's dress-up do and added a big bow, a jarring contrast to those indelible images Americans had stored: Jackie in the blood-stained pink Chanel suit, Jackie heavily veiled in black. Her ingénue makeover screamed that she was a survivor, and told us that her life had to move away from that point.

Jill is no baby when it comes to self-preservation, either. She feigns faithfulness to George, but already has her eye on her next male, who says he's married "sometimes." He produces commercials and offers her a job in Egypt, based mainly, the scene implies, on her wide-eyed deliciousness and the length of her legs. Jill's ease in this pose suggests that she might never move on. Perfectly cast, Goldie Hawn has been trading on the silly baby-blonde persona she initiated on *Laugh-In*, but reality may finally force her towards middle age. At the 2002 Academy Awards, her adult daughter Kate Hudson's presence punctuated, perhaps punctured, Hawn's insistence that she be the constant nymph. (Hawn has starred in films that spoof our culture's obsession with youth, like *Death Becomes Her* (1992) and *First Wives Club* (1996).

Change, not stasis, excites Jackie Shawn (Christie), George's ex-steady and Lester's current mistress. Jill's sexiness emanates from baby-ish tendrils and wisps, but Jackie's depends on with-it sophistication. Jackie's before state could never be called plain, but it could be described as blurry. Her hair and clothing overpower her, illustrating the too much, too late exhaustion of sixties style (recently foisted on us). Lots of heavy hair buries Jackie's fine features, lots of necklaces clutter her bosom, lots of soft, full bell bottoms recall the fatal flaw of that style: a millimeter too short, and you look really stupid.

When George meets Jackie by chance in Lester's office, he doesn't like what he sees. "Who's doing your hair?" he asks, critically. "Nobody much," Jackie shrugs.

That remark spurs Jackie's makeover and displays George's talent. Sticking a blow dryer, pistol like, in his jeans, he leaves a dripping client at the salon to ride to Jackie's rescue, a Pygmalion knight on a motorcycle instead of a white charger. Jackie parodies the Princess who must be rescued. She's a bitchy Rapunzel, locked in an elegant trysting place with three tiny Pekes for guards.

Jackie (whom Lester wants to keep her hidden from his wife, Felicia) wants *out*. Her short-term goal is to look "absolutely great" at Lester's election-eve party, to which George will escort her. George convinces her he can transform her, telling her she looks "like a tart." Uttering warnings that she doesn't want "short hair," Jackie lets him have his way with her hair, even though he has uttered the five words most women dread: "I have to cut it." Cutting it, in this case, means shaping it into a now familiar look. George works like a sculptor chipping away superfluous marble to transform Jackie's too much of a good thing into a minimalist's dream. When he's done, a long, geometric, Vidal Sassoon bob frames her perfect features.

Longer in the front, shorter in the back, swingy, and bangy, this look has never died. For Sassoon, it helped create a worldwide empire of shops and products and turned him into a celebrity. Sassoon and his wife Beverly, the perfect Sassoon model, even appeared on talk shows, popularizing the ways in which the scraggy excesses of sixties hair could be rendered mod. This may have been a good thing for Vidal, but for George, playing Pygmalion to Jackie spells major temptation. The after Jackie appraises her reflection as if she is a piece of merchandise. Clad in a towel,

Shampoo (Columbia, 1975) This tightly framed shot makes us feel the heat a makeover can generate. Once lovers, Jackie Shawn (Julie Christie) and George Roundi (Warren Beatty) now try to maintain a client-stylist relationship. But how long can that last? George's quintessential Beverly Hills hairdresser sexiness (played with a generous dash of Jon Peters) says that he's thinking about more than his blow dryer, as he leans in to lock eyes with Shawn. Her seductively open-legged pose and her look of satisfaction with her swinging after haircut make it clear that she'll accept what George offers. But the doorway that opens behind Jackie foreshadows her exit. Flaunting her after glamour, she will discard George's passion for Lester's cold cash.

she turns from side to side, catching this angle of her neck, that slice of cheek. Finally, she shrieks in approval, "You're a genius!" Aroused by praise, George lowers Jackie to the bathroom floor, but Lester intrudes, to be halted only by the mysteries of the boudoir. In the funniest scene in the film, George and Jackie gain time to recover their sangfroid by convincing Lester that Jackie's new do will be ruined if he lets the steam out of the bathroom.

Jackie's haircut sets the wildest part of her free, proving that less *is* more. From the moment that George clips Jackie out of her before malaise, everything seems to fit. Her after wardrobe underscores the change. Consider the gown Jackie chooses for Lester's big election night bash, a spangled, long-sleeved, black sheath, austere in the front, but WOW in the back, cut so low that it nearly reveals her beautiful derrière.

Jackie's new hair swings, and so does she, using the election night party that Lester hosts as her coming out. No debutante, however, would sport that gown or utter the words that made her character famous. When an amorous older man asks Jackie what she would *really* like, she positively leers at George and says, "I'd like to suck his cock." And then she climbs under the table and *does* it. Later, she and George do more, right where Lester can see them, at a psychedelic Hollywood bash. Instead of discarding Jackie for her faithlessness, Lester rewards her. By the film's end, he has decided to leave his wife, Felicia, and marry Jackie.

Jackie's final appearance showcases her complete transformation. The perfect hair tops a mod wedding outfit of white turtleneck, mini-skirt and white go-go boots. George has helped her discard that rippling hair and flapping cloth, and she has seized the power her new look gives her. Too bad for George, who has decided, too late, that he loves her. In the Pygmalion myth, Venus took pity on the sculptor by giving his creation life. Only Lester takes pity on George. Reviewer Richard Blake accurately complains that it's hard to feel any empathy for any of these characters, who "sell themselves to the highest bidder and get what they deserve" (73). Both ingénue and mistress crave perfect hair, and, in both cases, they believe perfection can trigger financial stability. *Shampoo* makes the futility of their upward climb clear. Felicia (Grant), Lester's wife, has everything the others want: wealth, status, carefully-tended beauty. In her before look Felicia could walk through Saks today and attract very little attention; plenty of women flash their expensive accessories—fur coat, designer sunglasses—like badges, and plenty of women still have that shoulder-brushing hair style with its wispy bangs. Felicia, however, wants what she cannot have: youth. (Her quest has an element of parody; Grant is about thirty-five, hardly an aged parent.)

Felicia feeds on George's sexual energy. For her, sensation comes first, hair second; she is less interested in being made over than in making it. *Shampoo* opens in the dark with the sounds of Felicia and George having sex. Felicia directs the activity, telling George where to place his hands and when to move. Felicia continues to drive George, and she will not be denied. Ordering George to come to her palatial home to "comb her out," she delays that particular attention. Instead, fully clad in curlers and a mink coat, she pulls him onto her satin-covered bed to insure her physical satisfaction first.

Although he must be exhausted (having first "done" Jackie, and then having bedded Felicia's daughter, Lorna), George delivers sex and a comb-out, making Felicia look "great" for Lester's party, the last time she appears in the film. George doesn't recreate Felicia, as he does Jackie, but he does sharpen her already stylish look. In an early scene that helps establish his compulsion to tend beauty, George looks into the salon mirror, cupping Felicia's head in his hands, lifting her chin and her hair. Satisfied with what he sees, George makes everyone in the shop look, too, confirming that she looks "great." Ominous portents color this scene. The salon provides a background of huge headshots. Out of these black and white photos leer Felicia's competition—gorgeous, young models. George foreshadows Felicia's future when he raises and tightens her chin and cheeks, mimicking the action of a facelift, surely Felicia's next step. Felicia surveys herself analytically, the marketing agent for a declining product.

George cuts Felicia's hair into a style similar to Jackie's, just shorter and less extreme. Her after look turns her into an older version of Lester's mod mistress. Although no one ever mentions the similarity, at the election night bash, Felicia (who wears glittering white to contrast with Jackie's glittering black) repeatedly studies Jackie, suggesting that she sees the likeness. Felicia disappears from the film after the party, yielding the field, but not all the goods, to Jackie. Felicia's final reward, which she makes clear to Lester, will be to suck him dry.

There's a paradigm here—the older the woman, the shorter the hair—and it fits the continuum of female roles *Shampoo* establishes: daughter, ingénue, mistress, wife. At the opposite end of the continuum, Felicia's daughter, Lorna (Fisher), reinforces the rigidity of the pattern; she's too young and confident to worry about her very long hair, which is carelessly tied back under a kerchief. This blasé Beverly Hills kid, who wants to know if George is gay, seeks revenge upon her mother. Although George invites her to "stop in at the shop" (an invitation he issues to every woman) and says he would like to do her hair, Lorna dismisses his powers of transformation, claiming that she has never been to a salon. (Two years later,

Fisher would be made over into the equally salty princess Leia in *Star Wars* (1977), whose feistiness overcame those gross coils of hair.)

When George says Lorna has her mother eyes, Lorna responds vehemently, "I'm *nothing* like my mother." Lorna's scenes, however, show a young Felicia, already bored by her tennis lessons and palatial mansion. Like her mother, she has rapacious appetites. Felicia doesn't have much finesse, but she adopts a pretense of affection for George. Lorna is more direct. "Want to fuck?" she asks him, after providing him first with a feast of leftover food. Lorna may not be interested in a makeover, but her greedy behavior forecasts a future not too different from her mother's.

None of these Galateas have much to recommend them. Conversation? Minimal. Interests or family connections? Who knows? Friendships? When the women interact, which happens infrequently, wariness inflects their conversations and behavior. Competition does not breed closeness. The *Shampoo* women might as well be statues for all the interior they reveal. Pygmalion's not very likeable either. When George tries to explain his womanizing, he tells Jill that he finds all women "beautiful" and irresistible. Yet, what could you call a man who juggles women like oranges and never listens to or remembers a word any of them say? Pymalion's misogynism fits George like a pair of his tight jeans. Jay Cacks finds the end "a betrayal," because it "excuses George" (5). At least the conclusion embodies typical seventies ambiguity, and *Shampoo* rejects a "ragshop" happy ending. Instead, it describes an endless cycle of sculpting and resculpting worthy of a circle in Dante's *Inferno*.

Up Close and Personal *(1996)*

Shampoo reveals the danger of chasing an eternal makeover; if you obsess over surfaces, you become nothing but the shell you so frantically tend. A less risky film, *Up Close and Personal* promises an interior view, but concentrates on image. Directed by Jon Avnet, the Pygmalion and Galatea story between Tally Atwater (Michelle Pfeiffer) and Warren Justice (Robert Redford) shoots for high drama but hits a low makeover mark.

Leonard Maltin calls the film "a paraphrase of *A Star Is Born*," recognizing *Up Close and Personal*'s debt to the 1937 hit starring Fredric March and Janet Gaynor. (The first *A Star Is Born* remake in 1954 starred Judy Garland and James Mason, and another in 1976 featured Barbra Streisand and Kris Kristofferson.) *Up Close and Personal* follows the same narrative line as *A Star Is Born*, but an essential difference makes it a closer fit for the Pygmalion sub-genre than its forerunners.

A Star Is Born goes like this: Norman Main, a male star past the zenith of his career, discovers a young woman, Esther, trying to break into the business. He gives her a big chance, and then watches her meteoric rise. Desperately in love, the two marry. After that, Main experiences a meteoric fall (due to alcoholism). The two continue to love one another, even though their rising and falling positions pull them apart. No one will take a chance on him, and Main is reduced to answering his wife's phone, like a secretary. To boost his self-esteem, Esther uses her power to get Norman a job. This doesn't work. When she wins an award, Main makes a disastrous, drunken appearance at the ceremony. Finally, his fear of dragging her down drives him to suicide. Esther becomes a heroic emblem of fame touched by never-ending love, a sainthood that only increases her popularity.

Up Close and Personal follows that trajectory. Warren Justice (Robert Redford), once a big time network reporter and Washington insider, has been done in by his unimpeachable honor and a lying source—his second wife. Brought low, Justice now produces a small time news show in Miami. He discovers Sally Atwater (Michelle Pfeiffer), a raw novice with big career dreams. Justice christens her Tally and "tests" her to see if she's tough enough. When she demonstrates spunk, he grooms her for bigger news markets. During the grooming, they have an affair, which culminates in a romantic vacation in Key West.

Atwater moves up, first to Philadelphia, where she replaces an older, more experienced female anchor (Stockard Channing). Justice gives up his Florida job and comes to her aid when she feels shaky. They marry. When Justice looks for something meaningful to do, he discovers the depth of his ostracism. No one, not even his "friends," will hire him. Tally gets him a job, but as usual, Warren's moral principles collide with the "entertainment" view of news.

Meanwhile, Tally happens to be inside a prison when the convicts riot, and she provides exclusive coverage. Because of her performance, she gets a big network offer. As she prepares to move up, Justice decides to freelance and gets killed in a melee in Panama while pursuing a politically explosive story. The film closes as Tally gives the main address at a network banquet. She delivers her righteous reminder about the purpose of news casting in front of a giant screen bearing Warren's face.

Back this story up with a soundtrack featuring Celine Dion singing "Because You Loved Me," while Pfeiffer and Redford cavort in the Keys, and you have a winner, right? *Wrong.* Many weaknesses trouble this film, but the biggest problem is the twist *Up Close and Personal* gives to its *A Star Is Born* storyline. In all the other versions, Norman Main discovers, but *does not* remake the female star. The Garland-Mason version includes a great scene in which the studio tries to cram Garland into its starlet mold, dying her hair blonde and caking on the makeup. Mason quietly undoes the crass makeover, returning Garland to herself. Norman recognizes the female lead's raw talent. He places her in the way of notice, and she takes over from there. Unfortunately, that's not quite the way it goes in *Up Close and Personal*. Sally Atwater has guts and attractiveness, but Justice must labor overtime to give her everything else, including her name.

We have to admit that the chance to gaze at Redford pulled us into the theater for this one. We applaud what his Sundance Film Festival has done for the industry, but his golden aura, not his role as industry benefactor, made us plunk down our dollars and stock ourselves with popcorn. An iconic star, Redford has chosen many roles that suggest his fascination with monolithic characters: Sundance in *Butch Cassidy and the Sundance Kid* (1969), beautiful, funny, dangerous, dead, the bad boy every good girl lusted for; Hubble Gardner (1973) in *The Way We Were*, so waspishly gorgeous, so brilliant, so detached; Jay Gatsby in *The Great Gatsby* (1974), eternally faithful, dancing that endless waltz with Daisy; Bob Woodward in *All the President's Men* (1976), all political passion, corduroy, and tousled gilt hair that asked to be pushed back; Denis Finch-Hatton in *Out of Africa* (1985), gatekeeper of the African plains, trying to stop time as he made love to Meryl Streep. What a compendium of virtues: courage, humor, spontaneity, intellect, honor, faithfulness, sexuality.

We won't be adding Warren Justice (oh, the heavy-handedness of his name) to that hallowed list. In *Up Close and Personal*, Redford once again plays a god-like character, but Justice tries to *be* God and comes across more like a too strict father than an irresistible lover. This Pygmalion hacks his Galatea into shape with a sledgehammer, not a delicate chisel, and she seems to relish the beating.

The hacking begins as soon as Sally Atwater walks into the station. Redford mouths abrupt orders at her without looking her way. "Try to keep up, sweetheart," he barks back at her as he and the others sweep from a room, leaving her to follow. Sally balks at the "sweetheart," but she doesn't complain enough about all the injustices Justice delivers, and their number is legion. For starters, when Warren chastises Sally for slipping on her press credentials in the studio, she rips them off, dumping the contents of her ugly purse on the floor. Horribly embarrassed, she drops to the floor to reclaim her stuff, including a tampon. Warren helps her, but when two other employees enter the office, he rises. Poor Sally scampers around on her hands and knees, while Warren takes a good, long gander at her posterior. This Pygmalion makes Henry Higgins look like a feminist. Screenwriting pair Joan Didion and John Gregory Dunn, who also wrote the screenplay for the Streisand and Kristofferson version of *A Star Is Born*, give Justice terse dialogue, often at Atwater's expense. When she dumps her purse, for example, Justice utters an ironic, "Oh, that's good." Even after they begin to fall in love, he can't resist a cheap shot that reveals her ignorance. An agent has told Tally that her voice is "full of money." "Hemingway, right?" Justice baits her. Of course Tally doesn't recognize the line from *The Great Gatsby*. (Redford played the title role.) Justice claims to have been "testing" his new hire, but when a character's this arrogant, it's hard to redeem him.

Atwater gets no pithy dialogue, but she's so "deliciously low" that she has little to say anyway. Pfeiffer's before inflects the makeover convention that insists on a beautiful star who masquerades as plain. Janet Maslin begins her *New York Times* review by summing up Pfeiffer's transformation: "In *Up Close and Personal*, Michelle Pfeiffer morphs gorgeously from tacky would-be-television-news-talent at a local Miami station to sleek, glamorous network swan."

As Maslin notes, Pfeiffer's playing *cheap*, not ugly. Not as sleazy as Vivien in *Pretty Woman*, she's closer to Tess in *Working Girl*, with a scruffy perm that should have died in the eighties, loud jewelry, big-shouldered, bright jackets, and discount store pumps. She looks wrong, wrong, wrong. We wish we could report that Justice lifts her out of her fashion-victim misery when he notices her smarts, but her face, not her brain, entices him to raise her up. Sally has been languishing at the phone desk, making coffee, picking up Warren's dry-cleaning and longing for a shot at stardom. Since his boss wants a weather spot, Justice gives Sally a chance. Dressed in a yellow slicker and goofy sunglasses, she freezes in front of the camera, her state of shock partially brought on by Justice, who gives her a new name while she is on-air.

He types Tally, not Sally, into the teleprompter, and the anchor cues her: "Here's Tally!" Who's that? Sally wonders while her eyes wander to Justice instead of the camera. She rebounds in time to save the spot, but no one could call her performance a success. Justice, however, looks at her face on his monitor and declares that "she eats the lens." That sounds obscene, and Justice uses obscenity when he comes to Tally's apartment that evening. He announces that on the strength of her lens eating, he's promoting her to reporter: "I'll bet you thought I came to fuck you," he taunts her as he leaves.

Who could resist such charm? Tally does react because this couldn't be a late twentieth-century film if she didn't say anything. She accuses Warren of getting a "rush" when he makes her feel stupid. She rages at him for playing Daddy Warbucks when her sister needs some help. All Tally's tough talk, however, doesn't change the balance of power. Browbeaten, like Eliza in *My Fair Lady,* Tally defers to Warren's experience. She has anger, but he's got history, literature, and business savvy at his command, and he uses them like clubs. His agenda always trumps her complaints. Gradually, she concedes that father knows best. (In 1996, Redford was 59 to Pfeiffer's 39.)

First, Justice dresses her, taking her to a classy boutique (shades of *Pretty Woman)* where he oversees her selections with the help of the stylish owner. He insists that Tally cut her hair, although, initially, she refuses. Tally's makeover trims away excess clutter, like Jackie Shawn's in *Shampoo.* She emerges wearing a short, body-skimming, pale pink dress with a matching jacket, a chin-length, layered bob (serious hair, like Tess McGill's) and some quiet jewelry. Her first makeover renders her much more professional, but she's not even close to Paula Zahn yet. Before her second makeover, Justice has to work on her apparently empty mind.

Henry Higgins taught Eliza how to pronounce words correctly. Justice teaches Tally to think the way he does. In his background check of her credentials, Justice discovered that she has no experience. Perhaps, for him, Tally's emptiness is her greatest draw. What fun would it be to hire a woman he couldn't mold? He becomes her teacher and boss, an uneasy combination. Only once, Justice suggests that Tally read some national newspapers instead of *People* magazine. Only once, we see her studying news coverage from the past—all the clips are of Justice. Only once, she listens to Spanish tapes. Besides these glimpses, no evidence proves that Tally does anything to educate herself, except sit at the feet of her Pygmalion. Like some Athenian sage, Justice offers blurbs of wisdom while he points out the mindlessness of all Tally's stories, criticism she accepts without a whimper.

Justice manipulates Tally's first successful story, a live feed from Miami Beach, where two Colombian deck hands have jumped ship and drowned only a few feet from freedom. Tally and her photographer, Ned (Glenn Plummer), arrive on the scene to find Warren pacing the beach. He shoves Tally into the knot of reporters surrounding a spokesperson as if she is a child. He yanks her back out again to get the details of the story. "Let's see what you've got," he challenges her, and then he tells her what *he's* got. His view, his words, and his information become "her" story. Justice glows with pride at her performance, and why shouldn't he? He thinks it, says it, and, voilà, it emerges from Tally's mouth. He continues manipulating her work, hanging around while she's covering a story, letting her watch while he masterfully edits her pieces. In this environment they fall in love, like one of those smarmy grad school romances in which an older, male professor plays God for a female student.

The power balance in *A Star Is Born* gives the female lead more weight because of her obvious talent. Garland and Streisand, particularly, light up their productions. Does Tally have talent? In her first chance to prove it, she can't operate without Warren. After her move to Philadelphia, she tries to imitate the bright female anchor (Channing) by filling her stories with policy and statistics, a style that doesn't fit because research is never her forte. (Why can't she look things up?) Tally does nothing to resist a second physical makeover when a focus group finds her too blonde and too edgy for Philadelphia. This time she emerges with dark hair and a deeper-toned wardrobe; this makeover implies that seriousness resides in brunettes. Tally doesn't comment about the drastic change in her looks, but then she never mentions her changed name. Alone and lost, she sits at her desk after hours, playing solitaire.

Like Eliza Doolittle, Tally is a "good girl," less anguished than Jessica Savitch, the real newscaster whose life inspired this story. Savitch's rise to fame included parties and drugs, and it ended in her tragic death. Roger Ebert comments on the sweeping changes to the screenplay, originally titled *Golden Girl*: "*Up Close and Personal* is so different from the facts of Savitch's life that if Didion and Dunne still have their first draft, they could probably sell it as a completely different movie." Maybe a little grit would have made this formulaic film feel more like life. Free from bad habits, or many human connections, Tally inhabits a closed circle containing herself and Justice. Yes, she has a sister, but Luanne (played by Pfeiffer's actual sibling, Dedee), appears in too few scenes to make her real. Tally has no women friends, although two slight conversations encourage us to believe that she becomes friends with Joanna (Kate Nelligan), Justice's second wife. Tally alludes to a romantic past, but she has no visible ex-lovers, and only one man, a sleazoid anchor at the Miami station, makes a pass at her. Tally's as pristine as a statue or an unwrapped gift.

Only Warren can unwrap her. When he appears in Philadelphia, she rolls around on the floor with him like a lovesick teen. She depends on him for professional sustenence and sexual relief, and with his guidance, she rebounds. At first, his guidance consists of calling every story she has done in Philadelphia "shit." He accuses her of losing her identity. Tally speaks the truest words in the film, claiming that she cannot know who she is because he "invented" her. Warren refuses this responsibility. A

Up Close and Personal (Touchstone, 1996). With a television news set between them, Tally Atwater (Michelle Pfeiffer) and Warren Justice (Robert Redford) gaze at each other. The positioning's not coincidental. Broadcast news always *is* between them; in fact, it's the *raison d'être* for their relationship. Justice's stance, hands on hips, good side to the camera, indicates the power balance here. He's the God; Tally, leaning in, is the supplicant.

series of clips follows, meant to show that Tally can deliver on her own. Although she looks more relaxed, she's no Judy Woodruff, and she still has Justice at her side, doesn't she?

Warren's mentoring continues after their marriage. Even Tally's exclusive prison story explores an angle Warren suggested to her on their honeymoon. Their positions during the lockdown could be a metaphor for their relationship. Tally's trapped inside, and, like a puppeteer, Warren controls the live feed to the network. During the broadcast, Justice types a list of points *he* would cover if he were inside. Tally addresses each one, almost before he types it in. Her quickness is supposed to demonstrate her growth, but it also shows how completely she has become Justice's creature. Her prison coverage replicates his coverage of the Beirut marine base bombing, a tape she studied. She's perfect now.

In *A Star Is Born*, poor Norman has a flaw: alcoholism. Justice's flaw, his exacting sense of justice, makes him admirable, but not very human. The screenplay feeds us contrived reasons to empathize with him—his wife betrayed him, he lost a child—but isolated bio bytes hardly mediate the

Up Close and Personal (Touchstone, 1996). Justice has already given her a new name and a new look, which apparently isn't enough. When Tally reaches a bigger venue, she's remade again. She and Marcia McGraff (Stockard Channing), like bookends of brunette credibility, balance the Philadelphia news team.

Warren Justice we see. Norman Main's self-created exit makes everyone sad, but Justice's gutsy pursuit of a dangerous story lifts him into journalistic sainthood. In *Up Close and Personal*, Pygmalion, not Galatea, is made of cold marble. The last scene shows Tally standing at a podium before a huge screen bearing a closeup of Justice's face. Joanna, Justice's first wife, gazes sorrowfully up at Tally from the audience. They have become the vestals guarding his holy image.

That closeup of Redford, hanging like Big Brother above the network elite, provides a not so subtle clue to the focus of *Up Close and Personal*. The film begins with an extreme closeup of Pfeiffer and includes forty-six other closeups of her face, her legs, etc. All that face time might lead to the assumption that it's her film, Tally's story. But who is Tally? Eliza Doolittle has the insight to realize she has been altered almost beyond recognition. Except for her outburst in Philadelphia, Tally doesn't seem to notice, or to care that she's become a reflection. All those closeups confirm something we already knew: Pfeiffer is beautiful. About Tally Atwater, they say she's a face and an assemblage of parts. Janet Maslin thinks the romance between Justice and Atwater lifts the film out of disconnectedness, but we agree with Desson Howe, who believes that "for the most part Pfeiffer and Redford, who spend a lot of lovin' time lying around on beds, beaches, and TV studio floors are reduced to a collective, supine idiocy." *Collective* works well as a term to describe this Pygmalion tale in which the creator, even more self-adoring than Henry Higgins, makes a female clone of himself, not an independent woman.

Miss Congeniality *(2000)*

Unlike the other Pygmalion makeover films in this chapter, *Miss Congeniality* does not depend upon a romantic relationship between its Galatea and Pygmalion. Shaw would have liked the ending, which pairs Gracie Hart (Sandra Bullock) with Eric Matthews (Benjamin Bratt), a colleague *her own age*, who respects her smarts and comes to see her beauty as a result of the transformation she undergoes. Also unlike the others, the story hints that through her makeover Gracie, a misogynistic Galatea, gets to know and like other women. These differences sound encouraging, but a good cast and good intentions can't make *Miss Congeniality* anything but awful. Is it comedy? It isn't funny. A crime thriller? It isn't suspenseful. The film's muddled identity and thin plot squander any chances of originality, but its statements about gender and transformation put it in a Pygmalion category of its own.

Miss Congeniality begins in a school playground where some nine or ten-year-old bullies are pounding one of their classmates. Across the playground, a little girl puts down her Nancy Drew book and comes to his aid, punching out the main bully and calling him a "girl." For this, she is scorned by the boy she saves, who says that the others will see him as a bigger wimp. In frustration, she punches him out, too. Little Gracie has braids, sloppy clothing, and dark-rimmed glasses. The next scene shows us that this is true for grown-up Gracie Hart. She has become an FBI agent who says about herself, "I am the job." A glimpse of an undercover operation, however, shows Hart following her instincts instead of orders. Because of this tendency, her boss (Ernie Hudson) sticks her with paperwork although she's intelligent and resourceful. Hart has male buddies (other agents) but no female friends, and she regards any trait that could be interpreted as female with derision. A coded message from a terrorist alerts the FBI to the possibility that he might strike at the Miss United States beauty pageant. Put in charge of the case, Eric Matthews recruits Gracie to go undercover as a pageant contestant. She refuses, but is forced to comply. The aging pageant host, Stan Fields (William Shatner), and the pageant director, Kathy Morningside (Candice Bergen), reluctantly agree to place Gracie in the top five if she has a complete makeover. Morningside enlists Vic Melling (Michael Caine) to do the reshaping. In a blitz of a makeover, the obviously gay Melling gives Gracie a new hairdo, makeup and wardrobe, and some tips on poise. He continues mentoring her at the pageant.

Masquerading as Gracie Lou Freebush from New Jersey, she meets and befriends Miss Rhode Island (Heather Burns) and a few other "contestants." She participates in the pageant events, and Eric Matthews begins to notice her romantic possibilities. Gracie suspects Morningside of vengeance when she learns the director will be replaced. When the FBI leaves the location, certain that they have caught the terrorist, Hart leaves the FBI, and stays to protect the contestants. The convoluted plot, with several lame red herrings, leads to the arrest of Morningside and her son just as the new Miss United States is crowned. Because of her heroism, the contestants choose Hart as Miss Congeniality, and she leaves with a sense of herself as a woman.

Sometimes we make a game of trying to decide why actors choose certain roles. The reasoning behind the choices made by some of *Miss Congeniality*'s higher profile stars seems pretty clear. Michael Caine probably accepted the role of Victor Melling because he rarely refuses offers, as his more than 133 film credits show. The brevity of their roles and the largesse of their salaries must have seduced William Shatner and Candice Bergen. (*Miss Congeniality* had a budget of $45 million.) Still, it's hard to watch the actress who made Murphy Brown a household name in such an anti-feminist film. Bergen's character, Cathy Morningside, confirms every nasty thing one might think about an ex-beauty queen turned pageant coordinator. Benjamin Bratt might have been lured by the chance to do comedy (instead of blow-'em-ups) and to work with Bullock.

What about Sandra Bullock? Perhaps the comedic concept—Gracie Hart gets girly—sounded engaging to her. After all, she plays the same character over and over again. She produced this film with Katie Ford, but it's hard to believe that she could read the screenplay by Mark Lawrence, Katie Ford, and Caryn Lucas, and *still* choose to play Gracie Hart. Neither the dialogue nor the direction by Donald Petrie does anything to lift the characters out of dreadful stereotypes.

For example, Bullock can claim the most disturbing, gender-bending before state in makeover films. Most befores thinly veil stars with those familiar signifiers we have learned to read as plain. Gracie Hart has the standard Charlotte Vale collection: the masses of unruly, dark hair, the heavy brows, the glasses, the baggy clothes. Her posture would make

Emily Post weep, and she swaggers instead of walking. She's also bereft of any people skills. Wesley Morris calls Bullock "Eliza Doolittle in sweats," but she's way worse than that. *Miss Congeniality* adds grossness to the before formula: matted hair, a grimy face, disheveled clothes, a laugh like a pig snort, and an appetite to match. That Gracie can negotiate the professional world without drawing stares strains credulity. She most resembles a street person, but it's not poverty or madness this before is getting at. As Morris also notes, she's "a mannerless, styless brute."

Watch Gracie masticate rare steak and a side of spaghetti with her mouth open. Take a look at her stripped-down bachelorette pad with a punching bag suspended from the living room ceiling. Notice that when she cooks for herself, she tosses a frozen steak, still wrapped, into the microwave. See her settle an argument with a violent wrestling match. Subtle hints? No way. Sandra Bullock isn't playing *plain*, she's playing a disgusting, stereotypical *male*. The tomboy has grown up into a tomman, or something like that. Other female agents look more normal, but they stay on the periphery. Gracie Hart stands alone, front and center, as a warning. If you are too smart, too strong-willed, too aggressive and too absorbed in your job, you might end up like Gracie: a hermaphroditic loner.

Obviously, Hart needs an industrial-strength makeover, and that's just what the film delivers. Vic Melling begins the process by lunching with Hart, whom he calls "Dirty Harriet," and by delivering some etiquette tips. (Don't chew with your mouth open, etc.) After lunch, he demonstrates the way a lady should walk and is much more proficient at "gliding" than Hart. On the plane to Texas, the pageant location, Hart watches pageant tapes and practices emoting, a sight Melling declares both "painful and grotesque." Things get tougher at makeover central, an airport hanger, where rendering Gracie female takes on a *Mission Impossible* ambience. A voice announces operations, like hair removal, over a loud speaker, while a drum tattoo sounds in the background. As punishment for all those years of maleness, Gracie must endure the full range of salon experience.

Vic Melling never snaps Gracie's glasses in two; they just disappear. But the unmistakable mean edge of this makeover recalls *Now, Voyager* and the *Princess Diaries*. Like the makeover subjects before her, Grace feels pain and loses control. Beauty technicians comment derisively about predictable characteristics, Hart's hair and eyebrows. The stylist untangling her hair requests a drill, and other operators wax her every body part, including the backs of her fingers. "There should be two," Vic says about her eyebrows, although a rewind shows that Gracie never had a unibrow.

Miss Congeniality (Castle Rock, 2000). (*Top*) Positioned in front of those posters of past beauty queens, her "before" look presents a frightening contrast. Flat-haired, unsmiling, and drably clothed, she can't hope to aspire to be anything but Matthews's work buddy. (*Bottom*) Eric Matthews (Benjamin Bratt) knows he's an "after" hottie, so what's a girl who isn't up to his glitzy standards to do? FBI agent Gracie Hart (Sandra Bullock) can only duke it out with him.

Gracie learns starvation as a condition of femininity. While the fifty or so beauty operators needed to transform this hard case nosh on fat-laden goodies, she gets a stalk of celery. All this is funny, but not *that* funny. Hart's painful makeover does everything it can to reinforce the idea that she was unacceptable, really disgusting, or as Eric Matthews puts it, "a car wreck," before.

Revealed in her after state, Hart walks out of the hangar a stereotypical pretty woman. She struts to the strains of "Mustang Sally," clad in a short, skin-tight, blue dress and beige heels with ankle-straps. Her hair? They've styled it in the mandatory side-parted, slightly highlighted long fall. Her makeup? Understated, with arched brows and pale pink lips. Hart manages to carry off the changes easily, except for the shoes. She falls off the heels way too many times for the gag to stay funny.

When we watched the film for the first time, we thought it would make a turn after the makeover. The heart of the film, we hoped, would show Gracie, included in the closed circle of pageant contestants, discovering that these girls, so often taken at surface value, have depth. Although Gracie suggests this, calling the other contestants "smart, terrific people" at the end of the film, not much substance leads to that conclusion. The contestants Hart meets are shallow, ego-driven, and stupid. Miss Rhode Island (Burns), for example, the single contestant with a more developed character, has the IQ and the maturity of a six-year-old. No matter what the screenplay implies, form reinforces the film's true content, as the camera does plenty of ogling at the women preparing for pageant activities. Male attitudes toward the contestants also help undercut the film's purported "beautiful women can be great people" message. As preparation for the mission, FBI agents assume a bachelor party air as they use a computer simulation to undress agents (both male and female) who might fit the undercover assignment. Later, watching the feed from the camera Gracie wears, the agents act as if the assignment equals a visit to Hooters. Although Agent Matthews develops increased sensitivity to Gracie, he still whoops it up when Hart's hidden camera gives him a butt or breast shot of one of the other women.

Not disturbing enough for you yet? Consider the film's subtext that homophobia is funny, and that homosexuals themselves are a screech, too. We are obviously supposed to find it amusing that a queen teaches Hart how to become a beauty queen. Throwing sweeping hand gestures with every line, Caine camps it up as Vic Melling, whose wardrobe favors coordinated pocket squares, a heavy gold Rolex and ice cream colors in suits, shirts and shoes. Hart addresses Vic as "Yoda" and "Henry Higgins," but agent Matthews calls him "you old fruitcake" and avoids his touch like the plague. At first, Matthews won't even lunch with Melling and Hart because Melling exudes waves of poorly concealed admiration for the young male agent, who fits his idea of beauty much more precisely than Hart does. At the end of the film, Matthews cringes when Melling gets him in backstage during the crowing ceremony by explaining, "He's with me," and calling him "Muffin."

In another attempt to get a guffaw, the screenplay has Miss New York (Karen Krantz) breaking free to speak to the audience as the top ten are whittled to the top five: "I just want to let all the lesbians out there know," she screams, "that if I can make it to the top ten, so can you!" As guards drag her from the stage, she adds, "Tina, I love you baby!" and a lovely audience member jumps up to shout, "Oh, God, I love you, Karen!" This little interlude gives Miss Morningside a chance to roll her eyes in horror, and it sets up Stan Fields (Shatner) with a one-liner. Fields breaks for a commercial with this announcement: "And we'll be right back with our final five lesbians ... interviews." Funny, no?

No. Think through this context back to Hart's exaggerated before state and to her exaggerated makeover, and you can imagine another warning: Don't cultivate any behavior that might smack of gender confusion. A gay man, like Melling, makes an okay target for comedy, but looking like a dyke gets you ridicule and punishment.

Melling tells Hart how proud he is of her near the end of the film, but, again, there's little content to support the idea that these two get to know and like each other. Hart confesses to Melling that she has reasons for her pose as a tough loner, but she never reveals the reasons. Hart has no family or friends, and that playground shot at the beginning of the film provides the only clue to her background. *Miss Congeniality* truly does miss any congeniality it might have intended. Instead the film presents a gender-loaded Pygmalion makeover story characterized by nastiness and innuendo.

Miss Congeniality does, at least, escape the guru problem. In most cases (George Roundy's another exception) Pygmalion becomes Galatea's lover although he's old enough to be her father. Hollywood eternally insists that twenty- or thirty-year gaps between romantic leads don't matter, if the age and experience are on the man's side. The Pygmalion schema, the male "teaching" the female, lends itself to this premise.

The mythical Pygmalion sculpted his perfect woman from scratch, and life's spark came from a god, not from him. In each of these Pygmalion films, the "poor" creator has to work with previously flawed material—an already living woman (marble would behave better). From this circumstance comes the darkest of many negative implications—that the female character's speech, or attire, or hair, or walk or behavior is so horrid that she can't fix it herself.

From the corrections the Pygmalion characters make, viewers can infer the formula for a "perfect" woman. She should be ladylike and well-spoken, but not educated beyond limits set by her creator. Her hair should be perfect, and she shouldn't need specific compliments, but be content with general assurances that she's "great." She should accept wardrobe tips, and she should reflect the values of her creator. If possible, she should resemble a contestant for the Miss World competition, tall, big-busted, long-legged. Can a woman like that be created? Well, maybe.

The Stepford Wives *(1975)*

The most extreme retelling of the Pygmalion myth, *The Stepford Wives*, directed by Bryan Forbes (who directed *The Slipper and the Rose*), stays close to its literary source, Ira Levin's 1972 novel of the same title a lean, evocative best seller that reads like a screenplay. Tired of noisy New York, Walter Eberhart (Peter Masterson), his wife, Joanna (Katharine Ross), and their two children move to Stepford, a safe, quiet community within commuting distance. Joanna wonders if it isn't too quiet. A semi-professional photographer and a member of NOW, she can't find one of the gorgeous Stepford women who's concerned about more than the glory of Lemon Pledge.

Finally, a like-minded woman finds Joanna. Determined to increase their ranks, Bobbie Markowe (Paula Prentiss) and Joanna try to raise a little consciousness. Their house-to-house canvassing unearths only one candidate, Charmaine (Tina Louise), who loves tennis and astrology, and who bitches about her husband's desire for kinky sex.

Unlike Joanna, Walter likes Stepford where he's included in the thriving Men's Association with its no-women-allowed policy. When Joanna protests, Walter claims he can change it from inside, and he spends more evenings with the men instead of with the family. Joanna finds the Men's Association president, Dale Coba (Patrick O'Neal), cold, and the others insipid. She's embarrassed, but pleased, when one of them, a famous artist, sketches an idealized portrait of her. Another club member asks Joanna for help with a linguistic project. Calling himself "Henry Higgins," he explains that he wants to create a computer program that can place speakers geographically by their pronunciation, and Joanna agrees to tape a lengthy word list for him.

Joanna works on her photography, and she and Bobbie keep griping

The Stepford Wives (Columbia, 1975). (*Right*) BEFORE: Intent on getting her shot, Joanna Eberhart (Katharine Ross) raises her Nikon. She's focused on finding a place in the professional world. The loveliness of concentration, apparent in this before shot, has nothing to do with surface beauty. Joanna's hair tumbles, uncoiffed, over her shoulders and down her back; her face is bare of makeup. It's her ability to detach from the trivia of daily tasks that irritates her husband and the other Stepford men. (*Below*) AFTER: After her murderous makeover, Joanna's formulaic beauty and vacant look make her just another Stepford wife. Here, they  form a phalanx of happy shoppers—demure, big-busted, and totally witless— just the way the Stepford men like them.

and playing tennis with Charmaine. They panic, however, when Charmaine comes back from a weekend with her husband changed into a glamorous hausfrau. She gives up tennis, astrology and her maid, and she cleans compulsively. Joanna and Bobbie stop joking about the Stepford wives. They suspect something serious: nerve gas, or chemicals in the water. What could be affecting the women so profoundly?

Both women plan to move, but before that happens, Bobbie returns from a weekend with her husband a busty, beautiful, boring version of herself, fixated on brewing coffee. Now completely spooked, Joanna researches past newspapers to find that Stepford once had a thriving women's group with prestigious speakers like Betty Friedan. She also discovers that Dale Coba, nicknamed Diz, once worked for Disney, creating animated figures that functioned like live humans.

She agrees to seek psychiatric help, but Joanna knows the truth; the detailed sketches and the "linguistic project" fit her discovery. The Stepford wives don't act like real women because they aren't; they're robots the men have created and programmed. Joanna runs. The men catch her and take her to visit Bobbie, who will cut her finger, the men tell her, so that Joanna can see she still bleeds. Bobbie waits for Joanna with a "big knife." The last chapter reveals a changed Joanna, dressed to the hilt and beautifully coiffed, shopping contentedly with the other Stepford wives.

William Goldman stays close to Levin's spare narrative, changing or adding to make the truth of the tale a little less ambiguous. For example, telling glances, scraps of phone conversation, and a scene that shows Ed, Charmaine's husband, shaken by the transition from real wife to dummy, underscore male involvement in the scheme. The most crucial additions and changes in the adaptation sharpen the contrast between before and after and confirm Joanna's knowledge that the Stepford wives are robots.

An added opening scene foreshadows plot direction and alerts us to Joanna's engagement with her photography. Waiting to leave New York, she sits in a station wagon with her children while her husband sees to final details. Joanna notices a man awkwardly carrying a nude female mannequin across a busy street. She's out of the car and shooting in a second. Joanna, before, a committed observer of life, misses very little.

The Stepford wives observe nothing, and an added scene demonstrates the surreal experience of trying to converse with them. Joanna has managed to gather four women (plus Bobbie and Charmaine) for a consciousness-raising session. She leads by complaining mildly about her husband, and Charmaine follows, bitterly accusing her husband of never loving her. Bobbie, animated and engaged, listens. The others, however, sit like the zombies they are, staring blankly ahead, smiling serenely.

Finally one of them confesses that she didn't manage to bake anything the day before. The others console her with the suggestion that she switch to Easy-On Spray Starch. "If time is your enemy," one busty beauty pontificates, "make friends with Easy-On—that's all I can say." The other Stepford wives chime in passionately, extolling the virtues of Easy-On. Joanna, Bobby and Chamaine, defeated, don't try this anymore.

In this scene, and in the rest of the film, costuming and camera work underscore the contrast between before, the real women, and after, the Stepford wives. Katharine Ross, who memorably played Elaine Robinson in *The Graduate* (1967) and Emma Peel in *Butch Cassidy and the Sundance Kid* (1969), give Joanna a hippie edge. Joanna negotiates sedate Stepford in bell-bottoms and midriff-baring halters, usually with a cigarette in hand. When she wears a dress, it fits like a t-shirt, emphasizing her flat-chested bralessness. Joanna lets her long hair cascade down her back, or she bundles it carelessly on top of her head. Ross is a beautiful woman (fulfilling the Hollywood "before" convention), but, as Joanna, one of her attractions is her nonchalance about her appearance. The camera helps define Joanna's character; the many close-ups of her emphasize the planes of her rather angular face instead of her prettiness. Paula Prentiss's pre-makeover Bobbie Markowe favors zany overalls and patchwork jeans, and the gorgeous pre-makeover Charmaine doesn't mind being sweaty and disheveled after a good game of tennis. Their freewheeling style contrasts absolutely with the Stepford wives' garden party perfection. All these big-busted, long-legged robots wear what the Stepford men see as "womanly": perfect makeup, fluffy, high-maintenance hairdos, and long, ruffled dresses. Often they top off their color-coordinated ensembles with ribbon-trimmed leghorn hats.

Levin shows us Joanna Eberhart's "replacement" in the supermarket only, but Goldman adds a chilling scene that gives us an earlier glimpse of the almost-finished robot. Katharine has been cornered at the Men's Association, and in her terrified run from Dale Coba, she stumbles upon a replica of her bedroom. Before the dressing table sits the robot, combing its shiny, Dynel hair. During this scene, the camera cuts from the robot to close-ups of Joanna's face, juxtaposing real and artificial woman. The robot, clad in a green, nylon see-through shift, has huge breasts and slim hips. Her doll-like face is a clever caricature of Joanna's, but her eyes, pools of darkness with no whites, make her a terrifying figure. She walks towards Joanna twisting a nylon stocking. In the film, Joanna's replacement kills her.

Some contemporary reviewers read *The Stepford Wives* as a seventies satire on the emptiness of American housewives. We agree with Peter

Straub, who argues that the men, trapped in adolescence, who "yearn to translate their fantasies of sex with Playmate-style lollapaloozas into reality" are Levin's real target (xi). After all, *The Stepford Wives* proposes that men would *murder* to get compliant Barbie dolls as wives instead of real women.

This horror tale reverses the Pygmalion myth; the creators replace real women with statue-like dolls. Yet, *The Stepford Wives* may not be so distant from the other films as it seems. It's easy to imagine the male FBI agents in *Miss Congeniality* filling out order forms for Stepford's products, and to see egocentric Warren Justice accompanied by a big-busted Tally, programmed to praise his anti-establishment bent with her full, luscious lips. George Roundy would sigh in relief over a woman whose hair stayed put, and even Henry Higgins might prefer an android Eliza who would not throw his slippers. The paradox of the Pygmalion myth lies in males yearning for female perfection. When male creators try to craft perfect fantasy objects, and they always do, the women they alter become less interesting, and less real. (Paramount plans to offer audiences the chance to see the most cautionary Pygmalion tale again. A new version of *The Stepford Wives* starring Nicole Kidman as Joanna Eberhart is due to be released spring 2004.)

Ovid's "Pygmalion" includes the touch of Venus, a mythic component all of these makeover films delete, opting for complete male control of the transformations. It's a relief to turn from these problematic Pygmalion stories to makeover films about more mature women who practice transformation for their own purposes, and who extend the rich selves they uncover to the lucky and loving others around them.

• *Six* •

The Mirror Inside

The best transformations make you feel more like yourself, not less so.

—Cindi Leive, Editor-in-Chief, *Glamour*

Most men drool when they think of Jamie Lee Curtis, star of *A Fish Called Wanda* (1988), *Trading Places* (1983), *True Lies* (1994), and *The Tailor of Panama* (2001). The striking, statuesque daughter of Janet Lee and Tony Curtis screamed "object of male fantasy" from her screen debut in John Carpenter's 1978 slasher flick, *Halloween*. Scantily clad and crouching, terrified, Curtis's Laurie Strode created the prototype for all those future victims of knife-wielding, masked stalkers. Ten years later, her sex appeal *and* humor delighted male audiences in Charles Crichton's farce, *A Fish Called Wanda*. Then, in *True Lies*, one of the most talked about films of 1994, Curtis performed a strip tease for Arnold Schwarzenegger that was simultaneously funny, provocative, and humiliating. Men cheered. Feminists cried. Jami Bernard called it "the biological link between the mother and the whore that every sexually tormented male has been looking for" (77). In short, Jamie Lee Curtis has been an icon of female beauty for more than twenty years.

But in the September 2002 issue of *more* magazine, the now-forty-three-year-old mother of four insisted on de-glaming for the camera. The photo that smiles back at us from the first page of her "True Thighs" layout is Jamie *au naturel*—no makeup, oily hair, tummy rolls, thick thighs and calves, and slumping posture. She had a point to make: "Glam Jamie, the Perfect Jamie, the great figure, blah, blah, blah…. I don't want the unsuspecting forty-year-old women of the world to think that I've got it going on. It's such a fraud. And I'm the one perpetuating it" (qtd. in Wallace 92). Wearing an unflattering black sports bra and spandex briefs, Jamie skewers her glamorous image. No trace of Pygmalion's Galatea, that male fantasy come to life, exists in this first photo. Curtis wants readers to know that the fabulous physique is a dangerous fake—dangerous because it invites women to believe they're somehow lesser if they don't fit that perfect physical image, dangerous because it annihilates women's self-confidence. "I'm trying really hard to take the veil off the fraud, to be real, to start with me," she says (qtd. in Wallace 92).

The story of Curtis's transformation from screen diva to author of children's books that deal with issues such as self-esteem and creative expression serves as the perfect entry point for our discussion of midlife makeover films. Through her own journey, Curtis turns the mirror inside, reflecting back an interesting woman at peace with herself, a woman who shares her talents and discoveries with others, and one who (unlike those frustrated and frustrating male creators of fantasy objects) seems quite comfortable with the reality that female perfection doesn't exist.

Looking through some of Curtis's photographed self-portraits, Amy Wallace came across one of the actress's favorites: "a black-and-white shot of [a] mirror, broken into shards on the ground ... her face reflected in one tiny sliver" (94). "You have to find me," Curtis told her. "I'm in there" (qtd. in Wallace 94).

In *Alice Doesn't Live Here Anymore* (1974), *Moonstruck* (1987), *The Mirror Has Two Faces* (1996), and *My Big Fat Greek Wedding* (2002), the heroines are all middle-age women searching for themselves amidst broken shards of mirror. They've experienced physical and mental abuse, death of a loved one, jealousy, and looming spinsterhood. The shard, when they find it, reflects a dual persona; these women are vulnerable *and* tough—tough enough to make themselves over their way, for their own reasons. They become much more than just physically beautiful women. Like Charlotte Vale, that first midlife makeover—and like the real Jamie Lee Curtis—they understand, almost instinctively, that beauty might be empowering, but it means nothing without humanity. And these characters never lose their humanity, no matter how beautiful they become. Their makeovers act as a portal to self-exploration and independence, and, in each case, the after simply reflects and enhances the beautiful person inside before. Alice Hyatt, Loretta Castorini, Rose Morgan, and Fortoula Portokalos are women of substance. As editor-in-chief Cindi Leive writes in *Glamour's* "first-ever" makeover issue (January 2003), "The best transformations make you feel *more* like yourself, not less so" (22).

Alice Doesn't Live Here Anymore *(1974)*

Directed by a young Martin Scorsese (the current don of gritty, tough, provocative films like *Goodfellas* and *Gangs of New York*), *Alice Doesn't Live*

Here Anymore speaks for its time. Women, caught between opposing forces of traditional roles and new opportunities, muddled over whether to clean closets or help bring home the bacon. Some followed the voice of emerging feminist leaders, ripped off their aprons, and ran out their beautifully painted suburban doors. Others opted for cookies and car pools, feeling too unwilling or too guilty to leave their male-feathered nests. And some, like Alice Hyatt (Ellen Burstyn), the heroine of *Alice Doesn't Live Here Anymore*, were thrust, scared and unprepared, into the world to make their own way. Whatever the situation women found themselves in, they were in transition, and Scorsese's film, as the title indicates, has something important to say about a woman in transition. Unfortunately, its message almost gets lost amid the counterculture fallout of the 1970s.

Few makeover films exist at all from this period. In fact, there seems to be a long stretch between the mid-sixties and the late eighties when women's fare, in general, dropped off the Hollywood radar screen. There may be several reasons for this that took root in the chaotic sixties. The assassinations of Jack and Bobby and Martin sent the entire country into a downward spiral. The Vietnam War escalated. Race riots swept Watts and Los Angeles. The Middle East became a tinderbox. And hippies with flowers in their hair objected to it all. Music moved from surf to soul to electrified folk to psychedelic. Films followed suit. They went from big and splashy—like *Spartacus* (1960), *Lawrence of Arabia* (1962), *Cleopatra* (1963), *The Sound of Music* (1965), *Doctor Zhivago* (1965), and *Camelot* (1967)—in an attempt to bring back television audiences, to dark and serious—like *The Wild Angels* (1966), *Bonnie and Clyde* (1967), *The Graduate* (1967), *Rosemary's Baby* (1968), *Midnight Cowboy* (1969), and *Easy Rider* (1969)—to reflect a generation defining itself in opposition to its parents.

In this era of dissent and rebellion, the makeover genre virtually disappeared. Women were too busy trying to climb the corporate ladder and make an equal buck to make themselves into some guy's vision of ideal beauty. Inspired by Betty Friedan, founder of the National Organization for Women and author of *The Feminine Mystique*, the book that became a manifesto for equal rights, women who had sacrificed their own dreams for their husbands and their families yearned for something more fulfilling and went after it with style and gusto. Friedan had held the mirror up to an entire American society, exposing all the faulty wiring of a culture that maneuvered to stifle the spirit of intelligent women and keep them happily polishing their furniture. Hollywood, as it often does, took its cue from this political, economic, and social climate.

But there was an unexpected twist. As Molly Haskell suggests, the growing strength of the women's movement in real life created a back-

lash against women in film in general. Others noted the same trend. Giannetti and Eyman write:

> The masculinization of American movies coincided with the rise of the
> feminist movement. Militant feminists like Jane Fonda fueled the move-
> ment, which was growing more vocal in its demands for justice. Several
> film critics wondered if there was a correlation between the growing stri-
> dency of feminism with the increasing brutalization of women in movies
> [*Flashback* 403].

With a new, more permissive production code in place, Hollywood sub-
stituted violence and sex for romance. Movies like *Klute* (1971) and *Looking for Mr. Goodbar* (1977), for example, are cautionary tales designed to
show women that independence comes with a big, sometimes lethal, price
tag. Falling right between these two films, *Alice Doesn't Live Here Anymore*, tinged with elements of violence and sexism, implies that some
women aren't ready for independence when it does come knocking.

Hollywood had already started to edge out female characters with
films like *Butch Cassidy and the Sundance Kid* (1969) where the main story
line focuses on the relationship between two attractive male characters,
in this case Robert Redford and Paul Newman. This new kind of love, or
buddy film, continued into the eighties as Redford and Newman morphed into Mel Gibson and Danny Glover in the *Lethal Weapon* series, and
the white male action adventure heroes and military commandos of the
Reagan era all but quashed women's fare at the boxoffice. To compete
with tough guys played by Clint Eastwood, Sylvester Stallone, and Arnold
Schwarznegger, female characters were fetishized, like Sigourney Weaver
in *Alien* (1979) or Goldie Hawn in *Private Benjamin* (1980).

The rare glimpses of the makeover genre were revisionist, like *Shampoo* (Chapter 5), which depicts women in a constant state of narcissistic
transformation inspired by their scissor-wielding lothario of a hairdresser,
George Roundy (Warren Beatty). Woody Allen's revisionist romantic
comedy *Annie Hall* (1977) also shows woman in transformation, but here
our heroine's quest is not so much physical as it is intellectual. Annie's
mantra is "You don't think I'm smart enough," and so she sets out to make
herself over from a Midwestern, gum-chewing, insecure babe-in-the-
woods to a hip, sophisticated, insecure Californian. And *Grease*, which
we also discuss in "The Ladder of Class," took the physical makeover in
a new direction: from girl-next-door to greaser.

Though enormously successful, these films represent virtually all the
makeover fare to be found until the late eighties when *Moonstruck* (1987)
and *Working Girl* (1988) opened the door to a tidal wave of makeover

movies that appeared throughout the 1990s, in a more female friendly political administration, and seem to be holding their own amidst today's proliferation of war films.

Alice Doesn't Live Here Anymore is one of those rare 1970s makeover movies, but it accurately represents the plight of women at the time. Its complexity, realistic style, tone, and ambiguity are largely the work of the film's director. In his book *The Cinema of Martin Scorsese*, Lawrence S. Friedman tells the story of how Ellen Burstyn, a star with considerable clout at the time, ended up hiring a "man's" director for her "woman's" film.

Martin Scorsese had just finished directing *Mean Streets* (1973), starring Robert DeNiro and Harvey Keitel. Scorsese, who grew up on Elizabeth Street in Little Italy, was working with familiar territory: street hoods in New York's Lower East Side. What did he know about a frumpy housewife living in Socorro, New Mexico, with an abusive truck driver for a husband and a precocious 11-year-old? What did he know about her longing for the good old days in Monterey, California, where she dreamed of being a singer? Did he have the sensibilities to deal sensitively with women's issues? Burstyn thought Scorsese was just what her project needed. "I thought Scorsese would be perfect for *Alice*, which needed to be roughed up. I wanted to make it the story of women today, with our consciousness as it is now, not a Doris Day film," she said (qtd. in Friedman 52). Burstyn's desires and Scorsese's intersected at the right time and place. He was ready for a challenge. "I wanted to make a film which was completely different and yet rough, the way I always like it. Rough in camera movement, rough in impact" (qtd. in Friedman 52).

Thus, the visions of Ellen Burstyn, star, and Martin Scorsese, director, merged into an uneasy little romantic comedy about broken dreams and compromise with a complex mix of both unsettling and satisfying makeover conventions. But, as Friedman points out, "In its awareness and manipulation of convention, spontaneously freewheeling camera work, quirky takes on human relationships, and sudden outbursts of unpredictable violence, *Alice* is vintage Scorsese" (54).

Scorsese begins in Alice's past, with Alice's dream to be a singer. In this opening scene, reminiscent of *The Wizard of Oz*, a young Alice, dressed much like Judy Garland as Dorothy, walks into the shot singing "You'll Never Know." It's evening as she approaches her home, an old farmhouse. Through the window, she watches her mother serving dinner. "I can sing better than Alice Faye. I swear to Christ I can … and if anybody doesn't like it, they can blow it out their ass." The language coming from such an angelic looking child shocks and later explains where

Alice's son, Tommy (Alfred Lutter), gets such a foul mouth. Her fierce determination to be more than her mother leads our false expectations for her. The whole scene is shot in low-key lighting with red filters over the lens, creating an almost suffocating feel that continues long after Scorsese's abrupt transition to Alice 27 years later, living in New Mexico in a tiny house, waiting on a loutish husband (Billy Green Bush) and a smart-ass son. Tall hedges surround her little home, alluding to a sleeping beauty entombed there. The red filters and cramped rooms inside suggest a woman trapped, a woman who has sacrificed her dreams and now lives to serve others. Her matronly figure, cheap calico housedress with ruffles, and stringy short hair, signify that Alice hasn't much time or energy to spend on herself. Though she cries to her friend and neighbor about her unhappy marriage, nothing here indicates that Alice has the courage or will to change things, and it's disturbing to twenty-first century viewers to witness her solicitous behavior toward her temperamental, macho spouse and desperate turn to tears to get any warmth from him.

Her husband's sudden death in a trucking accident, the catalyst of the film, should be both relief and opportunity for Alice, but she's become so dependent on a man to take care of her that she's afraid to strike out on her own and seize the moment to pick up the dream buried deep inside. Through tears, again, she will later tell Flo at Mel & Ruby's Café, "I got sidetracked. I was so afraid of Donald, always trying to please him. I don't know how to live without a man." Her admission is troublesome to us, but a realistic situation for many women in the mid-seventies. Donald's death liberates Alice, but, as Scorsese points out, she would never have left him on her own (Friedman 55). A male trigger still determines Alice's fate.

Perhaps Alice realizes what we begin to suspect: her talent, minimal at best, will not take her very far. The film seems to beg the questions: What happens when we are given the opportunity to realize our dreams? Is it easier or more comforting to *talk* about what we could have been rather than *do* something about it? What do we do with the possibility that those old dreams may not manifest into the success we imagined? Are we really as good as we think we are? Alice's real problem is not the death of her husband, or the need to earn a living for herself and her son. It's the fear of not being able to live up to her own dreams.

Yet her dreams are all Alice has to fall back on. "The only job I ever had was singing," she tells neighbor Bea. Cut to Alice—still plain and frumpy—now sitting at her piano practicing. No longer so sure of her talent, she remarks to herself, "It ain't Peggy Lee." We're not so sure, either. Neither is her son, Tommy, who listens from outside the window, with growing skepticism. Even this 11-year-old knows his mother's not going to set the world on fire. She's a mediocre pianist with a thin little voice, but she packs up her son and sets out for Monterey.

Several critics have pointed out that *Alice Doesn't Live Here Anymore* is a road movie. The rising action takes place between Sorocco, New Mexico, and Monterey, California—between Alice's unhappy past and her uncertain future. But for someone who wants to get to Monterey in a hurry, Alice takes a bewildering route. From New Mexico, most people would take Route 40 West to 15 South to 10 West, which turns into Highway 101, a direct shot into Monterey. Not Alice. She stops for awhile in Phoenix to make some money and then ends up in Tuscon—a path that almost brings her circling back to where she started. A journey that takes two, maybe three, days tops, turns into weeks for Alice and Tommy.

This is significant when we consider Alice's inner journey. She sets out in pursuit of her dreams, of necessity, not choice. Along the way she realizes she's not as good as she once thought. She has no other marketable skills, except those connected with service and housework. She becomes what she said she never wanted to be: a waitress. And she foregoes her rather shaky plans for another man, albeit a more sensitive man who stands ready to abandon his own dream and leave his beloved ranch to "take" her to Monterey, to the extreme West and the Promised Land, if she still wants to go. She doesn't. It would seem that Alice hasn't traveled very far. It would appear that she's headed right back to a life of solicitous servitude.

Alice is like a slave who's just been told she's free at last. Where will she go? What will she do? How will she, after all these years, live as an independent person? She is, after all, a repressed victim of a time when media blitzed society with messages designed to keep women at home, stoking the family fires. For many women in 1974, the very nature of their independence was problematic, and Alice's plight coalesced their fears.

When Alice turns the mirror inside on her journey of self-discovery, it tends to first reflect more of what she is not, rather than what she is. While on the road, the lighting is still dim and stifling as she and Tommy move from one cramped motel room to another, suggesting Alice's state of mind. She feels trapped, cornered, and afraid. For the first time in a long time, she must rely on herself and she has no confidence in that self. Her initial makeover is phony, artificial. When Alice stops in Phoenix in order to make some money, she spends money she doesn't have on a new look—a lounge singer's look. She comes back to the motel dressed in a tight, polyester, bright green V-neck dress, white shoes, and a scarf. Her straight hair has been permed and fluffed and sprayed, her makeup overdone. "I'm trying to look like I'm under 30 so I can get a job," she wails. (She's 35.) But the overall effect is hard and unnatural. Tommy shuts the door in her face.

The first lounge owner has a different reaction. She asks for an audition, and he asks her to turn around. "Turn around? Why don't you look at my face? I don't sing with my ass," she counters as she runs out. (There's still some spark and grit here.) But after looking for a job all day, in bar after bar where the only light filters in through the doorways, Alice stumbles exhausted into the establishment of the kindly Mr. Jacobs. He doesn't even have a piano, but touched by her tears and desperation, he gives her an audition in another bar down the street and hires her because he feels sorry for her. As Friedman points out, "Whether her tears are spontaneous or strategic, they suggest that success for women is directly proportionate to their skill in manipulating men" (56).

Cut to Alice performing an adequate, but certainly not stellar, rendition of "I've Got a Crush on You." She seems as uncomfortable in her new skin as her songs seem out of touch with the times. Her performance does, however, attract a younger man, Ben Eberhardt (Harvey Keitel), who wheedles a date and then sex from the lonely Alice. She's even thinking about staying in Phoenix, much to Tommy's chagrin, when Ben turns out to have a wife, a son with a hearing problem, and a violent temper. In typical Scorsese style, Ben viciously attacks his wife in front of Alice, makes a shamble out of her motel room, and then terrorizes her and Tommy. Alice packs up her dreams once more and heads out on the road in her slacks, shirt, scarf, and "lucky" ball cap that her neighbor in Sorocco gave her.

How she ends up in Tuscon is a mystery, but, once there, she can't find a lounge gig so she takes a job as a waitress in Mel & Ruby's Café. (This part of the film spawned the television sitcom *Alice*.) Unhappy about compromising her dreams, Alice gets off to a shaky start at Mel's, especially with Flo, the good-natured but foul-mouthed I've-been-around-the-block-a-time-or-two-honey waitress. "You don't like me very much, do you?" Flo asks. "No, not much," is Alice's direct answer. Soon, however, they end up collapsing in laughter over some remark Flo makes and become fast friends.

In one lovely scene, we see them in close up, talking, sunning their faces. A pull out long shot shows them sitting in chairs in the back lot of Mel's diner, side by side. Alice needs female friends, and she knows it. Early in the film, we witness her loving friendship with Bea in Sorocco. They help each other through tough times. Later, Alice gives a cherished shawl to a poor, elderly woman at her garage sale; she's sympathetic to

Ben's abused wife; and she bonds with Flo and Vera, her sister waitresses. Alice may claim that she doesn't know how to live without a man, but it's her female friends who give her strength.

Two things are especially noticeable once Alice reaches Mel's. First, Alice's harsh makeover softens out. Her hair is back to its original style but now looks clean and pretty. Sometimes we see her in her pink uniform, her hair held back with a white, wide headband. Her makeup is toned down, and, when not working, she wears slimming, flattering casual jeans and t-shirts. She is becoming more like the person inside, not less. Second, the lighting changes. The low-key lighting, so pervasive in the first half of the film, and so illustrative of Alice's confusion and hard times, finally transitions into high-key at Mel's. This change signifies a shift in Alice's mood and circumstances. No longer isolated, Alice now finds herself surrounded by people who care about her, people she cares about, too.

She also meets David (Kris Kristofferson) at Mel's. David's actually a good guy who falls for Alice at first sight. We later learn that he's divorced. His wife took the kids. And it has taken him years to realize his dream of owning a sizeable ranch nearby. A bit gun shy at first because of her previous disasters with men, Alice takes it slow with David, but they're soon spending lots of time together at his ranch. In their scenes together, he is gentle and caring. At one point, he even asks her, "Which do you want? Do you want to go home? Or do you want to sing?" He seems to care about what matters to Alice most.

David also spends quality time with Tommy, who has taken up with the local bad girl, Audrey (Jodie Foster). Tommy is out of control. He's a good kid, but mouthy and prone to follow Audrey's lead when it comes to drinking and shoplifting. David and Alice's romance seems destined for the altar until David gives Tommy a much-needed smack on the bottom for not listening to him or his mother. Alice, protective of her son and scared David will turn into Donald, or, worse yet, Ben, leaves him after a huge fight. He later shows up at the restaurant to get her back. "I don't give a damn about that ranch," he says in front of all the customers. "You want to go to Monterey? I'll take you to Monterey. Let's go."

According to Friedman, the lines were Kristofferson's idea. The film was turning into one of those Doris Day flicks that Burstyn and Scorsese were trying to avoid. "The realistic intensity of the breakup dissolves into the parodic staginess of their makeup: Alice and David fall into each other's arms, cheered on by an applauding lunchtime crowd at Mel's" (58). The studio wanted a happy ending, but Burstyn and Scorsese wanted more realism, more ambiguity. David's lines reinforce the notion that he's not like the others and provide a window of opportunity for Alice to follow her dreams.

Interestingly, it's the mother and son relationship that's privileged here. The movie does not end with the scene between David and Alice in Mel's. Instead, Alice and Tommy are walking, arm in arm, down the street talking about the future. Both want to stay in Tuscon—and both want to give David another chance. Some critics read this ending as a cop-out, an affirmation that Alice will return to her former state of wife and mother, chief cook and maid. They have a point if we read the film with today's raised consciousness. However, *Alice* speaks for its time. If Alice does marry David, the film stays true to the consciousness of women at the time who felt that marriage and motherhood were the only jobs they'd been trained for. Besides, Alice is not the same woman we met at the beginning of the film. She has made herself over into a stronger, more attractive, more self-assured image of the person inside.

One other key point in the scene provides an ironic clue that Alice may still pursue her singing career. She and Tommy are walking away from us, the audience, and toward a building called The Monterey. Is it a nightclub? Will she notice it? Does it mean that she has finally reached Monterey via Tuscon? Remember, David has previously asked: "Which do you want? Do you want to go home? Or do you want to sing?" Can she have both in Tuscon? We don't know. It would seem that Burstyn and Scorsese found their ambiguous ending, and a more realistic one for the times.

Moonstruck *(1987)*

From the moment it begins, *Moonstruck* asks viewers to enter its irresistible motion. First, you enter a night with a moon too huge to be real, "a monster moon" (Kempley), hanging over New York City. Next, like visiting an empty stage set, you watch while a worker walks across the quiet, dark Met plaza to hang a poster for *La Bohème.* Then, the sun rises, and you follow the truck carrying the sets for *La Bohème* through the streets. By the time you meet *Moonstruck's* heroine, Loretta Castorini (Cher), who walks, unseeing, past that very truck, past a romantic, horse-drawn hansom cab, and through Brooklyn streets that pulse with energy, you want to scream at her: "Hey you! Watch out! Something's about to happen!" Director Norman Jewison offers his viewers a privileged vantage point throughout *Moonstruck,* and it makes for an involving, satisfying ride. Before you know her problem, you instinctively *know* Loretta's problem. She's detached from the life swirling around her. Although she doesn't take a road trip, like Alice Hyatt, Loretta's on the same kind of journey, a search for a state of mind that will bring her harmony.

A thirty-something widow, Loretta's preparing to settle for a marriage of convenience to Johnny Cammareri (Danny Aiello), a fortyish bachelor still tied to his mother's long apron strings. (She lives in Sicily.) Fearing the bad luck that ended her first marriage in tragedy, Loretta's obsessed with getting everything *right*: the right proposal, a ring, a ceremony, a reception. She's sure her city hall marriage doomed her and her first husband.

Of course, everything begins to go *wrong*. Before Johnny flies off to Sicily to watch his aging mother die, he asks Loretta to invite his estranged brother Ronny (Nicolas Cage) to the wedding. When Loretta meets Ronnie, a passionate, tortured baker, sparks fly. Ronny, too, has been wounded in love (and in life—he's missing a hand). Loretta tries to refuse Johnny's advances, but she quickly gives in, and, in fact, welcomes them. "I've been dead," he tells her. "Me too," she answers. Ronny takes her directly to "the bed." Horrified by their behavior, Loretta nevertheless agrees to attend *La Boheme* with Ronny as a farewell gesture of goodwill.

Loretta's not the only Castorini in turmoil. Her father, Cosmo (Vincent Gardenia), a wealthy plumber, has a serious case of male menopause and a mistress (Anita Gillette) to make him feel better. Loretta's mother, Rose (Olympia Dukakis), knows Cosmo's straying, and desperately tries to figure out why "men chase women." Stir into this rich mix Loretta's grandfather (Feodor Chaliapin, Jr.) who, along with his five dogs, lives with Cosmo, Rose, and Loretta, and her loving aunt and uncle, Rita and Raymond Capomaggi (Julie Bovasso and Louis Guss). These family members witness, but don't always understand, the travails of the Castorinis.

Loretta sheds her gray, lifeless widow's weeds and drab hair for a dynamite dress and dazzling locks, and one night of opera and Ronny slays any notion she had of marrying Johnny. Ronnie convinces Loretta that life *can't* be made "right," but must be lived as it is, full of error and confusion. The next morning, everyone meets around the Castorini breakfast table. Rose tells Cosmo to break off his affair, and he agrees. Johnny returns from Sicily to report that he can't marry Loretta—it would kill his mother, who still lives. Ronny proposes to Loretta, who accepts. Even Johnny joins in the final toast—"A la famiglia," that ends the film.

Critics, like Pauline Kael, enjoyed *Moonstruck*, but generally they admired its zaniness and zest. Kael calls it a "loony fugue," and a "screwball ethnic comedy" ("Loony" 1162), while Rita Kempley dubs *Moonstruck* a "big, beautiful valentine of a movie" (1). Few critics, however, notice what we consider the heart of the film: Loretta's makeover. Loretta, before, is hardly Charlotte Vale, although her character does display some of

Charlotte's before signifiers: her thick, gray-streaked, dark hair is bundled into a knot; her heavy brows overpower her narrow face; her dull, dowdy clothing looks as if it was chosen from a catalogue for aspiring missionaries. She wears virginal white underwear (surely from Sears) and ugly knee socks under her boots. Every detail screams neglect. Loretta's neat, clean, and bland, locked into a look that reflects her refusal to engage life.

This role, for which she won the Best Actress Oscar in 1987, reverses reality for fashion-crazed Cher, who charmed us with her straightest of the straight hair and widest of bell-bottoms when she and Sonny Bono ruled the pop charts in the late sixties. Her stint on the *Sonny and Cher Comedy Hour* in the early seventies made the world aware of her potential as a comedian and spawned her love of Bob Mackey gowns too wild for the rest of us. That wildness manifested itself on Oscar nights for years, when half the fun of watching was waiting to see how much Cher you *could* see. (She won her appearances at the Academy Awards with film performances worthy of note, like those in *Silkwood* (1983), *Mask* (1985), and the *Witches of Eastwick* (1987) Cher's fondness for outré fashion and wildness lit up her videos, like "If I Could Turn Back Time" (1989), which featured a glimpse of tattoos on a well-toned posterior. Cher has always cultivated an outrageous, changing, never bland, identity.

Loretta, however, doesn't see life, and, literally, doesn't see herself. As she performs her accountant's duties for a customer who is a florist customer, she sits before a mirrored wall. She scoffs at men wasteful enough to send expensive roses, and, even when the florist hands her a single, red rose, she doesn't look up at herself. In one of those privileged moments, we see the sweetness of her smile, and, in the mirror, watch her brush the rose across her cheek. Is she really so practical, after all? Later, after Johnny proposes (in the "right" way), Loretta sees him off. When she catches her reflection in the airport window, she checks her teeth for bits of food. We, however, see the moon, the really big moon, shining down, like a portent of change.

Ronny *sees* Loretta, and in a welcome switch from the usual makeover format, his vision precedes Loretta's makeover. Unlike all those near-sighted Princes who only recognized Cinderella when the slipper fit, Ronny recognizes Loretta's true self before her transformation. She sees him right back, and each of them tell each other's life, a true mirror moment, in which Loretta calls Ronny a "wolf," stupid for turning away from love, and Ronny calls Loretta "stupid yourself" for doing the same thing. John Patrick Shanley won the Academy Award for Best Original Screenplay for this dialogue, which sounds like real people speaking with heightened sensibilities. In the light of the moon, Ronny knows Loretta already looks "like an angel," and in the moonlight coming through the slats of the blind, they look alike, gypsy brother and sister, or soul mates.

It's in the afterglow of this moment that Loretta has her makeover. Alice Hyatt goes after her lounge singer wannabe look out of necessity. Why does Loretta decide on a change? You could say it's for Ronny, but he already adores her. You could say it's a whim. Loretta, still under the spell of the moonlight, turns into the "Cinderella" beauty parlor (well, of course) when she sees a fashionable photo in the window. You could say it's for the beauticians, who get to do what they've wanted to do for years. "She's gonna take out the grey," the women in the shop crow, overjoyed.

A happy hour or two full of chatter follow. A little color, a little eyebrow shaping, and Loretta leaves the store looking better than beautiful. The beauticians watch her leave, and you sense their happiness that Loretta is in motion, not standing still. She's *energy*, not entropy. Her curly hair bounces, and her walk becomes a stroll. (She's surprised at the reaction of some male bystanders who admire her.) Even her ordinary clothes look newly stylish because the woman who's wearing them feels good. She *looks* at things, like a gorgeous wine-colored dress in a boutique window. Norman Jewison opts not to let us see her buy the dress, but we see Loretta alone at home, seeing herself changed. This moment tells us that the makeover was for her.

Alone in the house for a rare hour or so, Loretta finds some jazz on the radio, pours herself a glass of wine, and sits on the floor by the fire, looking at her wine-colored dress, her extravagant shoes, and, finally, herself. No, this isn't a *Josie and the Pussycats* encouragement to head for the mall. Loretta's hungry for beauty; she strokes the soft fabric of the dress and admires the glitter of the jewels on her velvet shoes. Roger Ebert mentions that the tone of *Moonstruck* is "a certain bittersweet yearning" and it's certainly apparent in this scene. Loretta approaches the mirror slowly, still wearing that white slip. Shyly, appraisingly, she watches herself as she applies a deep red lipstick. She has discovered that "she is still capable of love" (Ebert).

Loretta's after has a dramatic reveal. As she steps from a cab, the camera sweeps from her outstretched foot to her mass of curls; it's that Casey Robinson shot, the tilt up that showed viewers the "new" Charlotte. We know Loretta by this time, so the shot doesn't feel exploitative; there's no lingering to ogle, just a glance, and an accompanying musical accolade. The first chord of *La Boheme's* overture sounds as Loretta's slipper hits the plaza. Ronny and Loretta have come to see Puccini, but this is the "opera" we've been prepared for. Ronny's made himself over, too. He has

Moonstruck (MGM, 1987). (*Top*) BEFORE: After a night of glamour, Loretta Castorini and Ronnie Cammareri shed their formal clothes for everyday attire. In this shot, their similar expressions and mirrored posture indicate their closeness. Their love is a true union, not just a one-night fling triggered by *La Bohème*. In the final scene of *Moonstruck*, they sit at the Castorini kitchen table as if they belong there, which, of course, they do.

(*Bottom*) AFTER: With her opera lover's first night look, and her raised wine glass, Loretta Castorini (Cher) could be any sophisticated Lincoln Center regular. But Loretta's glamorous makeover doesn't render her blasé. Lifted into the romantic evening by her after look, Loretta responds to Ronnie Camareiri (Nicolas Cage) with desperate passion worthy of any operatic heroine.

slicked back his wild hair, and he wears a tuxedo with a dazzling white shirt. "You look beautiful," he tells Loretta. "So do you," she replies. He thanks her for "her beautiful dress," and her hair—a unique moment in makeover films. Ronny knows that Loretta's special look is a gift, part of a special event. Loretta's never been to the Met, and her wonder makes the audience see it anew, those gem-like chandeliers that rise, that Chagal mural. *Moonstruck* makes viewers yearn to be part of that crowd, looking their best, going to see something wonderful for the first time. (Loretta also sees something not so wonderful, her father with his mistress, but that doesn't spoil the evening.)

Can the moonlight last? In the family kitchen the next morning, Loretta wears sweats with her hair bundled back and has a love bite on her neck, but the glow's still there; it's softer. "Ma, I love him awful," she tells her mother about Ronny. "That's too bad," her mother commiserates. Between them runs a consistent current of tolerant understanding that viewers know will continue.

Ronny, too, is back to his ordinary, funky look, with that crazy hair and intimidating black-gloved hand, but he fits right in. It's that sense of belonging that characterizes *Moonstruck*. Loretta's rebirth makes the family feel whole again. Charlotte Vale tells Jerry that they shouldn't "ask for the moon," but Loretta and Ronny ask for the moon, the chance to try for happiness, and get it.

Norman Jewison gives us a last, privileged look that says volumes. The camera leaves the family in the kitchen and travels around the living room and front hall, lingering on family photos. It stops on an aged, oval portrait of a man and a woman, surely the progenitors of the current Castorinis. Their wise peasant faces tell us just where that Castorini resilience comes from. They smile with a lust for life, a willingness to throw their lives across the ocean, to risk remaking themselves in the new world. In 1987, at the end of the Reagan era, this film reminds us that America's amazing powers of renewal comes from all kinds of families, not only those who came here on the *Mayflower*.

The Mirror Has Two Faces *(1996)*

In one respect, Barbra Streisand, who directed and stars in *The Mirror Has Two Faces*, reminds us of Audrey Hepburn: it's hard to make either of these women look bad, and they never quite disappear into their characters. The camera loves those exquisitely angular faces, and no matter what characters they play they always end up looking and acting like, well, Audrey and Barbra. When Hepburn starred as the middle-aged Marion opposite Sean Connery's aging Robin Hood in Richard Lester's 1976 revisionist, *Robin and Marion*, audiences couldn't take their eyes off of her, even though she was covered in grime and wore filthy smocks for most of the film. In 1983, Streisand made herself into a young man in order to get an education in *Yentl*, a film she produced, co-wrote, directed, and starred in. Even dressed as a boy, it was hard to disguise those gorgeous eyes, high cheekbones, and distinctive nose and mouth. In her third time out as director and star, Streisand chose another makeover movie, and, though she tries hard to be the frousy before, she still looks pretty— just an unadorned version of herself, the glamorous Barbra she becomes by the film's end. The real life Barbra always made a point of not changing herself. She refused to get a nose job and often poses in profile.

In *The Mirror Has Two Faces*, Streisand plays Rose Morgan, an English professor at Columbia University. Like Loretta in *Moonstruck*, Rose has a successful occupation but still lives at home with her mother, Hannah (Lauren Bacall), who's afraid of growing old and losing the one thing that's gotten her by in life—her looks. Photographs of her (actually of Bacall) as a stunning young woman stare self-assuredly and unselfconsciously back at us from almost every shot in Hannah's apartment, where her low-key lighting and strategically placed mirrors give her the illusion of youth. She won't even go out with Mr. Jenkins because of how it would look. "The mother's dating and the daughter stays home alone?" she asks.

Hannah's obsession with age requires constant feeding, too. Over dinner, she tells Rose about her day as a beauty consultant. (She performs makeovers on the less fortunate.) "I had one customer come in looking for a makeover. She needed one. Dyed blonde hair. Blue eyeshadow. Ash brown foundation. Hideous…. She was shocked when she found out how old I was." Bacall—who won a Golden Globe Award for Best Supporting Actress, a Screen Actors Guild Award for Best Supporting Actress, an Academy Award nomination for Best Supporting Actress, and a British Academy of Film and Television Arts Award for Best Supporting Actress—enacts the most believable character in the film, a woman awakening, late in life, to the fact that her whole life has been about maintaining an illusion.

Hannah also constantly compares Rose to her beautiful sister, Claire (Mimi Rogers), who has just snared Rose's love interest, Alex (Pierce Brosnan). The fickle Claire doesn't even love Alex. She later tells Rose, "If he weren't gorgeous, rich and straight, I wouldn't even have bothered."

Like her mother, Claire is all about appearance, but she does her sister one good deed, though her motives (like the real point of this movie) are unclear. Guilt? Pity? We don't know why she sends Rose's photograph and phone number in response to Gregory Larkin's lonely hearts ad.

Larkin (Jeff Bridges), a math professor at Columbia, has a somewhat unusual problem. He's tall and handsome and intelligent, but he can't sustain a relationship. Sex always gets in the way of respect and friendship. After he meets Rose, he explains: "I go crazy when I want someone sexually. I go out of my mind." His friend, Henry (George Segal), tells him he can't have sex and chew gum at the same time. Gregory's shortness of breath, dizziness, and weak-kneed reactions to beautiful women come across as a bit exaggerated and unrealistic, but, to give screenwriter Richard LaGravanese (*Bridges of Madison County*) the benefit of the doubt; they simply may be a way of externalizing or showing what happens to some men internally when they come face-to-face with physical beauty.

Sex has kept Gregory from focusing on his work. It's taken him 14 years to write his book on the twin prime conjecture. Like Alice Hyatt in *Alice Doesn't Live Here Anymore*, Gregory says he got a little "sidetracked." But, ultimately, it's the mathematical world that makes sense to Gregory, and he wants to settle down with someone he's not sexually attracted to. Rose is the one for him, especially after he attends her lecture on courtly love, which plays out more like a stand-up comedy routine than a real scene from academe.

Standing before a classroom full of eager, attentive, responsive students, Rose looks like the stereotype of a female professor: no makeup, hair pulled away from face, long skirt, long, baggy sweater, sensible shoes, and glasses. Yet this before image never seems exaggerated. She's plain, not homely. Though not stylish, her clean hair falls softly to her shoulders, and her nondescript ensemble never detracts from her message. She's talking about romantic versus platonic love. "A wedding is the final scene of the fairy tale. They never tell you what happens after. They never tell you that Cinderella drove the Prince crazy with her obsessive need to clean the castle and that she missed her day job." In the Middle Ages, she explains, courtly love—a passionate relationship that was never consummated—"took sex out of the equation, and what was left was a union of souls. Sex was the fatal love potion that led to madness, despair, or death."

Unfortunately, Gregory doesn't stick around for the punch line. He leaves, buoyed by Rose's affirmation of his own equation. He never hears Rose's last question: "Why do people want to fall in love, when it has such a short shelf life?" Her students come up with a few profound answers, but her answer, she says, is much simpler: "Because while it does last, it feels fucking great!" Her students burst into applause (talk about unbelievable). They like her before, so Rose is not an invisible makeover heroine.

Rose is a romantic. She wants to hear the philharmonic in her head when she kisses a man. She loves old romantic comedies, like *It Happened One Night* with Claudette Colbert and Clark Gable. She would rather watch baseball than go out on a date with a guy she's not attracted to. While she waits for Mr. Right, she bonds with her friend, Doris (Brenda Vaccaro), over food and spinsterhood. In one scene, Rose reveals her dreams about love to Doris: "I'd love it if someone knew me, really knew me. What I like. What I'm afraid of. What kind of toothpaste I use. I think that would really be wonderful." This scene foreshadows her relationship with Gregory, who does come to "really know" her and she him.

On their first date, Gregory watches fascinated as Rose loads her fork with the perfect combination of food to form the perfect bite. He takes notes on how she orders, what she likes and what she doesn't like. Rose "gets" his theory on prime numbers immediately. After another date, an animated Gregory paces back and forth as Rose sits on a bench listening to his new theory about relationships. She tries to interrupt, but Gregory keeps talking:

> I'm not interested in sex ... I, too, believe that it's the emphasis on sex that keeps people separate and alone.... Romance is a myth, a manipulation. Relationships that are based on romantic love are worthless.... This addiction to beauty and perfection created by advertising feeds on people's pathetic desires.... The media tells us what's beautiful and what's not.... Two people *can* marry out of respect, love, and trust.

Hmmm. Except for that first line, Gregory seems to have a point here. Rose doesn't buy it, but she says nothing and continues to see Gregory platonically.

A scene sequence shows Rose giving Gregory a makeover in the classroom. He *asks* for her advice out of his respect for her success. "You're too detached. Relate more to the students. You teach like you're having a math party and you only invited yourself," she tells him. We later see him using baseball, something else Rose has explained to him, to clarify complex calculus problems and establish a better rapport with his bored students. In one shot, Gregory teaches Rose how to play backgammon (both wear glasses here). Over a three-month period, they spend a lot of time together; they get to know and respect each other. Talk replaces kissing and touching. In fact, their dialogue led Roger Ebert to write in his review of the film: "It's rare … to find such verbal characters in a movie, and listening to them talk is one of the pleasures of *The Mirror Has Two Faces*."

He's right. A movie about an intelligent, middle-aged couple in love is a rare thing in Hollywood. Courtly love and calculus? Puccini and prime numbers? Here's a real merger of the arts and sciences. But the talky script also underscores the communication problems between the sexes. Here are two people at the top of their professions, in the business of communicating ideas and concepts, yet they, like the rest of us, still battle with the "men are from mars, women are from venus" syndrome. Gregory is confused about what women want from a man. Rose has bought into the beauty myth, or what women think men want. It's like a meeting of two preconceived notions, and for two intelligent people, this dilemma plays out too long and gets lost in the film's dizzying array of issues: courtly love versus romantic love, mother and daughter relationships, jealousy, self-esteem, internal and external beauty, what happens after the fairy-tale. Like the grandfather in *Moonstruck*, we're a little confused, too. In spite of the film's flaws, however, we found some well-acted scenes that speak to the process of merging the inner and outer self—and the process of coming back to life.

Two scenes in particular illustrate a reawakening for both Rose and Hannah. After Gregory proposes to Rose, she comes through the door and turns to face the mirror. "Well, well, well," she says to herself in disbelief. Hannah can't believe the news either, and, when she finds out that marriage means no sex, she's appalled, she says so, and then sits on the sofa with her back to Rose, who stands behind her. Behind Rose hangs a painting of Madonna and child.

> Why do you do that? Why do you make it sound so pathetic? You had a life, a husband who adored you. Why don't you want me to have just a little bit of that? I'm getting older, too, Mom. Why can't you be happy for me? But you can't, can you, because you're scared to death of being alone. And you're jealous because a man wants me—a good-looking man wants me.

Rose leaves Hannah sitting alone on her sofa in a darkened room.

In a later scene, the scene that probably won Bacall the Academy Award for Best Supporting Actress, Hannah admits that she is jealous of Rose. Rose has just returned home after her attempt to seduce her husband ends in humiliation and rejection. Again, she faces the mirror inside the door. "What are you doing here?" a sleepy Hannah asks. "Was I pretty as a baby?" Rose asks her. The question initiates a mother and daughter talk that changes both their lives. In her silk pajamas, Hannah stands by the window. Without makeup, we can see every unforgiving line on her face (still magnificent after all these years). Rose sits on the sofa, in tears, asking, "How did it feel? Being beautiful. Having people look at you with such admiration, looking at yourself in the mirror with such appreciation?" Cut to a lengthy closeup on Hannah. She pauses. "It was wonderful."

The scene continues the next morning. Hannah hasn't slept. "That's an awful thing to do to a woman my age—leave her alone with her thoughts," she tells Rose, who sits at the table opposite her mother. "You really love him. It's obvious. I never felt that," Hannah confesses. Hannah finally drops the façade and communicates with her daughter about her own marriage and then shows Rose a picture of a beautiful little girl. Rose thinks it's Claire. "That's not Claire. That's you. You're father adored you. He never felt that way about Claire. Only you."

The photo and her mother's admission give Rose the courage to change, and Rose's question forces Hannah to think about her own life and how she will spend the rest of it. She finally agrees to go out with Mr. Jenkins. These two scenes give the film weight and substance and believability as mother and daughter turn the mirror inside in an effort to save their relationship.

Gregory actually falls in love with the person Rose is, the inner Rose, the before Rose, though he doesn't know it. His proposal is romantic, even if his reasons for marrying Rose aren't. "Rose, when I look at you, I see a woman unlike any I've ever known before—your mind, your humor, your passion for ideas.... I feel as if when I'm with you, I'm home," he tells her. The key word here is "see." Gregory does see Rose, the person. He likes the before. In one restaurant scene, he's kind and considerate, ordering what she likes, enjoying her enjoyment of the perfect bite. He looks at her lovingly, and when she excuses herself to go to the restroom, he rises and his knees buckle. When Rose tries to seduce him one night, he gives into passion only momentarily and rejects her out of fear that they will lose what they have together. "Most people never get to where we are with the sharing and respect."

Rose's attempts to make herself over to seduce Gregory are clichéd. She's taken advice from her sister who wouldn't recognize a real relationship. She pours Gregory wine, lights the candles, and opts for sexy music instead of the baseball game. She wears a black negligee that shows off her cleavage, which, prior to this, has been hidden under layers of flannel granny gowns and chenille robes. She looks pretty, and Gregory obviously finds her alluring, but, after some steamy, passionate kissing, he leaves her lying in a heap on the floor. He's confused. He's disappointed. He thought they had a deal. He took precautions to make sure that there would be no physical attraction. Rose locks herself in the bathroom with her own reflection in the mirror to reinforce Gregory's words. She throws a towel over the mirror, weeps, waits until he falls asleep and leaves him. Gregory leaves for a three-month European book tour, but keeps calling, to no avail.

This incident and her mother's confession lead to Rose's makeover, which comes about three-quarters of the way through the second act. In another scene sequence, we see Rose exercising, changing her diet (from Hostess snowballs to carrots), getting highlights in her hair, and having a pedicure. Now these are things that Hannah can help her with, so we see mother and daughter bond over which shade of nail polish to use. Her mother has validated the idea that Rose can be beautiful again. Scenes of Rose's transformation are intercut with scenes of Gregory trying desperately to reach her by phone. She won't take his calls.

The new Rose has a sleek look: lots of form-fitting black suits with short skirts that show off her shapely legs. She wears heels and low cut sweaters to class. Male students give her the eye. "What?" she asks them. "I have breasts—and they can't be the subject of your next term paper." (We don't know any academic who would dress like this for class or make references to her breasts.)

Rose controls her makeover, and, like Loretta, she relishes her new look. But there's a downside here. At first she alienates her friend Doris, still dowdy and dumpy. Cheeseburgers in the middle of the day bloat her. Doris's face falls. Realizing her hurtful comment, Rose trades half of her salad for half of Doris's cheeseburger. Nice save.

When Gregory returns home, Rose is waiting. She's planned an intimate dinner, a staged event to introduce her new self. In a typical makeover revelation, Gregory comes in, turns his back to pour a drink, and Rose enters. Instead of the tilt up from sexy shoes to new coif, director Barbra does a tilt down. Gregory does a double take, mouth agape, as he takes in her hightlighted hair, her curvy figure in a tight black dress, her shapely legs, and black heels. Rose assumes a flirtatious pose, a bit too manipulative. Here's the gist of their conversation:

GREGORY: What happened to you?
ROSE: Nothing. I just made a few changes.
GREGORY: What did you do to your hair?
ROSE: I lightened it.
GREGORY: And your face. You're wearing makeup!
ROSE: Yeah. Well, women do wear makeup from time to time, Greg. It's not like I had surgery or anything, although my mother offered.

GREGORY: You lost weight, too.
ROSE: Well, thank you.
GREGORY: What have you done?
ROSE: What have I done? I'm wearing makeup. I've lost a few pounds. I
    didn't name names before a Senate committee.

When Gregory says he feels betrayed, Rose zings him with "What difference does it make what I look like? You never looked at me anyway." He obviously has, else he wouldn't recognize the changes. But Rose is on a roll now. She likes the way she looks, and she's sorry that it's upset his mathematical equation. As she gets ready to leave again, her speech reminds us of what Ronnie says to Loretta in *Moonstruck* about love being messy:

> I settled for something I didn't want. I think your theories about rela-
> tionships are total bullshit. I believe in love and lust and sex and
> romance. I don't want everything to add up to some perfect equation. I
> want mess and chaos. I want someone to go crazy out of his mind for
> me. I want to feel passion and heat and sweat and madness. I want
> valentines and cupid and all the rest of that crap. I want it all.

Gregory is speechless, especially after Rose tells him she doesn't love him anymore and walks out. It seems all the more manipulative because we know she doesn't mean it. The whole scene has been a snare, a trap, a scheme to show Gregory just how wrong he was to reject her, and somehow we like her less for her behavior here.

Perhaps Rose is just cutting loose. The makeover has brought her back to life, and she's not afraid to look good, despite her sister's warning: "Now you'll spend an extra hour in front of the mirror every morning and every night. And now you'll be the one to walk into a room and scan it for who looks better than you and who doesn't. And, as the years go by, the numbers change. One day you'll walk into a room, and you're the last woman any man notices." Claire's notion of beauty pits woman against woman in competition for a man's favor. Rose is too smart to buy into that.

Perhaps it's the revenge element of the makeover genre that kicks into high gear here. Gregory has hurt Rose, and, instead of reaffirming her makeover (which has given her confidence and reassurance that she was always beautiful) as a good thing, he's angry. She's turned into the thing he most fears: a beautiful woman who will eventually dump him. In addition, Rose gets her revenge on Alex for marrying Claire, who soon tires of him and walks out. Alex invites Rose over for a romantic dinner, but in the middle of their passionate moment, she realizes that she doesn't

The Mirror Has Two Faces (TriStar, 1996). (*Left*) BEFORE: Like Audrey Hepburn before her, Barbra Streisand can never look plain. Even in her before state, with baggy clothes and glasses, she commands our attention with her photogenic features and larger-than-life persona. Her Professor Rose Morgan, already attractive inside and out, just *thinks* she's not as beautiful as her mother (Lauren Bacall) and her sister (Mimi Rogers). In this scene, she has an auditorium full of students eating out of her hand. (*Right*) AFTER: Rose's makeover, triggered by husband Gregory's (Jeff Bridges) bizarre rejection of her sexual advances and her mother's affirmation of her beauty, takes its own strange turn to diva extraordinaire. Her pose goes beyond self improvement to sexual challenge, reminiscent of Mae West's lines to Cary Grant in *She Done Him Wrong*: "Come up. See me. I won't tell." By the final scene, Rose has softened her "I'll show him" stance. Throwing an old chenille robe over new silk pajamas, she finds a compromise between her pre and post makeover modes and meets her husband halfway.

want Alex. "I always thought I wasn't good enough for you," she laughs. "But you are, you are good enough for me, Rose," Alex pleads. "But Alex, *you're* not good enough for *me*," she zings as she makes her exit.

It takes Gregory's meltdown to satisfy Rose. He wails to his friend, "Henry, I love Rose. I love the old Rose, the one with no makeup and baggy clothes who loves the perfect bite. I thought she was quite beautiful." He ends up screaming her name in the middle of the street below her apartment at 6:00 A.M. like Stanley Kowalski in *A Street Car Named Desire* and wrestling with the doorman. "He's insane," Hannah says to Rose. "I know. Isn't it wonderful?" she laughs as she goes down to save him. She has thrown her old chenille robe over her new silk pajamas, to signify her compromise between the old Rose and the new. "God, you're beautiful," Gregory tells a grateful, tearful Rose as he apologizes for his stupid behavior. "I don't care if you are pretty. I love you anyway." They end up dancing in the street in a scene that seems to go on forever while Puccini's *Turandot* swells under the action and transitions into Streisand's and Bryan Adams's duet, "I Finally Found Someone."

In the end, *The Mirror Has Two Faces* shows how two people help each other fit and shed their preconceived notions about the opposite sex. It's like they know the answer to the problem, but they have to figure out how to arrive at that answer, step by step. Gregory won't listen to his physical reaction to her, and he doesn't trust what he sees in women. Rose isn't listening to herself, and the mirror's not telling her the truth—that she is already beautiful. Rose's before and after are close. What she really adds is glamour, like the star herself. Her compromise between the before and the after at the end of the film tells us that she has come to terms with who she is, and Gregory's acceptance of her outward appearance suggests that he has learned to trust. Like Ronnie and Loretta, they end up getting it all.

My Big Fat Greek Wedding *(2002)*

The story of how *My Big Fat Greek Wedding*, directed by Joel Zwick and written by and starring Nia Vardalos, made it from the stage to the big screen reads like a fairytale. Once upon a time in Winnipeg, Canada, there lived a young, geeky Greek girl named Nia Vardalos with "bangs and glasses from her eyebrows to her chin" (*Nightline*). Her family was big and loud and greek, and everybody knew everybody else's business. The little Greek girl grew up to become a member of the famous Second City comedy troop and told lots of stories about her big, loud, Greek family on the stage. Her well-meaning producer would say, "Try some lipstick, you don't have to be the ugliest person in the room" (qtd. in Onstad).

Geeky Greek girl moved to Los Angeles, turned her schtick into a one-woman play, and people, including busloads of Greeks, came from far and wide to see it. They loved it so much they came back again and brought their friends. Nia's play was so successful that people would say, "This should really be a movie." So she wrote a screenplay, but the big, bad Hollywood producers and agents wanted to change everything. Too Greek. Who cares about Greek? Let's make it about Italians. *You* want to star?! No way. We need Jennifer Lopez. One "mean, evil" producer said: "You're not pretty enough to be a leading lady, you're not fat enough to be a character actor. You're Greek—who cares?" (qtd. in Onstad). They waved big, fat checks in front of Nia, saying, "You're not going to get a better offer" (*Nightline*). But Nia held her Greek head high and held out for just the right producer who would be faithful to her work. One night a famous actress named Rita Wilson, also Greek, who was married to a more famous actor, Tom Hanks, came to see the play. Rita loved Nia's play so much that Nia gave her the screenplay. Rita took the script home to her powerful husband, who came the very next night to see the play for himself. He liked it so much that he called Nia and said, "We're gonna make your movie." Nia stayed cool. "I would like to play the lead role," she told Tom. "Yes, of course, we know. You're going to play the lead role," he assured Nia (*Nightline*). Nia's independent movie was made for $5 million. After six months, it grossed over $200 million (Grossman 129). Geeky Greek girl got the leading role and the last laugh, and everybody lived happily ever after—and a lot richer. But sometimes, Nia says, she still feels like "that girl with the bangs and the glasses" (*Nightline*).

There's not one false moment in *My Big Fat Greek Wedding*, probably because Hanks took a chance, respected the material, and stayed true to Nia Vardalos's vision. The film is, after all, a condensed version of her own family and experiences. "I took 20 years of my life, and I squished them into the year of the movie," she told Ted Koppel on *Nightline*. Her real husband, Ian Gomez, has a bit part as Mike, and many of her family members are extras in the film. Most of the main roles, however, are played by a marvelous ensemble of character actors who represent composites of Nia's real relatives.

Nia herself plays Fotoula Portokalos, a thirty-something "frump girl" whose decision to go to college literally brings her back to life. The wonderful thing about this film, which makes it a fitting conclusion for our makeover canon, is that Vardalos is not conventionally beautiful. She's not a stunner. She's an average-looking woman, and most of the women sitting in the audience can relate to her. She plays a character who chooses to control her own destiny and make herself over, first by going to college and then by changing her appearance, gradually and believably. Her outward transformation comes to reflect the beautiful person she is inside, but we recognize her as a real person, someone we might know, not a goddess. As Roger Ebert wrote in his review, "Five minutes into the film, I relaxed, knowing it was set in the real world, and not in the Hollywood alternative universe where Julia Roberts can't get a date" ("Greek Wedding").

Set in Chicago, not Winnipeg, the movie follows "Toula" who works in her family's Greek restaurant, Dancing Zorba's, as a seating hostess because that's what nice Greek girls who don't get married do. She also still lives at home (complete with Greek columns and Greek statues) with her father, Gus (Michael Constantine), who believes every word has a Greek derivative and every physical ailment can be cured by spraying it with Windex, and her mother, Maria (Lainie Kazan), a warm, wise woman who exudes her own kind of wisdom: "The men may be the head of the house, but the women are the neck, and they can turn the head any way they want." Her brother, Nick (Louis Mandylor), also lives at home and cooks at the family restaurant, but he longs to be an artist. Perfect sister Athena (Stavroula Logothettis) has followed the expected path for Greek women to marry Greek boys, make Greek babies, and feed everyone until the day they die.

Toula has aunts, uncles and 27 first cousins alone, and though they all show up for family functions, they are mostly represented by a few characters. Andrea Martin (also a Second City alumna) plays Aunt Voula, Gerry Mendicino plays her husband, Taki, and the cousins are all rolled into their children: Nikki (Gia Carides) and Angelo (Joey Fatone of 'N Sync). The camera work might not be fancy in this film, but the soft dissolves from one scene to the next tie this big, loud, rowdy family inextricably together. The movie opens in darkness and rain. We see Toula and her father through the windshield of his sleek, black Cadillac as he pulls up in front of Dancing Zorba's. A subtitle tells us that it's Chicago, 5:00 A.M. Windshield wipers obstruct any clear view of Toula, but we can make out a big, uncovered yawn, drab and stringy dark hair, and glasses. Her father looks over at her and says the first words in the film: "You better get married soon. You starting to look old." Gus, obsessed with the fact that his daughter is over thirty and not married, will repeat this line several times throughout the first act of the film. Toula does look old. As she helps her father open the restaurant, we see a woman who has stopped caring about herself. Her wet hair hangs in clumps, her ears are covered with red muffs, her face is totally void of makeup, and she's wearing thick, dark glasses. She removes a rumpled sweater only to reveal a rumpled white blouse.

Toula's voiceover sets up her story: "When I was growing up, I knew I was different. The other girls were blonde and delicate, and I was a swarthy six-year-old with sideburns." A flashback shows those blonde and delicate girls making fun of Toula as a child and refusing to sit with her at lunch. More flashbacks show Toula at different stages of her life, but they all illustrate the idea of "otherness." She had to attend Greek school; other girls didn't. Being Greek has made Toula different, and, in her mind, not better. "You should be proud to be Greek," her father tells a twelve-year-old Toula who rolls her eyes.

The exposition introduces the rest of the family as they move in and out of the restaurant. They are loud and colorful compared to Toula, who wears an unflattering, nondescript, loose-fitting brown blouse and slacks and remains in the periphery of the frame as she pours coffee for customers. A child's barrette holds her limp hair to one side. Toula watches her family from the sidelines, taking everything in. She loves them, but she looks at them sometimes with tolerant amusement and sometimes with embarrassment.

In a corner booth, we see her father conferring with Maria, Voula, and Taki about Toula. He's embarrassed that she's not married yet and that she's looking so old. As they assess Toula's appearance, Voula says, "She not so bad." Nobody's convinced, not even Voula. Gus wants to send his daughter to Greece so she can pick out a nice Greek husband. Outside in the back alley, Toula pulls out a brochure for college, crumples it up, and then puts in back in her pocket. In a voiceover she says, "I wish my life were different. I wish I were braver, or prettier, or just happy. But it's useless to dream because nothing ever changes."

An invisible fairy godmother must have overheard her wish because in the next scene, we see Prince Charming enter in the form of tall and handsome Ian Miller (John Corbett). Ian is an English professor, and a more sweet, kind, endearing, worthy prince we've yet to find in filmdom. Ian has come into the restaurant with his colleague, Mike (played by Vardolas's real life husband), who wants to fix him up with any number of women who, to Ian, all look the same. Like Toula, Ian just goes through the motions. "My life was boring," he later tells Toula. "And then I met you. And you're interesting and beautiful and fun." Still later he will tell her that she brought him back to life.

Unlike other heroes of the makeover genre, Ian actually *sees* Toula in the before state. She's not invisible to him, and he's certainly not invisible to her. She can't take her eyes off of him as she pours coffee into his cup instead of Mike's and makes him laugh by telling him she's his very own "private Greek statue." But Ian isn't the catalyst for Toula's makeover. She doesn't make herself over for him; she does it for herself.

Toula approaches her father about going back to school to take some computer classes so that she can update their system. "Don't you want me to do something with my life?" she asks. "Yes. Get married and make babies!" he yells in frustration. It's Toula's mother who argues her daughter's case, and when we see Toula next, she's striding confidently, happily out of Harry S. Truman College. Vardalos explained why she included this scene to Ted Koppel:

> I was ... not exactly cool. I don't think I'm cool now. But I'm a little cooler. But I went to college, and I found out who I was when I was there. I really discovered that I could fit into society, or maybe not fit, but I could kind of get along. And so I wanted to portray that this character goes to college and finds out who she is. Some of the reviews say she has a makeover, and I'm like no, no, no, no. That's not what happens. She goes to college and finds out who she is. And then she feels like enough of a person to attract Ian Miller [*Nightline*].

Bolstered by her decision to attend college, we see Toula's confidence grow. This, in turn, gives her the courage to start changing the way she looks outside. The point that Vardalos makes is that Toula controls what happens to her, and she makes those physical changes because she wants to, not because she wants to "get" Ian Miller. At this point, she has no idea whether she'll ever see this man again.

The next few shots show Toula's transition. We see her first at her mirror. Her hair is in curlers, and she is applying makeup and trying to insert contact lenses. Nobody breaks her glasses or tells her she would look better without them. *She* sheds the frumpy clothes. When Toula stands before a full-length mirror, she smiles at the reflection wearing a flowing pink print skirt, white shell and pink V-neck sweater. Her hair is curled and pulled back to show her attractive, strong features. Several more shots show her at school, looking pretty in an ice blue turtleneck sweater. "Blonde and delicate" girls smile at her and invite her to sit at their table. She's striking, and, next to her, they all look the same. The more confident Toula becomes, the more vivid the colors Toula wears, like beautiful reds and vibrant blues, as well as chic black. As in *Pleasantville* (1998), the color signifies a return to life.

Toula also moves to the center of the frame, signifying her shift from onlooker to full, active participant. Maria masterminds a plan for Toula to work at Voula's travel agency because she now knows computers, and it's here that Toula again meets Ian. He notices her through the window as she happily, and expertly, services customers over the phone and tends the business. They meet after a double slapstick routine and end up collapsing in a heap of laughter on the floor. "Do you want to have dinner with me?" he asks. "Yeah," she responds. No hesitation.

Their courtship is lovely, funny, and fraught with cultural angst. On their first date, Ian discovers that Toula is the woman at Dancing Zorba's. "You're that waitress," he muses. "I was going through a phase.... I was frump girl," she tells him, hesitatingly. And here comes the line that made *us* fall in love with this man: "I don't know frump girl, but I remember you." He doesn't care who she was. He doesn't care that no one in her family has ever dated a non–Greek. He thinks she's beautiful and funny. Her father, on the other hand, is mortified. He trots out a series of increasingly bizarre Greek suitors, but Toula wants Ian.

Ian also wants Toula. In a beautiful scene, the two lie on his bed. Moonlight streaming through the blinds throws light and shadows across Toula's face. She looks gorgeous and happy. Ian lies on top, his head at her waist. "I love you," he whispers. "Will you marry me?"

Their announcement throws her father into a tizzy. "How can she do this to me?" he wails. As Maria calms him, we see Toula in a blue, flowing nightgown on her porch, listening to her parents, looking every inch a living incarnation of the statue of Aphrodite, goddess of love and beauty, that stands silently behind her.

Ian, willing to do whatever he must to appease Gus and make Toula happy, gets baptized in the Greek church. When Mike says, "I guess her family has you by the short hairs," Ian just smiles and nods happily. His love is unconditional. "You're a part of your family. I love you. I'll do whatever it takes," he gently tells Toula. The baptism scene, like so many other scenes in the movie, is subtly layered. While Ian stands stripped down to his undershorts in what appears to be a child's play pool, being oiled up and immersed in water, Toula stands next to her brother, Nick, and says, "Any minute he's going to look at me and say, you're so not worth this." Her brother smiles, looks at his sister, and whispers, "Yes, you are." One of the great joys of watching this movie is this affirmation of family affection.

The differences between Ian's family and Toula's becomes hilariously clear when Zwick juxtaposes shots of the couple partying with the boisterous Portokalos clan, who can fill up a room quickly, and the Millers. Ian is an only child, and his parents Rodney (Bruce Gray) and Harriet (Fiona Reid) remind us of that famous television couple, Ozzy and Harriet, not only in the sound of their names. Harriet looks like she stepped right out of a Talbot's catalog with her slacks, sweater sets, and pearls. Miller calm, order, and silence counters Portokalos chaos. Ian and Toula sit facing his "white toast" parents in perfect balance as they make polite small talk. When Harriet wants to hold the reception at their country club, Ian matter-of-factly tells them that they will get married in Toula's church, since religion is important to them and it never has been to the

Millers, and the reception will be held at Aphrodite's Palace. Rodney and Harriet smile and nod politely. By the end of the film, they have been completely embraced by the Portokalos's, with a little help from a lot of ouzo.

It's easy to see why this Prince Charming comes to life when he meets Toula and her family. They tease him, play tricks on him, swarm him, smother him with kisses, feel his hair, teach him to dance, and accept him. Vardalos confesses that there are definite parallels between the fictional Ian Miller and her husband. "My husband is the type of person that can ... get rolled over by my family. And he just gets up, shakes himself off and goes, 'what happened?' And he's fine.... I think that John Corbett ... was able to portray this unconditional love, without losing his masculinity that the real Ian has" (*Nightline*).

The poster for the film shows Corbett as Ian in his tuxedo, tie undone, looking lovingly at Toula, who is smiling and truly beautiful in her wedding dress as she holds her family back behind her. The tagline reads: "Love is here to stay ... so is her family." It represents what Desson Howe of the *Washington Post* calls the movie's "tremendously sweet spirit" ("*Greek* Aisle" WE43). And part of that sweet spirit comes not only from Toula and Ian's relationship but also from the female relationships in the film.

Unlike *The Mirror Has Two Faces*, the bonds between Toula and her mother, grandmother, sister, aunts, and cousins are never in question. There's no jealousy or pettiness here. In one scene, Toula sits on her bed worried that her marriage to a non–Greek is killing her dad. Maria comes in, sits next to her daughter, and weaves a story about her hard life in Greece into a moral: don't let anybody tell you how to live your life. Gently, she says, "I gave you life so that you could live it." Just then, Toula's grandmother comes in with a box filled with mementos and photographs of her as a young woman. She reaches underneath, takes out a crown of dried flowers that she wore for her own wedding, and places it on Toula's head. The end of the scene shows three generations of women reflected like a beautiful portrait in a mirror.

On the morning of Toula and Ian's wedding, the Portokalos kitchen is filled with all the Portokalos women in various stages of dress. Mustache creame, tweezers, curlers, zit concealer, nail polish, hair brushes, panty hose—they all fly in a flurry of arms and elbows as they help each other and Toula get ready. The women pass Toula's wedding dress from hand to hand, and when she turns to face the mirror, she's in frilly layers of white from head to toe. "I look like a snow beast," she declares. The dress, the makeup, the hair are all overdone, but Toula, whose self-motivated makeover seems natural and never over the top, finds the patience to indulge her family without hurting their feelings; consequently, her bridesmaids happily walk down the isle in their vampy, low-cut, form-fitting, ice-blue dresses, and Toula floats toward Ian in a white lacy bubble. Her side of the church overflows with relatives, while his family takes up a paltry four isles.

The actual wedding ceremony takes up less film time than the reception, where the real cultural blending of families and Gus's gracious capitulation to the inevitable occurs. He stands before the minions of Portokalos relatives and the Millers, who have been encircled, and delivers a touching, funny toast to the bride and groom. Portokalos means orange in Greek. Miller means apple. They are all different, but, in the end, they are all fruit. He embraces his daughter and Ian and gives them the deed to a house, the one right next door to his.

By the reception, Toula has wiped off much of the makeup and removed most of the bows and trim from her dress. She and Ian sit with ease and contentment, and, as they rise to dance, Toula's aunt Voula says to her husband, "Ah, Taki, he *looks* Greek." Toula's courage, her resolve, her makeover, which blends the best of the Greek world and the world outside, have not only bridged two cultures but have also brought her back into the circle of family and into life. A swish pan to six years later shows the cycle beginning again as Ian and Toula send their daughter off to Greek school.

The female characters in this chapter—Alice Hyatt, Loretta Castorini, Rose Morgan, and Fotoula Portokalos—assure us that America is still a melting pot of cultures, and their stories offer hope that we can still turn out successful movies about middle-age women and the issues and concerns that affect them. More importantly, these women represent a more realistic subgenre of makeover movies. None of the actresses who portray these characters are conventionally beautiful. Ellen Burstyn, Cher, Barbra Streisand, and Nia Vardalos can be striking, but they're not classic beauties. Real women can relate to them as people not unlike themselves. Their makeovers are not so overdone as to render them unrecognizable. Jamie Lee Curtis would be proud. There's not a fraud in the group. These characters wear their makeovers comfortably because they've used the mirror inside to create them.

Conclusion:
Mapping the Makeover

We have reached the open sea, with some charts...
—Francis Crawford, *Checkmate*

Our attempt to map the terrain of important makeover films is far from an assertion that their time has passed. The success of *Maid in Manhattan* (2002) probably assures their continuation. Some critics of the makeover genre might say it *should* be put to rest. Female viewers, they might claim, watch these films for the guilty pleasure of it; we know *Pretty Woman* isn't good for us, but we can't resist the desire to see a Cinderella reality where a wretched life, like Vivian Ward's, can be transformed by a new hairdo, gorgeous clothes and a wealthy lover who becomes her Prince. Perhaps we've become so desensitized to what Laura Mulvey calls *"to-be-looked-at-ness,"* that we no longer read destruction in all the gazing directed at makeover heroines (19). Or maybe we're all taken in by the big lie: that pouffing out Ann Hathaway's (*The Princess Diaries*) hair, beefing up her brows, handing her the dark rimmed glasses, and dressing her in baggy clothes renders her plain, in need of some *serious* work. (Hathaway's featured, by the way, in *Glamour's* January 2003 "Make Me Over!" Issue, getting multiple makeovers. Hathaway says she "dresses like a Stepford wife one moment and Alanis Morissette the next"[108]).

At their worst, makeover films seek to calcify beauty and its reverse into a rigid set of signs, like the before and after code repeated again and again. Or, like *Josie and the Pussycats*, they incite us into frenzied acquisition, commanding women to be good little capitalists, to buy more expensive clothes and shoes, like the ones in Hathaway's *Glamour* shots, as a means of approaching perfection. Or, like the films in the Pygmalion chapter, they try to make us believe in the damaging, ancient assumption that women's bodies are essentially unacceptable, and must constantly be tended. These films imply that women can't be trusted to orchestrate their own changes. Control must be handed over to someone else. Gracie Hart, for example, a woman who hasn't internalized the beauty codes, gets a punishing makeover administered by a crew of technicians who ridicule her as they work. To attempt a combination of mental and physical perfection, "inadequate women," like Tally Atwater, must undergo strenuous courses of improvement, usually overseen by those lords of culture, males.

Certainly, there's proof that many real women harbor anxieties about themselves and their bodies, and that plenty of "helpers" avidly await a chance to "fix" what's wrong. That "Make Me Over!" issue of *Glamour* capitalizes on such feelings, "helping" women who worry about being too heavy, unstylish, or even "dirty," to new looks (*Style* 115). (Shades of Dr. Jaquith—all the befores who wore glasses were without them in the *Glamour* afters.) Confirming the pervasiveness of such anxiety, a recent *People* poll reported that 80 percent of the women questioned "said images of women on TV and in movies, fashion magazines and advertising make them feel insecure about their looks" (Dam 114). But not only ordinary women anguish over surface appearance.

Even celebrities considered beautiful and desirable by the rest of us think they should be closer to perfection. Kate Winslet, star of *Titanic* (1997), *Sense and Sensibility* (1995), and *Iris* (2001), recently permitted *GQ* to airbrush a picture of her that was to appear on the magazine's cover. *GQ* editor Dylan Jones said of the photo: "Various parts have been improved, including her stomach and legs" (E5). This Pygmalionesque remark characterizes blatant falsehood as an "improvement" on reality and assumes the right to make Winslet's "parts" fit a proscribed, male view of female beauty. It's surprising that Winslet, whose film choices— especially the nude scenes in *Iris*—suggest a confident, independent spirit, would lightly endorse the change. In a reversal of Jamie Lee Curtis's "True Thighs" attempt to appear, for once, as herself, Winslet allowed the "makeover" to stand for her.

But to think that women watch, adore, and don't question the destructive makeover messages and all the "perfect" images they see posits a passive audience. That same *People* poll finds that many women resent the insinuation made by all those poreless faces and svelte bodies, and that they understand the artifice involved: "We are looking at ourselves in the mirror," one woman commented, "and comparing ourselves to women who … [have] had the best of what Hollywood can do to make them look great" (116).

Surely those who return, again and again, to makeover movies—even bad ones, like *Pretty Woman*—are drawn by more than guilty pleasure, or by the parade of "improved" female stars. Even a flawed narrative can disclose a germ of truth. Consider the case of playwright and screenwriter David Henry Hwang, who gives us an example of the way an audience and an artist can reclaim a stereotypical text. Hwang, who remembers watching the film version of Rodgers and Hammerstein's *Flower Drum Song* (1961) as a teenager and enjoying what seemed to him to be "one of the few positive portrayals of people who looked like me" (Phillips). Later, Hwang understood why a stereotypical view of the tensions between generations of Asian Americans, authored by two non–Asian Americans, troubled many viewers. During his college years "[*Flower Drum Song*] became something to be demonized," Hwang commented (Phillips). But something still drew him, and other Asian Americans, to that work. Now, Hwang's written a "more conflicted" version of the musical that retains the original songs while it alters the clichéd story. Hwang expected more "flak" about the changes, but he philosophizes, "I think people are able to have some perspective on [*Flower Drum Song*]—accept it as an artifact of its time, appreciate what was useful and important about it, and what was creaky and stereotypical about it." Hwang calls his reworking of *Flower Drum Song* "having a conversation with it" (Phillips).

Hwang is not the only reclaimer of reviled texts. In "The Search for Tomorrow in Today's Soap Operas," Tania Modleski discloses a "possible feminist aesthetic" for soap operas (43). Critics generally relegate these narratives, characterized as melodramas, much like the label "weepy" attached to *Now, Voyager,* to the category of guilty pleasure. Surely, women who watch them are mindless victims of the sticky pull of packaged romance. Modleski, however, suggests that female viewers know how to *use* soaps for their own purposes. She also asks television writers and feminist artists to see daytime drama as a starting point for creation and investigation; they "*don't* have to start from nothing: rather, they can rechannel and make explicit" the implied critique of "masculine power and masculine pleasure" (46). Both Hwang and Modleski see future possibility in stereotypical narratives; both understand the identification that draws their audiences.

We believe that many women watch makeover films for similar, complicated reasons that go beyond familiarity with the plot, whether it's fueled by the creaky and stereotypical before and after codes, which we identify and trace, or by the accessory-triggered moment of recognition, as shown by an old shoe (or a tiny slipper), which we discuss in the Cinderella chapter. We shake our heads at the persistent patterns of female-to-female insensitivity and downright meanness. (Remember, most of these films were authored and directed by men.) We revel, a *little* unhealthily, in those payback moments, when the heroine, like Tess Mcgill, gets well-deserved revenge. We acknowledge that these films are, indeed, artifacts of their times, and we look for differences, like Danielle de Barbarac, Cinderella with a *real* name, to tell that us the times are changing.

At their best, these films can provide us with useful and important ways of thinking about ourselves, not just familiar forms and predictable outcomes. We can see ourselves in them, sometimes trapped, sometimes liberated by the moment of change. No matter what the "happy" endings imply, the crux lies in the tension between internal and external identity acted out on the screen. Watch Alice Hyatt's painful journey to a new self, defined by her relaxed, happy face and softer look, and her amazing effort seems worth the outcome. View films written and directed by female artists, like Amy Heckerling's *Clueless* (1995) and Nia Vardalos's *My Big Fat Greek Wedding* (2002), whose inventive reworkings of makeover plots tell us this is far from an exhausted narrative. Empathize with characters like Loretta Castorini and Fotula Portokalos who encourage us to risk transformation that might trigger happiness more permanent than any mascara.

We live in a culture that clamors for female perfection. Avoiding that siren song of self that begins and ends with surface appearances, each of us can take from makeover films what we need to create a map of discovery. Following our "maps," which might resemble self-authored poems of voyaging, we can "sail forth to seek and find" (Whitman, "Untold Want"), using the past to envision a more affirming future.

Our discussion ends here; we hope you will continue it.

Filmography

The films are arranged by release date. Principal characters are listed in alphabetical order.

Pygmalion

Released 1938; *Running Time:* 96 minutes

Producer: Gabriel Pascal for MGM; *Directors:* Anthony Asquith and Leslie Howard; *Screenwriter:* George Bernard Shaw; *Cinematographer:* Harry Strandling, Sr.; *Editor:* David Lean; *Art Director:* John Bryan; *Set Designer:* Laurence Irving; *Costume Designer:* Ladislaw Czettel; *Music:* Arthur Honegger

Cast: Jean Cadell (Mrs. Pearce); Everley Gregg (Mrs. Eynsford-Hill); Wendy Hiller (Eliza Doolittle); Leslie Howard (Professor Henry Higgins); Wilfrid Lawson (Alfred Doolittle); Marie Lohr (Mrs. Higgins); Leueen MacGrath (Clara Eynsford Hill); Esme Percy (Count Aristid Karpathy); Scott Sunderland (Colonel George Pickering); David Tree (Freddy Eynsford-Hill)

Now, Voyager

Released 1942; *Running Time:* 117 minutes

Producer: Hal B. Wallis for MGM; *Director:* Irving Rapper; *Screenwriter:* Casey Robinson; *Cinematographer:* Sol Polito; *Editor:* Robert M. Haas; *Art Director:* Robert M. Haas; *Set Designer:* Fred M. MacLean; *Costume Designer:* Orry-Kelly; *Music:* Max Steiner

Cast: Ilka Chase (Lisa Vale); Gladys Cooper (Mrs. Vale); Bette Davis (Charlotte Vale); Bonita Granville (June Vale); Paul Henreid (Jerry Durrance); John Loder (Elliot Livingston); Lee Patrick (Deb McIntyre); Claude Rains (Dr. Jaquith); Mary Wickes (Nurse Pickford)

Cinderella

Released 1950; *Running Time:* 74 minutes

Producer: Walt Disney for Disney; *Directors:* Clyde Geronimi, Wilfred Jackson, and Hamilton Luske; *Screenwriters:* Ken Anderson, Homer Brightman, et al.; *Editor:* Donald Halliday; *Directing Animator:* Marc Davis; *Music:* Mack David, Al Hoffman, Jerry Livingston, Paul J. Smith, and Oliver Wallace

Cast (Voices): Eleanor Audley (Lady Tremaine); Lucille Bliss (Anastasia); Verna Felton (Fairy Godmother); June Foray (Lucifer); Betty Lou Gerson (Narrator); James MacDonald (Gus, Jacques, and Bruno); Clint McCauley (Mice); William

Phipps (Prince Charming); Luis Van Rooten (King and Grand Duke); Rhoda Williams (Drizella); Ilene Woods (Cinderella)

Sabrina

Released 1954; *Running Time:* 113 minutes
Producer: Billy Wilder for Paramount; *Director:* Billy Wilder; *Screenwriters:* Samuel A. Taylor, Billy Wilder, and Ernest Lehman; *Cinematographer:* Charles Lang; *Editor:* Arthur P. Schmidt; *Art Direction:* Hal Pereira and Walter H. Tyler; *Set Designer:* Sam Comer; *Costume Designer:* Edith Head; *Music:* Frederick Hollander
Cast: Humphrey Bogart (Linus Larrabee); Francis X. Bushman (Mr. Tyson); Ellen Corby (Miss McCardle); Marcel Dalio (Baron St. Fontanel); Walter Hampden (Oliver Larrabee); Audrey Hepburn (Sabrina Fairchild); William Holden (David Larrabee); Martha Hyer (Elizabeth Tyson); Joan Vohs (Gretchen Van Horn); Nella Walker (Maude Larrabee); John Williams (Thomas Fairchild)

Funny Face

Released 1957; *Running Time:* 103 minutes
Producer: Roger Edens for Paramount; *Director:* Stanley Donen; *Screenwriter:* Leonard Gershe; *Cinematographer:* Ray June; *Editor:* Frank Bracht; *Art Directors:* George W. Davis and Hal Pereira; *Set Designers:* Sam Comer and Ray Moyer; *Costume Designers:* Hubert de Givenchy (Paris costumes) and Edith Head; *Music:* Adolph Deutsch, Roger Edens, Leonard Gershe, Ira Gershwin, and George Gershwin
Cast: Fred Astaire (Dick Avery); Michel Auclair (Emile Flostre); Robert Flemyng (Paul Duval); Virginia Gibson (Babs); Audrey Hepburn (Jo Stockton); Ruta Lee (Lettie); Kay Thompson (Maggie Prescott)

My Fair Lady

Released 1964; *Running Time:* 170 minutes
Producer: Jack L. Warner for Warner Bros.; *Director:* George Cukor; *Screenwriter:* Alan Jay Lerner; *Cinematographer:* Harry Stradling, Sr.; *Editor:* William H. Ziegler; *Production Designer:* Cecil Beaton; *Set Designer:* George James Hopkins; *Costume Designer:* Cecil Beaton; *Music:* Frederick Loewe
Cast: Jeremy Brett (Freddie Eynsford-Hill); Gladys Cooper (Mrs. Higgins); Isobel Elsom (Mrs. Eynsford-Hill); Rex Harrison (Professor Henry Higgins); Audrey Hepburn (Eliza Doolittle); Stanley Holloway (Alfred P. Doolittle); Wilfrid Hyde-White (Colonel Hugh Pickering); Mona Washbourne (Mrs. Pearce)

Rodgers and Hammerstein's Cinderella

Released 1965; *Running Time:* 84 minutes
Producer: Charles S. Dubin for CBS; *Director:* Charles S. Dubin; *Screenwriter:* Joseph Schrank; *Costume Designer:* George Whittaker; *Music:* Richard Rodgers
Cast: Pat Carroll (Prunella); Stuart Damon (Prince); Celeste Holm (Fairy Godmother); Walter Pidgeon (King); Ginger Rogers (Queen); Barbara Ruick (Esmerelda); Jo Van Fleet (Stepmother); Lesley Ann Warren (Cinderella)

Alice Doesn't Live Here Anymore

Released 1974; *Running Time:* 112 minutes

Producers: Audrey Maas and David Susskind for Warner Bros.; *Director:* Martin Scorsese; *Screenwriter:* Robert Getchell; *Cinematographer:* Kent L. Wakeford; *Editor:* Marcia Lucas; *Production Designer:* Toby Carr Rafelson; *Music:* Richard LaSalle

Cast: Mia Bendixsen (Young Alice); Ellen Burstyn (Alice Hyatt); Valerie Curtin (Vera); Jodie Foster (Doris/Audrey); Lelia Goldoni (Bea); Billy Green Bush (Donald); Harvey Keitel (Ben); Kris Kristofferson (David); Diane Ladd (Flo); Alfred Lutter (Tommy Hyatt); Vic Tayback (Mel)

Shampoo

Released 1975; *Running Time:* 109 minutes

Producer: Warren Beatty for Columbia; *Director:* Hal Ashby; *Screenwriter:* Robert Towne and Warren Beatty; *Cinematographer:* Laszlo Kovacs; *Editor:* Robert C. Jones; *Production Designer:* Richard Sylbert; *Art Designer:* W. Stewart Campbell; *Set Designer:* George Gaines; *Costume Designer:* Anthea Sylbert; *Music:* Paul Simon

Cast: Warren Beatty (George Roundy); Julie Christie (Jackie Shawn); Carrie Fisher (Lorna); Lee Grant (Felicia); Goldie Hawn (Jill); Jack Warden (Lester)

The Stepford Wives

Released 1975; *Running Time:* 115 minutes

Producer: Edgar J. Scherick for Columbia; *Director:* Bryan Forbes; *Screenwriter:* William Goldman; *Cinematographer:* Owen Roizman; *Editor:* Timothy Gee; *Production Designer:* Gene Callahan; *Set Designer:* Robert Drumheller; *Costume Designer:* Anna Hill Johnstone; *Music:* Michael Small

Cast: Tina Louise (Charmaine Wimperis); Peter Masterson (Walter Eberhart); Patrick O'Neal (Dale Coba); Paula Prentiss (Bobbie Markowe); Katharine Ross (Joanna Eberhart)

The Slipper and the Rose

Released 1976; *Running Time:* 127 minutes

Producer: Stuart Lyons for Paradine Co-Productions; *Director:* Bryan Forbes; *Screenwriters:* Bryan Forbes, Richard M. Sherman, and Robert B. Sherman; *Cinematographer:* Tony Imi; *Editor:* Timothy Gee; *Production Designer:* Ray Simm; *Art Director:* Bert Davey; *Costume Designer:* Julie Harris; *Music:* Angela Morley

Cast: Rosalind Ayres (Isabella); Lally Bowers (Queen); Richard Chamberlain (Prince Edward); Gemma Craven (Cinderella); Annette Crosbie (Fairy Godmother); Edith Evans (Dowager Queen); Michael Hordern (King); Margaret Lockwood (Stepmother)

Grease

Released 1978; *Running Time:* 110 minutes

Producers: Allan Carr and Robert Stigwood for Paramount; *Director:* Randal Kleiser *Screenwriters:* Jim Jacobs and Warren Casey (play); Allan Carr and Bronte Woodard; *Cinematographer:* Bill Butler; *Editor:* John F. Burnett; *Production Designer:* Philip M. Jefferies; *Set Designer:* James L. Berkey; *Costume Designer:* Albert Wolsky; *Music:* John Farrar and Barry Gibb

Cast: Eve Arden (Principal McGee); Frankie Avalon (Teen Angel); Joan Blondell (Vi); Edd Byrnes (Vince Fontaine); Sid Caesar (Coach Calhoun); Stockard Channing (Rizzo); Jeff Conaway (Kenickie); Didi Conn (Frenchy); Dinah Manoff (Marty Maraschino); Olivia Newton-John (Sandy Olsen); Barry Pearl (Doody); John Travolta (Danny Zuko); Michael Tucci (Sonny); Kelly Ward (Putzie)

Moonstruck

Released 1987; *Running Time:* 102 minutes

Producers: Norman Jewison and Patrick J. Palmer for MGM; *Director:* Norman Jewison; *Screenwriter:* John Patrick Stanley; *Cinematographer:* David Watkin; *Editor:* Lou Lombardo; *Production Designer:* Philip Rosenberg; *Set Designer:* Philip Smith; *Costume Designer:* Theoni V. Aldredge; *Music:* Dick Hyman

Cast: Cher (Loretta Castorini); Danny Aiello (Johnny Cammareri); Julie Bovasso (Rita Cappomaggi); Nicolas Cage (Ronny Cammareri); Feodor Chaliapin, Jr. (Grandfather); Olympia Dukakis (Rose Castorini); Vincent Gardenia (Cosmo Castorini); Anita Gillette (Mona); Louis Guss (Raymond Cappomaggi); John Mahoney (Perry)

Working Girl

Released 1988; *Running Time:* 109 minutes

Producer: Douglas Wick for 20th Century–Fox; *Director:* Mike Nichols; *Screenwriter:* Kevin Wade; *Cinematographer:* Michael Ballhaus; *Editor:* Sam O'Steen; *Production Designer:* Patrizia von Brandenstein; *Set Designer:* George DeTitta, Jr.; *Costume Designer:* Ann Roth; *Music:* Carly Simon

Cast: Alec Baldwin (Mick Dugan); Philip Bosco (Oren Trask); Joan Cusack (Cyn); Olympia Dukakis (Personnel Director); Nora Gunn (Ginny); Harrison Ford (Jack Trainer); Melanie Griffith (Tess McGill); Sigourney Weaver (Katherine Parker)

Pretty Woman

Released 1990; *Running Time:* 125 minutes

Producers: Arnon Milchan and Steven Reuther for Touchstone; *Director:* Garry Marshall; *Screenwriter:* J. F. Lawton; *Cinematographer:* Charles Minsky; *Editors:* Raja Gosnell and Priscilla Nedd-Friendly; *Production Designer:* Albert Brenner; *Set Designer:* Garrett Lewis; *Costume Designer:* Marilyn Vance; *Music:* James Newton Howard

Cast: Jason Alexander (Phil Stuckey); Ralph Bellamy (James Morse); Elinor Donahue (Bridget); Hector Elizondo (Barney); Richard Gere (Edward Lewis); Alex Hyde-White (David Morse); Julia Roberts (Vivian Ward); Laura San Giacomo (Kit DeLuca)

Clueless

Released 1995; *Running Time:* 97 minutes

Producers: Robert Lawrence and Scott Rudin for Paramount; *Director:* Amy Heckerling; *Screenwriter:* Amy Heckerling; *Cinematographer:* Bill Pope; *Editor:* Debra Chiate; *Production Designer:* Steven J. Jordan; *Set Designer:* Amy Wells; *Costume Designer:* Mona May; *Music:* David Kitay

Cast: Donald Adeosun-Faison (Murray); Twink Caplan (Miss Geist); Stacey Dash (Dionne Davenport); Elisa Donovan (Amber); Dan Hedaya (Mel Horowitz); Breckin Meyer (Travis Birkenstock); Brittany Murphy (Tai Fraiser); Paul Rudd (Josh); Wallace Shawn (Mr. Hall); Alicia Silverstone (Cher Horowitz); Jeremy Sisto (Elton); Justin Walker (Christian Stovitz)

Sabrina

Released 1995; *Running Time:* 127 minutes

Producers: Sydney Pollack and Scott Rudin for Paramount; *Director:* Sydney Pollack; *Screenwriters:* Samuel A. Taylor, Billy Wilder, Ernest Lehman, Barbara Benedek, and David Rayfiel; *Cinematographer:* Giuseppe Rotunno; *Editor:* Fredric Steinkamp; *Production Designer:* Brian Morris; *Set Designers:* George DeTitta, Jr. and Amy Marshall; *Costume Designers:* Gary Jones, Bernie Pollack, and Ann Roth; *Music:* John Williams

Cast: Fanny Ardant (Irene); Patrick Bruel (Louis); Miriam Colon (Rosa); Richard Crenna (Patrick Tyson); Angie Dickinson (Ingrid Tyson); Harrison Ford (Linus Larrabee); Lauren Holly (Elizabeth Tyson); Dana Ivey (Mack); Greg Kinnear (David Larrabee); Nancy Marchand (Maude Larrabee); Julia Ormond (Sabrina Fairchild); J. Smith-Cameron (Carol); John Wood (Tom Fairchild)

Up Close and Personal

Released 1996; *Running Time:* 124 minutes

Producers: Jon Avnet, Jordan Kerner, and David Nicksay for Touchstone; *Screenwriters:* Joan Didion and John Gregory Dunn; *Cinematographer:* Karl Walter Lindenlaub; *Editor:* Debra Neil-Fisher; *Production Designer:* Jeremy Conway; *Set Designer:* Dorree Cooper; *Costume Designer:* Albert Wolsky; *Music:* Thomas Newman and Diane Warren

Cast: Stockard Channing (Marcia McGrath); Joe Mantegna (Bucky Terranova); Kate Nelligan (Joanna Kennelly); Lily Nicksay (Star Atwater); Dedee Pfeiffer (Luanne Atwater); Michelle Pfeiffer (Tally/Sally Atwater); Glenn Plummer (Ned Jackson); Robert Redford (Warren Justice)

The Mirror Has Two Faces

Released 1996; *Running Time:* 126 minutes

Producers: Arnon Milchan and Barbra Streisand for TriStar; *Director:* Barbra Streisand; *Screenwriter:* Richard LaGravenese; *Cinematographers:* Andrzej Bartkowiak and Dante Spinotti; *Editor:* Jeff Werner; *Production Designer:* Tom H. John; *Set Designer:* Alan Hicks; *Costume Designer:* Theoni V. Aldredge; *Music:* Marvin Hamlisch and Barbra Streisand

Cast: Lauren Bacall (Hannah Morgan); Jeff Bridges (Gregory Larkin); Pierce Brosnan (Alex); Elle Macpherson (Candy); Austin Pendleton (Barry); Mimi Rogers (Claire); George Segal (Henry Fine); Barbra Streisand (Rose Morgan); Brenda Vaccaro (Doris)

Cinderella

Released 1997; *Running Time:* 88 minutes

Producers: Whitney Houston, Mike Moder, and Chris Montan for Disney; *Director:* Robert Iscove; *Screenwriter:* Robert Freedman; *Cinematographer:* Ralf D.

Bode; *Editors:* Casey O. Rohrs and Tanya M. Swerling; *Production Designer:* Randy Ser; *Set Designer:* Julie Kaye Fanton; *Costume Designer:* Ellen Mirojnick; *Music:* Richard Rodgers, Martin Erskine, and Danny Troob

  Cast: Jason Alexander (Lionel); Veanne Cox (Calliope); Natalie Desselle (Minerva); Victor Garber (King Maximillian); Whoopi Goldberg (Queen Constantina); Whitney Houston (Fairy Godmother); Paolo Montalban (The Prince); Brandy Norwood (Cinderella); Bernadette Peters (Stepmother)

Ever After

  Released 1998; *Running Time:* 121 minutes

  Producers: Mireille Soria and Tracey Trench for 20th Century–Fox; *Director:* Andy Tennant; *Screenwriters:* Susannah Grant, Andy Tennant, and Rick Parks; *Cinematographer:* Andrew Dunn; *Editor:* Roger Bondelli; *Production Designer:* Michael Howells; *Set Designer:* Judy Farr; *Costume Designer:* Jenny Beavan; *Music:* George Fenton

  Cast: Drew Barrymore (Danielle DeBarbarac); Megan Dodds (Marguerite DeGhent); Patrick Godfrey (Leonardo daVinci); Anjelica Huston (Baroness Rodmilla DeGhent); Jeroen Krabbe (Auguste DeBarbarac); Melanie Lynskey (Jacqueline DeGhent); Anna Maguire (Young Danielle); Jeanne Moreau (Grande Dame); Judy Parfitt (Queen Marie); Dougray Scott (Prince Henry); Timothy West (King Francis)

She's All That

  Released 1999; *Running Time:* 95 minutes

  Producers: Peter Abrams, Richard N. Gladstein, and Robert L. Levy for Miramax; *Director:* Robert Iscove; *Screenwriter:* R. Lee Fleming, Jr.; *Cinematographer:* Francis Kenny; *Editor:* Casey O. Rohrs; *Production Designer:* Charles Breen; *Set Designer:* Jeffrey Kushon; *Costume Designer:* Denise Wright; *Music:* Stewart Copeland

  Cast: Kieran Culkin (Simon Boggs); Elden Henson (Jesse Jackson); Dule Hill (Preston); Rachael Leigh Cook (Laney Boggs); Matthew Lillard (Brock Hudson); Jodi Lyn O'Keefe (Taylor Vaughan); Tim Matheson (Harlan Siler); Debbi Morgan (Ms. Rousseau); Anna Paquin (Mackenzie Siler); Kevin Pollak (Wayne Boggs); Freddie Prinze, Jr. (Zach Siler); Paul Walker (Dean Sampson)

Miss Congeniality

  Released 2000; *Running Time:* 109 minutes

  Producer: Sandra Bullock and Katie Ford for Castle Rock; *Director:* Donald Petrie; *Screenwriters:* Mark Lawrence, Katie Ford, and Caryn Lucas; *Cinematographer:* Laszlo Kovacs; *Editor:* Billy Weber; *Production Designer:* Peter S. Larkin; *Set Designers:* Barbara Haberecht, Randy Huke, and Leslie E. Rollins; *Costume Designer:* Susie DeSanto; *Music:* Ed Shearmur

  Cast: Candice Bergen (Kathy Morningside); Benjamin Bratt (Eric Matthews); Sandra Bullock (Gracie Hart); Heather Burns (Cheryl Frasier/Miss Rhode Island); Michael Caine (Victor Melling); William Shatner (Stan Fields)

Josie and the Pussycats

  Released 2001; *Running Time:* 98 minutes

Producers: Tony DeRosa-Grund, Tracey E. Edmonds, Chuck Grimes, and Marc E. Platt for MGM/Universal; *Directors:* Harry Elfont and Deborah Kaplan; *Screenwriters:* Richard H. Goldwater and Dan DeCarlo; *Cinematographer:* Matthew Libatique; *Editor:* Peter Teschner; *Production Designer:* Jasna Stefanovic; *Set Designer:* Johanne Hubert; *Costume Designer:* Leesa Evans; *Music:* John Frizzell

 Cast: Alan Cumming (Wyatt Frame); Rosario Dawson (Valerie Brown); Rachael Leigh Cook (Josie McCoy); Gabriel Mann (Alan M); Parker Posey (Fiona); Tara Reid (Melody Valentine)

Legally Blonde

Released 2001; *Running Time:* 96 minutes

 Producers: Ric Kidney and Marc E. Platt for MGM; *Director:* Robert Luketic; *Screenwriters:* Karen McCullah Lutz and Kirsten Smith; *Cinematographer:* Anthony B. Richmond; *Editors:* Anita Brandt Burgoyne and Garth Craven; *Production Designer:* Missy Stewart; *Set Designer:* Katherine Lucas; *Costume Designer:* Sophie Carbonel; *Music:* Rolfe Kent

 Cast: Selma Blair (Vivian); Jennifer Coolidge (Paulette Bonafonte); Matthew Davis (Warner); Victor Garber (Professor Callahan); Ali Larter (Brooke Windham); Oz Perkins (David); Meredith Scott Lynn (Enid); Holland Taylor (Professor Stromwell); Bruce Thomas (UPS Guy); Raquel Welch (Mrs. Windham Vandermark); Luke Wilson (Emmett); Reese Witherspoon (Elle Woods)

The Princess Diaries

Released 2001; *Running Time:* 114 minutes

 Producers: Debra Martin Chase, Whitney Houston, and Mario Iscovich for Disney; *Director:* Garry Marshall; *Screenwriter:* Gina Wendkos; *Cinematographer:* Karl Walter Lindenlaub; *Editor:* Bruce Green; *Production Designer:* Mayne Schuyler Berke; *Set Designer:* Casey Hallenbeck; *Costume Designer:* Gary Jones; *Music:* John Debney

 Cast: Julie Andrews (Clarisse Renaldi); Hector Elizondo (Joe); Caroline Goodall (Helen Thermopolis); Anne Hathaway (Mia Thermopolis); Heather Matarazzo (Lilly Moscovitz); Mandy Moore (Lana Thomas); Robert Schwartzman (Michael Moscovitz)

Confessions of an Ugly Stepsister

Released 2002; *Running Time:* 100 minutes

 Producer: Jan Peter Meyboom for Alliance Atlantic and ABC; *Director:* Gavin Millar; *Teleplay:* Gene Quintano; *Cinematographer:* Gerard Simon; *Editor:* Angus Newton; *Production Designer:* Roger Hall; *Set Designer:* Karen Brookes; *Costume Designers:* Eve-Marie Arnault and Penny Rose; *Music:* Cynthia Millar

 Cast: Stockard Channing (Margarethe); Mark Dexter (The Prince); Matthew Goode (Caspar); Jenna Harrison (Clara); Emma Poole (Ruth Fisher); Jonathan Pryce (Master Schoonmacker); Azura Skye (Iris); Trudie Styler (Fortune Teller); David Westhead (Piter Van Den Meer)

Maid in Manhattan

Released 2002; *Running Time:* 105 minutes

Producers: Elaine Goldsmith-Thomas, Paul Schiff, and Deborah Schindler for Sony Pictures; *Director:* Wayne Wang; *Screenwriter:* Kevin Wade; *Cinematographer:* Karl Walter Lindenlaub; *Editor:* Craig McKay; *Production Designer:* Jane Musky; *Set Designer:* Susan Bode; *Costume Designer:* Albert Wolsky; *Music:* Alan Silvestri

Cast: Ralph Fiennes (Christopher Marshall); Bob Hoskiins (Lionel Bloch); Jennifer Lopez (Marisa Ventura); Priscilla Lopez (Veronica Ventura); Marissa Matrone (Stephanie Kehoe); Tyler Posey (Ty Ventura); Natasha Richardson (Caroline Lane); Amy Sedaris (Rachel Hoffberg); Stanley Tucci (Jerry Siegel)

My Big Fat Greek Wedding
Released 2002; *Running Time:* 96 minutes

Producers: Gary Goetzman, Tom Hanks, and Rita Wilson for Miramax; *Director:* Joel Zwick; *Screenwriter:* Nia Vardalos; *Cinematographer:* Jeff Jur; *Editor:* Mia Goldman; *Production Designer:* Gregory P. Keen; *Set Designer:* Enrico Campana; *Costume Designer:* Michael Clancy; *Music:* Xandy Janko and Chris Wilson

Cast: Gia Carides (Nikki); Michael Constantine (Gus Portokalos); John Corbett (Ian Miller); Christina Eleusiniotis (Young Toula); Joey Fatone (Angelo); Ian Gomez (Mike); Lainie Kazan (Maria Portokalos); Stavroula Logothettis (Athena); Louis Mandylor (Nick Portokalos); Andrea Martin (Aunt Voula); Gerry Mendicino (Uncle Taki); Nia Vardalos (Fotoula Portokalos); Marita Zouravlioff (Teenage Toula)

Bibliography

Alice Doesn't Live Here Anymore. Dir. by Martin Scorsese. With Ellen Burstyn and Kris Kristofferson. Warner Bros., 1974.

Allen, Jean Thomas. "Introduction: *Now Voyager* as Women's Film: Coming of Age, Hollywood Style." *Now Voyager, Casey Robinson Screenplay*. Warner Bros. Screenplay Series. Madison: U of Wisconsin Press, 1984, 9–41.

Anderson, Jeffrey. "Do You Really Need to Wear Those Glasses?" *San Francisco Examiner*. Online. 31 Jan 02.

Archerd, Army. "Just for Variety." *Daily Variety*. Online. 25 Oct. 2000.

Bernard, Jami. *Chick Flicks: A Movie Lover's Guide to the Movies Women Love*. Seacaucus, N.J.: Carol Publishing, 1997.

Blake, Richard A. "Movies and Myths of America." *America*. 16 Aug. 1975: 71–3.

Broeske, Pat H. "Outtakes: No Gritty 'Woman.'" *Los Angeles Times*. 18 Mar. 1990, Calendar: 39.

Brook, Tom. "Teen Power Storms U.S. Box Office." BBC News. Online. 5 Mar. 1999.

Cabot, Meg. *The Princess Diaries*. New York: Harper Trophy, 2001.

Cacks, Jay. "Blow Dry." *Time*. 24 Feb. 1975: 4.

Carr, Jay. "Why Is Hollywood Bashing Women?" *Boston Globe*. 25 Mar. 1990: B30.

Cinderella. Dir. by Wilfred Jackson. Disney, 1950.

Cinderella. Dir. by Robert Iscove. With Whitney Houston and Brandy Norwood. Disney, 1997.

Clueless. Dir. by Amy Heckerling. With Alicia Silverstone and Paul Rudd. Paramount, 1995.

Confessions of an Ugly Stepsister. Dir. by Gavin Millar. With Stockard Channing and Azura Skye. Alliance Atlantic, 2002.

Curry, Jack. "Why We Always Fall for the Cinderella Story." *TV Guide*. 13 Oct. 1990: 17–19.

Dabbous-Sensenig, Dima. "Who Is the Prettiest One of All?" *Al-Raida*. XVI, 86–87 (Fall 1999): 40–47.

Dam, Julie K. L. "How Do I Look?" *People*. 4 Sep. 2000: 114–120.

Dunnett, Dorothy. *Checkmate*. New York: Warner Books, 1975.

Ebert, Roger. Rev. of *Clueless*. *Chicago Sun Times*. Online. 19 Jul. 1995.

_____. Rev. of *Legally Blonde*. *Chicago Sun Times*. Online. 13 Jul. 2001.

_____. Rev. of *Mirror Has Two Faces*. *Chicago Sun Times*. Online. 18 Sep. 2002.

_____. Rev. of *Moonstruck*. *Chicago Sun Times*. Online. 15 Jan. 1988.

_____. Rev. of *My Big Fat Greek Wedding*. *Chicago Sun Times*. Online. 19 Apr. 2002.

_____. Rev. of *She's All That*. *Chicago Sun Times*. Online. 8 Aug. 2002.

_____. Rev. of *Up Close and Personal*. *Chicago Sun Times*. Online. 1 Mar. 1996.

Eliot, Marc. *Walt Disney: Hollywood's Dark Prince*. Seacaucus, N.J.: Carol Publishing, 1993.

Ever After. Dir. by Andy Tennant. With Drew Barrymore and Anjelica Huston. 20th Century–Fox, 1998.

Farber, Manny. "Between Two Worlds." *The New Republic*. 2 Nov 1942: 577.

Friedan, Betty. *The Feminine Mystique*. New York: Dell, 1983.

Friedman, Lawrence S. *The Cinema of Martin Scorsese*. New York: Continuum, 1998.

Funny Face. Dir. by Stanley Donen. With Audrey Hepburn and Fred Astaire. Paramount, 1957.

Giannetti, Louis, and Scott Eyman. *Flashback: A Brief History of Film*. Engelwood Cliffs, N.J.: Simon and Schuster, 1986.

_____. *Flashback: A Brief History of Film*. 3rd ed. Englewood Cliffs, N.J.: Prentice Hall, 1996.

Giannetti, Louis. *Understanding Movies*. 8th ed. Englewood Cliffs, N.J.: Prentice Hall, 1999.

Gove, Alex. "Special Effects." *RedHerring*. Online. Dec. 1999.

Grease. Dir. by Randl Kleiser. With John Travolta and Olivia Newton-John. Paramount, 1978.

Greenberg, Harvey Roy. "Pretty Woman's Co-opted Feminism." *Journal of Popular Film and Television*. 9–13.

Grossman, Lev. "People Who Mattered 2002." *Time*. 30 Dec 2002-6 Jan. 2003: 114–131.

Hallett, Martin, and Barbara Karasek, eds. *Folk and Fairy Tales*. Perterborough, Ontario: Broadview, 1996.

Hamilton, Edith. *Mythology*. Boston: Little, Brown, 1942.

Harrison, Rex. "Preface." *Bernard Shaw: Selected Plays*. New York: Dodd and Mead, 1981, ix–xiii.

Haskell, Molly. *From Reverence to Rape: The Treatment of Women in the Movies*. 2nd ed. Chicago: U of Chicago Press, 1987.

Heilbrun, Carolyn. *Hamlet's Mother and Other Women*. New York: Columbia UP, 1990.

Hinson, Hal. Rev. of *Clueless*. *Newsweek*. Online. 19 Jul. 1995.

Howe, Desson. "Comic Cruise to a 'Greek' Aisle." *Washington Post*. Online. 10 May 2002.

_____. "*Pretty Woman*: Ugly Truths." *Washington Post*. 23 Mar. 1990, Weekend: N37.

_____. "*Up Close* and Predictable." *Washington Post*. Online. 1 Mar. 1999.

Hyland, William G. *Richard Rodgers*. New Haven: Yale UP, 1998.

Hutchy, Patricia. "A Utopian Cinderella." *Maclean's*. 111, 32. 10 Aug.1998: 50.

Josie and the Pussycats. Dir. by Harry Elfont and Deborah Kaplan. With Rachael Leigh Cook. MGM/UP, 2001.

Kael, Pauline. *For Keeps: 30 Years at the Movies*. New York: Penguin Books, 1994.

_____. "*Moonstruck*: Loony Fugue." *Reeling*. Boston: Little Brown, 1976, 1162–64.

Kelley, Karol. "A Modern Cinderella." *Journal of American Culture*. 17.1 (Spring 1994): 87–92.

Kempley, Rita. Rev. of *Moonstruck*. *Washington Post*. Online. 15 Jan. 1988.

Kronenberger, Louis. Introduction. *Pygmalion*. *Four Plays by George Bernard Shaw*. By George Bernard Shaw. New York: Modern Library, 1953.

La Ferla, Ruth. "Need a Ratings Boost? Bring on the Makeovers." *New York Times*. 30 Dec. 2001: 1–2.

Leive, Cindi. "Be Yourself, Makeover or Not!" *Glamour*. Jan 2003: 22.

Legally Blonde. Dir. by Robert Luketic. With Reese Witherspoon and Luke Wilson. MGM/UP, 2001.

Leibman, Nina. "Decades and Retrodecades: Historiography in the Case of *Easy Rider* and *Shampoo*." *The Mid Atlantic Almanac: The Journal of Mid Atlantic Popular Culture/American Popular Culture Association*. 2, 1993: 81–94.

Leibovitz, Annie. *Women*. New York: Random House, 2000.

Lerner, Alan J., and Frederick Loewe. *My Fair Lady. A Musical Play in Two Acts*. New York: Signet, 1956.

Levin, Ira. *The Stepford Wives*. New York: HarperCollins, 2002.

Lurie, Allison. *The Language of Clothes*. New York: Henry Holt, 2000.

"Magazine Airbrushes Images of Kate Winslet." *Youngstown Vindicator*. 12 Jan. 2003: E5.

Maguire, Gregory. *Confessions of an Ugly Stepsister*. New York: HarperCollins, 1999.

Maid in Manhattan. Dir. by Wayne Wang. With Jennifer Lopez and Ralph Fiennes. Sony Pictures, 2002.

Maltin, Leonard. *Leonard Maltin's 2003 Movie and Video Guide*. New York: Signet, 2002.

Maslin, Janet. Rev. of *Up Close and Personal*. *New York Times*. Online. 1 Mar. 1996.

Mayne, Judith. "Feminist Film Theory and Criticism" *Multiple Voices in Feminist Film Criticism*. Eds. Diane Carson *et al*. Minneapolis: U of Minnesota Press, 1994. 48–64.

The Mirror Has Two Faces. Dir. by Barbra Streisand. With Barbra Streisand and Jeff Bridges. TriStar, 1996.

Miss Congeniality. Dir. by Donald Petrie. With Sandra Bullock and Benjamin Bratt. Castle Rock, 2000.

Mitchell, Elvis. "Pygmalion for Another Fair Lady." *New York Times*. Online. 3 Aug. 2001.

Modleski, Tania. "The Search for Tomorrow in Today's Soap Operas." *Feminist Television Criticism*. Eds. Charlotte Brunsdon *et al*. New York: Oxford U P, 1997. 36–47.

Moonstruck. Dir. by Norman Jewison. With Cher and Nicolas Cage. MGM, 1987.

Morris, Wesley. "*Congeniality* Full of Mischief." *San Francisco Chronicle*. 22 Dec. 2000: C-3.

Morrow, Terry. "MTV Makeover Show Goes Only Skin Deep." *Youngstown Vindicator*. 10 Jan. 2003: D3.

Mulvey, Laura. *Visual and Other Pleasures*. Bloomington and Indianapolis: Indiana U P, 1989.

My Big Fat Greek Wedding. Dir. by Joel Zwick. With Nia Vardalos and John Corbett. IFC Films, 2002.

My Fair Lady. Dir. by George Cukor. With Audrey Hepburn and Rex Harrison. Warner Bros., 1964.

Now, Voyager. Dir. by Irving Rapper. With Bette Davis and Paul Henreid. MGM, 1942.

Now, Voyager. MGM Video. Cover.

Onstad, Katrina. "A Lucky Lady with a Big Fat Laugh, Nia Vardalos: 'Greek Chic.'" *National Post.* Online. 16 Aug. 2002.

O'Sullivan, Michael. "A Modern Day Fairy Tale Princess." *Washington Post.* Online. 3 Aug. 2001: WE37.

Paurich, Milan. "*Maid in Manhattan* Dusts Off a Tired Script." *Youngstown Vindicator.* 12 Dec. 2002: D8.

Phillips, Michael. "Let the Debate Begin." *Los Angeles Times.* Online. 16 Sep. 2001.

Polenz, Joanna Magda. "Pretty Woman Selected by Psychiatrists as Most Romantic Film of 1990." *PR Newswire.* 12 Feb. 1991.

Pretty Woman. Dir. by Garry Marshall. With Julia Roberts and Richard Gere. Touchstone, 1990.

"*Pretty Woman* Selected by Psychiatrists as Most Romantic Film of 1990." *PR Newswire.* 12 Feb. 1991.

The Princess Diaries. Dir. by Garry Marshall. With Anne Hathaway and Julie Andrews. Disney, 2001.

Prouty, Olive Higgins. *Now, Voyager.* Boston: Houghton Mifflin, 1941.

_____. *Pencil Shavings.* Worcester: Clark UP, 1985.

Pygmalion. Dir. by Anthony Asquith. With Leslie Howard and Wendy Hiller. MGM, 1938.

Rader, Dotson. "'I Always Knew I'd Find My Partner Some Day.'" *Parade Magazine.* 8 Dec. 2002: 4–7.

Richard Rodgers Fact Book. New York: Lynn Farnol, 1965.

Ripley, Amanda, and Maggie Sieger. "The Special Agent." *Time* 30 Dec. 2002-6 Jan. 2003: 34–40.

Robarge, Leslie. "How Does a Celebrity Make Herself Over?" *Glamour.* Jan. 2003: 108–111.

Robinson, Casey. *Now, Voyager: Casey Robinson Screenplay.* Warner Bros. Screenplay Series. Madison: University of Wisconsin Press, 1984.

Rodgers and Hammerstein's Cinderella. Dir. by Charles S. Dubin. With Lesley Ann Warren and Stuart Damon. CBS, 1965.

Rosen, Leah. "*The Princess Diaries.*" *People.* 56, 7. 13 Aug. 2001: 33.

Sabrina. Dir. by Billy Wilder. With Audrey Hepburn and Humphrey Bogart. Paramount, 1954.

Sabrina. Dir. by Sydney Pollack. With Julia Ormond and Harrison Ford. Paramount, 1995.

Scala, Elizabeth. "Pretty Women: The Romance of the Fair Unknown, Feminism, and Contemporary Romantic Comedy." *Film & History.* 29, 1–2 (1999): 34–45.

Scott, A.O. "*Miss Congeniality*: Operation Ugly Duckling: Fighting Terrorism in Heels." *New York Times.* 22 Dec. 2000.

Seger, Linda. *The Art of Adaptation: Turning Fact and Fiction Into Film.* New York: Henry Holt, 1992.

_____. *When Women Call the Shots: The Developing Power and Influence of Women in Television and Film.* New York: Henry Holt, 1996.

Shampoo. Dir. by Hal Ashby. With Warren Beatty, Julie Christie, and Goldie Hawn. Columbia, 1975.

Shaw, George Bernard. *Pygmalion. Four Plays by George Bernard Shaw.* Introduction by Louis Kronenberger. New York: Modern Library, 1953.

She's All That. Dir. by Robert Iscove. With Rachael Leigh Cook and Freddie Prinze, Jr. Miramax, 1999.

The Slipper and the Rose. Dir. by Bryan Forbes. With Richard Chamberlain and Gemma Craven. Paradine Co-Production, 1976.

Sontag, Susan. Introduction. *Women.* By Annie Leibovitz. New York: Random House, 2000, 19–36.

Soergel, Matt. "Drowning in a Sea of Tears." *Jacksonville.com.* Online. 18 Feb. 1998.

Stack, Peter. "*Clueless* Knows a Lot About Teen Spoof." *San Francisco Chronicle.* Online. 19 Wed. 1995.

The Stepford Wives. Dir. by Bryan Forbes. With Katharine Ross and Paula Prentiss. Columbia, 1975.

Straub, Peter. "Introduction." *The Stepford Wives.* By Ira Levin. New York: Harper-Collins, 2002.

"Style: Befores & Afters." *Glamour* Jan. 2003: 112–115.

Tartar, Maria, ed. *The Classic Fairy Tale: Texts, Criticism.* New York: Norton, 1999.

Taylor, Samuel A. *Sabrina Fair: or, A Woman of the World.* Dramatists Play Service, 1953.

"Teens as Targets? Adolescent's Media Tastes and Preferences." www.ci.appstate.edu. Online. 8 Aug. 2002.

Thomas, Kevin. Rev. of *She's All That. Los Angeles Times.* Online. 29 Jan. 1999.

Travers, Peter. Rev. of *Ever After. Rolling Stone.* 20 Aug.1998: 113.

Turan, Kenneth. "A Bubble-Gum Romp." *Los Angeles Times.* Online. 11 Apr. 2001.

Turk, Rose-Marie. "Fashion 89: How Plot of *Working Girl* Can Apply to Real-Life Role." *Los Angeles Times.* 13 Jan. 1989, View: 1.

Up Close and Personal. Dir. by Jon Avnet. With Michelle Pfeiffer and Robert Redford. Touchstone, 1996.

Vardalos, Nia. Interview with Ted Koppel. *Nightline.* ABC. WYTV, Youngstown. 21 Aug. 2002.

Wallace, Amy. "True Thighs." *more.* Sep. 2002: 90–95.

Whitman, Walt. *Leaves of Grass, and Selected Prose.* Ed. Sculley Bradley. New York: Holt, Rinehart and Winston, 1949.

Wilson, Elizabeth. "Audrey Hepburn: Fashion, Film and the 50s." *Women and Film: A Sight and Sound Reader.* Eds. Pam Cook and Philip Dodd. Philadelphia: Temple UP, 1993.

Winn, J. Emmett. "Moralizing Upward Mobility: Investigating the Myth of Class Mobility in *Working Girl.*" *Southern Communication Journal.* 66.1 (Fall 2000): 40–51.

Working Girl. Dir. by Mike Nichols. With Melanie Griffith and Harrison Ford. 20th Century–Fox, 1988.

Zipes, Jack. *Happily Ever After: Fairy Tales, Children, and the Culture Industry.* New York: Routledge, 1997.

_____. "Breaking the Disney Spell." *The Classic Fairy Tale.* Ed. Maria Tatar. New York: Norton, 1999, 332–352.

Index